THE
AMERICAN
PRESIDENTS:

☆ ☆ ☆ ☆

FROM WASHINGTON TO CLINTON

☆ ☆ ☆ ☆

JOHN PYNCHON HOLMS

Pinnacle Books
Kensington Publishing Corp.

PINNACLE BOOKS are published by

Kensington Publishing Corp.
850 Third Avenue
New York, NY 10022

Pinnacle and the P logo Reg. U.S. Pat. & TM Off.

First Printing: October, 1996
10 9 8 7 6 5 4 3 2 1

Printed in the United States of America

CONTENTS

☆ ☆ ☆

INTRODUCTION

It's been said that one of the greatest things about the United States of America is that anyone who dreams can become president. Unlike the monarchies of Europe, where bloodlines are more important than qualifications, the highest office in American politics has been held by shoemakers, soldiers, shopkeepers, sailors, tailors, senators, rich men, poor men, beggars, even thieves—and still it has survived.

Some have occupied the White House by accident, some by desire, some by request, some because it was necessary. What most have had in common is a firm commitment to do the best they can and a strong belief in the fundamentals of democracy, as defined by the founding fathers over two hundred years ago.

A few presidents have been extraordinary in their conviction, capacity, and vision, most have been able to do what has been required of them, and some have failed. But no matter the quality or ability of the man, the office has survived and grown stronger with each transition of power—irrespective of how wrenching or inspired it might have been.

What is implicit in the contract between the president of the United States and the American people is that the office will make the man or the man will make the office. But either way the office will remain as the highest level of service to the public that democracy can offer.

These profiles offer a look at the men who have been president, what they have accomplished, and who they were before being called to govern. They present a microcosm of the diversity, complexity, and success of the American experience and a validation of those men who envisioned a government of the people, by the people, and for the people so many years ago.

CHAPTER ONE
☆ ☆ ☆

GEORGE WASHINGTON

1732-1799

1st President of the United States
"The father of our country."

☆ ☆ ☆

SECTION ONE

BORN

February 22, 1732, at the Washington family home near Pope's Creek, Westmoreland County, Virginia.

TERMS SERVED AS PRESIDENT

1789–1793
1793–1797

POLITICAL PARTY

Federalist

PUBLIC LIFE BEFORE PRESIDENCY

The French and Indian War

The French and Indian War (1754–1763) over control of the fertile Ohio valley, thrust Washington into public life. He had joined the Virginia Militia and in 1753 was sent with a warning to the French commander at Fort Le Boeuf to stop encroaching on British-held territory. The result of this dangerous mission was his promotion, at twenty-two, to lieutenant colonel and recognition of his instinctive qualities of leadership and management.

Washington spent the majority of the campaign on the frontier and saw considerable action. In 1758 he was involved in the successful campaign against the French at Fort Duquesne.

He returned to Mount Vernon in 1758 and began work in earnest restoring and rebuilding the house and grounds. He also began to establish a group of influential and supportive friends who convinced him to enter the political arena, and he was elected to Virginia's House of Burgesses, in which he served from 1759 to 1774.

Virginia Politics

By 1769, Washington had become a reluctant but active and vocal leader in Virginia's opposition to British colonial rule. Initially he had hoped for some compromise because his family ties and his loyalty to England were strong. But it was clear that the British presence was becoming more and more oppressive and that some policies, including westward expansion and his indebtedness to financial agents in London, were affecting him personally. Washington was a delegate (1774–1775) to the First and Second Continental Congresses, and in June 1775 he was the unanimous choice as commander in chief of the Continental Army as the colonies prepared for war with Britain.

The American Revolution

Washington took command of the ragtag Continental Army outside of Boston on July 3, 1775. The city at the time was held by British forces. Over the next nine months he worked to train fourteen thousand enthusiastic but green recruits while trying to build a stock of armor, weapons, and supplies. After establishing cannon hauled down from Fort Ticonderoga on Dorchester Heights, he forced the British to evacuate on March 17, 1776. But the success was to be short-lived. During the defense of New York City he blundered by committing his forces to an undefendable position in Brooklyn during the Battle of Long Island. The army was forced to retreat north through Westchester County and then south through New Jersey deep into the forests of Pennsylvania. While the retreat was a brilliantly executed military feat, civilian and troop morale sank. By the end of the year enlistment was almost up for a number of the troops, and others were deserting in droves. Congress withdrew from Philadelphia, fearing British attack.

The young revolution was saved when Washington captured Trenton, N.J., on Christmas night in 1776 during a daring attack in which he and his troops crossed the Delaware River and overcame the enemy garrison. He soundly defeated the British in Princeton on January 3, 1777, but was badly beaten in September and October 1777 at Brandywine and Germantown in Pennsylvania. The Battle of Saratoga, in October 1777, was considered the major success of the year and was won not by Washington but by Benedict Arnold and Horatio Gates. This led to a brief struggle in Congress to replace Washington with a more successful commander, but the plan failed as Washington's popularity in Congress and the military prevailed. The army then settled down to wait out the winter at Valley Forge.

That the army survived those bitter months with little food and terrible living conditions is a testament to Washington's leadership and their own faith and courage.

The news that France, under the command of the Marquis de Lafayette, had joined the War of Independence in May of 1778 rallied the troops and made the horrible and unspeakably difficult winter at Valley Forge seem almost bearable. Through the spring and early summer, Washington, with the help of Prussian military expert Baron von Stuben, was able to return the army to fighting strength, and in June he attacked the British near Monmouth Courthouse as they withdrew to New York. Although the war would continue four long and grueling years, the tide had turned. Until the final victory at Yorktown on October 19, 1781, and the surrender of British general Charles Cornwallis, the American Army, aided by French troops and under Washington's command, was on the offensive. Independence for the colonies was merely a matter of time.

The Call to Leadership

After the war Washington resigned his commission and returned home. For the second time he began the task of restoring and expanding his beloved Mount Vernon. The experiments in agriculture that Washington undertook drew a steady stream of visitors, and the estate was well on its way to becoming as famous as its owner. He chose not to reenter local Virginia politics although his enormous popularity would have assured him any role he wished to play. Washington was content to work his lands, spend time with his family, and increase his wealth as a planter and farmer.

But he was too important and popular a public figure to remain out of the political arena for long. In May of 1787 he was chosen to head the Virginia delegation to the Constitutional Convention in Philadelphia, where he was unanimously elected presiding officer. Although he made few direct contributions, his quiet presence and support of strong central government were essential to the difficult and sometimes contentious process of drafting the new Constitution. After the document was sent to the states and ratified, George Washington was unanimously elected the first president of the United States.

CAMPAIGNS

First Election—1789

Washington was not anxious to assume the presidency, but he gave in to immense public pressure and agreed to run for election.

The electoral process involved no campaigning at all. Instead, the sixty-nine electors (some were chosen by state legislatures and some by popular vote) all cast one vote for General Washington on February 4, 1789. The Constitution gave each elector a second vote, with the runner-up becoming vice president. That role fell to John Adams, who told his wife Abigail that "my country has in its wisdom contrived for me the most insignificant office that ever the invention of man contrived or his imagination conceived."

The only real controversy centered on the matter of his official title. Congress considered such terms as "His Excellency," "Elective Majesty," "His Serene Highness," "Elective Highness," and "His Highness, the President of the United States and Protector of the Rights of the Same." But simplicity won the day and Congress chose "Mr. President."

Electoral Votes:
Washington 69
Adams 34

Second Election—1792

Although the opposition party, who called themselves Democratic-Republicans, was gaining power and support, there was, in fact, no serious opposition owing to Washington's almost universal political appeal. Washington and the Federalist party won a unanimous decision, carrying every state. Once again, John Adams came in second and remained in office as vice president.

Electoral Votes:
Washington 132
Adams 77

VICE PRESIDENT

John Adams (1735–1826) Massachusetts. Lawyer. (Served both terms.)

THE CABINET

Secretary of State:
  Thomas Jefferson (1790–1793)
  Edmund Jennings Randolph (1794–1795)
  Timothy Pickering (1795–1800)

Secretary of the Treasury:
  Alexander Hamilton (1789–1795)
  Oliver Wolcott (1795–1800)

Secretary of War:
  Henry Knox (1789–1794)
  Timothy Pickering (Jan.–Dec. 1795)
  James McHenry (1796–1800)

Attorney General:
  Edmund Jennings Randolph (1789–1794)
  William Bradford (1794–1795)
  Charles Lee (1795–1801)

Postmaster General:
  Samuel Osgood (1789–1791)
  Timothy Pickering (1791–1794)
  Joseph Habersham (1795–1797)

SIGNIFICANT EVENTS THAT OCCURRED DURING OFFICE——APRIL 30, 1789–MARCH 3, 1797

Bank of the United States—1791

Washington agreed with and supported many of Hamilton's fiscal policies, including: founding the Bank of the United States, assuming state debts and the establishment of an excise tax—policies to which Jefferson was vigorously opposed. Jefferson and the Democratic-Republicans used these differences of opinion to attack Washington and thereby build their own political base.

Whiskey Rebellion—1794

The rift between the Federalists and the Democratic-Republicans was intensified when Washington sent fifteen thousand militia into western Pennsylvania to enforce the alcohol excise tax on local farmers who refused to pay. The action firmly established the presence of the federal government and its right to levy taxes.

Jay's Treaty—1795

Washington signed, putting to rest outstanding differences between the United States and Great Britain. The signing firmly divided the Federalists and the Democratic-Republicans, who saw it only as surrender to English power.

Also:

First Supreme Court, federal, and circuit judges appointed—1789

First federal census; patent and copyright protection; authorization to move the capital to Washington, D.C.—1790

Bill of Rights added to Constitution—1791

Order of presidential succession and U.S. Mint in Philadelphia—1792

CONTRIBUTIONS TO AMERICAN HISTORY WHILE

PRESIDENT

Washington faced two major tasks upon taking office. One was to structure the executive branch of government so that future presidents would be able to carry out their responsibilities with a minimum of administrative problems. The second rose out of his awareness of the danger that regional and sectional differences could divide the nation and render the central government unable to function. To help establish this he personally toured the northern states in 1789 and then in 1791 visited the South.

A great deal of his time was spent attempting to mediate and settle the huge differences between Secretary of State Thomas Jefferson, who strongly favored states' rights, and Secretary of the Treasury Alexander Hamilton, who was convinced that the new nation needed a strong central government.

After reelection in 1792, Washington and his government faced its most difficult and dangerous crisis, arising out of the issue of American neutrality during the war between England and France. In his first inaugural address, Washington had firmly stated his belief in American neutrality and established a policy of isolationism. He was horrified by the brutality of the French Revolution and agreed with Hamilton that economic ties to England were essential to America's future. Thomas Jefferson, who was strongly pro-French and felt a debt to them for their involvement in the Revolutionary War, was outraged and objected strongly. These differences of opinion, however divisive, would, in fact, strengthen the two-party system as well as the concepts of government laid down in the Constitution.

☆ ☆ ☆

SECTION TWO

PERSONAL PROFILE

George Washington was a large and powerful man, at least 6′2″, weighing between 175 and 200 pounds. He was quite fit, with broad shoulders, large hands and feet, and muscular arms (a benefit of years of hard physical work on the lands of his beloved Mount Vernon). Considered handsome and well comported, he dressed in a conservative but fashionable style. A servant at his wedding noted that "there was no one at the party like the young Colonel, so tall and straight . . . and with such an air!"

He would lose most, but not all of his teeth to gum disease and was forced to wear false teeth for a large part of his adult life. He experimented with many different kinds of false teeth, including ivory, human, and animal in vain attempts to find a good fit. Contrary to popular legend, none were made of wood.

Washington was a man of enormous personal and public integrity. Honest, serious, and fair-minded to a fault, he was known to be extremely ambitious as well as tough and thorough in his dealings, public and private. He could be impatient and impetuous and had a quick temper, which he struggled his entire life to control.

Shy and quiet, he was uncomfortable in public situations, and his natural reserve tended to make him an ineffective public speaker. He seemed aloof and distant to those who did not know him. However, he had instinctive skills as a writer and was eloquent when working from a prepared text.

FAMILY BACKGROUND

Ancestors

Descended from King Edward III of England (1312–1377) through his paternal grandmother, Mildred Warner Washington.

Immediate Family

FATHER: Augustine Washington (1694–1743) English businessman and colonial planter and foundry owner who, over the years, acquired a huge amount of prime farmland near the Potomac

River in Virginia. He traveled back and forth between England and America so often that George, who was eleven when his father died, remembered him with kindness but did not know him well.

MOTHER: Mary Ball Washington (1709–1789) The second wife of Augustine Washington, Mary Ball was an orphan under the care of a family friend, George Erskine. She married Augustine shortly after the death of his first wife, Jane Butler. Mary bore four sons (including George) and one daughter. The relationship between Mary and George was difficult, and they were never close. She died, probably of cancer, during Washington's first term as president.

BROTHERS AND SISTERS: Half brothers—Lawrence (to whom George was very close) and Augustine by Augustine Washington's first wife, Jane Butler. Brothers—Samuel, John Augustine, and Charles. Sister—Betty.

CHILDHOOD AND EARLY YEARS

After the death of his father, George, age eleven, went to live with his half brother Lawrence at Mount Vernon, Lawrence's plantation on the Potomac. Lawrence was, by all accounts, a caring surrogate father for his half brother, and the major influence in young George's life. Lawrence's support helped set him on the path that would take him to the presidency.

When a dream of going to sea was also quashed by George's mother, he learned surveying, a trade much in demand in colonial Virginia, and eventually was appointed surveyor for Culpeper County in 1749. When Lawrence died of tuberculosis in 1752, George inherited his beloved Mount Vernon, and the estate would remain his home for the rest of his life.

EDUCATION

Washington had little formal education and did not attend college either in the colonies or in England (as was the custom among young men of his class and background, including his half brothers Lawrence and Augustine). This was possibly because his mother objected to the idea of his leaving home. However, at the family estate he did study mathematics, surveying, the classics, and proper manners.

MILITARY SERVICE

Virginia Militia (1752–1754, 1755–1758)
RANK: Major, promoted to colonel.

Commander in chief: Continental Army (1775–1783)
RANK: General

Washington's experience in the military led him to develop an uncanny ability to arbitrate without losing sight of his own goals. Washington applied to the battlefield and to public life what he had learned from land—success was a combination of good judgment and the ability to improvise.

RELIGION

Episcopalian

FAMILY LIFE

Marriage:

Although infected by a shyness among strangers and in large gatherings that made him mumble or left him tongue-tied, Washington was an incorrigible romantic and often expressed his affections in earnest, if somewhat stilted, poetry. Evidently, none of his attempts were particularly successful until he began to court Martha Dandridge Custis, a wealthy and attractive young widow with two small children. They were married on January 6, 1759, at the "White House," her estate northwest of Williamsburg, Virginia. After a short honeymoon there they moved permanently to Mount Vernon, where they were, by all accounts, a happy and loving couple.

Children:

None. However, Washington formally adopted John Parke Custis and Martha Parke Custis, Martha's children from her previous marriage.

HOBBIES

Billiards, cards, fox hunting, fishing, mule-breeding, reading, and nature walks.

POST PRESIDENCY

The last three years of Washington's life were spent with his family at Mount Vernon, where he took charge of the running of the estate. He received many guests and observed the political scene with great interest. The Washingtons entertained frequently and lavishly.

DIED

December 14, 1799, at Mount Vernon, probably of *inflammatory quinsy* (an early term for tonsillitis) which he contracted after conducting a working tour of his plantation on horseback in raw and inclement weather on December 12.

CHAPTER TWO
☆ ☆ ☆

JOHN ADAMS
1735–1826

2nd President of the United States

☆ ☆ ☆

SECTION ONE

BORN

October 30, 1735, at the family farm in Braintree, Massachusetts. Braintree was later changed to Quincy.

TERM SERVED AS PRESIDENT

1797–1801

POLITICAL PARTY

Federalist

PUBLIC LIFE BEFORE PRESIDENCY

By the early 1760s, lawyer Adams began to speak out against the British presence and influence in colonial affairs. In 1765 he wrote *A Dissertation on the Canon and the Feudal Law,* which denounced the infamous Stamp Act (taxation by the British without colonial representation). The publication of the pamphlet placed him instantly as a member of the growing resistance to British rule, and his skills as a lawyer and thinker made him a natural leader of the movement. He served as a member of the Massachusetts legislature from 1770 to 1774 and was a strong vocal supporter of the Boston Tea Party, which protested British taxation by dumping English cargo into Boston Harbor.

The Boston Massacre

When British soldiers, taunted by a stone-throwing mob, opened fire, killing three and wounding eight, the city of Boston was caught up in a frenzy of revenge. The British put the soldiers up for trial to appease the mob, and Adams, believing them to have been provoked and therefore innocent, took up the unpopular cause of their defense. It was a difficult decision because although he believed that revolution was inevitable, he also believed in the right to fair trial. The soldiers were acquitted. In the short run, Adams was denounced for defending the enemy, but in the end his firm stand on the importance of trial by law over passion was proved not only to be fair but correct.

The Continental Congress

In 1774, Adams was chosen as a Massachusetts delegate to the Continental Congress in Philadelphia, where he was an outspoken supporter of colonial self-rule, helped draft the Declaration of Independence, and championed the choice of Washington as commander in chief of the Continental Army. So active was he that even Thomas Jefferson, who would later become a bitter political rival, called him the "Colossus of Independence."

The Diplomatic Corps

In 1778 Adams was chosen to be an American commissioner to France, along with Benjamin Franklin. But his blunt and sometimes terse Puritan manner, along with his dislike of Franklin's manner, made him unsuited for the life of a diplomat, and he lasted in Paris less than a year. He returned to Massachusetts and helped draft the state's constitution.

In November 1779 he returned to Europe with his sons to help Franklin, along with French officials, seek a peaceful settlement with Britain. Still unable to work with Franklin, he went to Holland and gained Dutch recognition of American independence. He returned to Paris in October 1782 and was part of the negotiations that finally led to the Treaty of Paris of September 3, 1783, which recognized American independence.

In 1785 he was appointed as the first American minister to Britain. But, while both sides spoke of healing wounds and seeking common ground, the American victory still stung the British military establishment, and they made it an impossible task to build a new and equitable relationship between the two nations. Facing enormous difficulties, Adams requested that he be recalled.

The Vice Presidency

On his return to the United States in 1788, Adams, considered a hero and leading light of the fight for independence, was promptly elected vice president under the new Constitution, a job he considered symbolic and boring beyond redemption. With little to do, he spent his time considering the nature of democratic government and worked with Washington to create a sense of order and ritual that would lend stability and dignity to the governing system.

He was a supporter of Washington and Hamilton's case for strong central government and strong fiscal measures on the federal level. This would lead to intense disagreements with Jefferson and establish their political rivalry, which lasted for the rest of their lives.

Adams served two terms as vice president before his election as president.

CAMPAIGN

The Election–1796

The campaign of 1796 was the first real test of the American political system. Washington was such a venerated and heroic figure that the opposition, led by Thomas Jefferson, was forced to tread lightly during his two terms in office for fear of angering the American public. But when Washington retired the gloves came off, and the campaign of '76 set a tone that would become the hallmark of American politics for generations. The fight between Jefferson and Adams was brutal and bloody, with both sides doing their best to smear and obliterate the opposition. Adams was pictured as a toady who secretly longed to be king and Jefferson as an opportunist and potential dictator only interested in personal gain.

Underneath the bluster was the central issue that continues to drive American politics: are the needs of the people best served by a strong federal government or by the states?

In the end, political maneuvers by Hamilton to steal the presidency from both candidates backfired and Adams, with the support of his New England allies, squeaked out a narrow victory. Jefferson became the reluctant vice president.

Electoral Votes:
Adams 71
Jefferson 68

VICE PRESIDENT

Thomas Jefferson (1743–1826) Virginia. Lawyer.

THE CABINET

Secretary of State:
Timothy Pickering (1795–1800)
John Marshall (1800–1801)

Secretary of the Treasury:
Oliver Walcott (1795–1800)
Samuel Dexter (Jan.–May 1801)

Secretary of War:
James McHenry (1796–1800)
Samuel Dexter (1800–1801)

Attorney General:
Charles Lee (1800–1801)

Secretary of the Navy:
Benjamin Stoddert (1751–1813)

Postmaster General:
Joseph Habersham (1795–1797)

SIGNIFICANT EVENTS THAT OCCURRED DURING
OFFICE——MARCH 4, 1797–MARCH 4, 1801

The XYZ Affair (1797–1798)

When Adams took office relations with France were strained over harassment of American merchant ships and the call to war was sounding loud and clear. Adams held firm and insisted on negotiating a peaceful settlement. But when his envoys returned with a French demand of $250,000 in bribes to cease attacking American shipping Adams called for war.

The pro-French, Jeffersonian Republicans didn't believe the extortion attempt was real and demanded proof. Adams refused, citing executive privilege but relented after substituting the names of the French agents with the letters X, Y, and Z and the battle cry "Millions for defence, but not a cent for tribute" rang throughout the land. During the conflict, Adams signed the Alien and Sedition Act (1798), which limited immigrants' chances of becoming citizens, made it easier to deport unnaturalized aliens, and limited freedom of the press. By 1802 the act had been repealed.

Adams knew that the nation wasn't ready for war with France

and continued to seek a negotiated solution. After two years of what was called the "Quasi-War" France signed the Convention of 1800 and recognized U.S. neutrality.

The Fries Rebellion—1799

Like Washington, Adams was forced to use federal power against a citizens' group who refused to pay federal taxes. A Pennsylvania farmer named John Fries led an armed rebellion, was caught and sentenced to hang for treason, but Adams granted him a pardon in 1800.

CONTRIBUTIONS TO AMERICAN HISTORY WHILE

PRESIDENT

Perhaps Adams's greatest accomplishment was the orderly transition of power both in the beginning and end of his single term of office. Washington's extraordinary popularity and almost godlike status raised real questions about whether or not the system of change ordered by the Constitution would actually work in practice. Adams succeeded in maintaining and strengthening the role of the president and entrenched the concept of the office as more important than the man.

 ☆ ☆ ☆

SECTION TWO

PERSONAL PROFILE

At 5´6˝ Adams was short and stocky as a young man and as he grew older was described as portly. He was weak and in poor health for almost all of his life, constantly afflicted with a string of minor and major illnesses, including chest pains, colds, headaches, bad digestion, and, finally, palsy. Like Washington, Adams lost most of his teeth to gum disease. Unlike Washington, he refused to wear dentures, which later affected his ability to speak clearly.

Adams was a New England Puritan in the truest sense, reserved to the point of seeming aloof and distant. Like Washington, he was uncomfortable in public situations. He believed deeply in the rights of man and individual freedom but remained uncertain throughout his life whether or not the masses were capable of governing themselves. It has been suggested that his ambition fueled his paranoia and that he took attacks from those who opposed him very personally, often falling into deep depressions.

With his family he was generous and loving, showing a warmth that was often lacking in his public life.

FAMILY BACKGROUND

Ancestors

Descended from John and Priscilla Alden, *Mayflower* Pilgrims. The Adams family settled in Braintree as early as 1640.

Immediate Family

FATHER: John Adams (1691–1761) The father of the second president was a hardworking farmer and leather worker who also found time to be actively involved in the religious and political life of Braintree as a selectman, officer of the law, tax collector, and a deacon of the church. His honesty was above reproach and his commitment to the welfare of the community spurred Adams to pursue a life in politics.

MOTHER: Susanna Boylston Adams (1709–1797) Adams didn't spend much time in his diaries and journals writing about his mother, and little is known about her beyond the fact that she was subject to fits of temper and argued with her husband over his community duties and his concern for Braintree's less fortunate. She shared, however, her husband's respect for education and the power of knowledge and encouraged her son to go to college. She remarried after her husband's death and seemed to further remove herself from the family.

BROTHERS AND SISTERS: Peter Boylston Adams, who became a farmer and captain of the Braintree militia; Elihu Adams, who died of fever while serving as an officer during the Revolution.

CHILDHOOD AND EARLY YEARS

Although subject to poor health and vision, young John seems to have loved the outdoor life and spent more of his childhood playing games and pursuing his passion for hunting instead of learning. In fact, he seemed bored with school and seemed to have little respect for the local teachers. His mother and father, who taught him to read as a child and wished him to become a minister, were aware of his intelligence and afraid he would settle for the life of a colonial farmer rather than seek a proper education to further himself.

EDUCATION

Adams became the first of his family to go to college, enrolling at Harvard in 1751. While at Harvard he chose the law as a course of study and by 1762, after a period of teaching school, he began what would become a successful practice.

MILITARY SERVICE

None

RELIGION

Unitarian

FAMILY LIFE

Marriage:

Adams married Abigail Smith (1744–1818) on October 25, 1764, at her family home in Weymouth, Massachusetts. All accounts show them to have been an extremely happy and contented couple. Well suited in temperament and supportive of each other, the couple thrived during the course of their fifty-one-year marriage. Because of illness during childhood, Abigail received almost no formal education, but her appetite for literature and philosophy coupled with her native intelligence and determination led her to become one of the most learned and intellectually competent first ladies in the history of the presidency. Her concern and vocal support for the liberation of women in society marks her place in history as one of the earliest American advocates for women's rights.

Children:

Abigail Adams (1765–1813); John Quincy Adams (sixth president) (1767–1848); Charles Adams (1770–1800); Thomas Boylston Adams (1772–1832)

HOBBIES

Daily walks, cards, reading, drawing, and fishing.

POST PRESIDENCY

Adams returned to his home and devoted the next twenty-five years of his life to correspondence with old friends and reading a wide variety of books and journals. As his vision failed his family would read to him. He cast one of Massachusetts's fifteen electoral votes for the reelection of James Monroe in 1820. He lived to see his son, John Quincy, elected president.

DIED

July 4, 1826, at Quincy, Massachusetts, at ninety years of age. During the last months of his life Adams was unable to leave his house. Near the end he was confined to bed. On the morning of the fourth, while the country celebrated its fiftieth birthday in nearby Boston, he lapsed into a coma. Around noon he awoke and spoke his last words—"Thomas Jefferson still . . . (survives)?" (In fact, Jefferson himself had died just a few hours earlier.) He then slipped back into a coma, rallied briefly, but passed away of heart failure and pneumonia during the early evening hours. He was buried beside his wife Abigail at the Congregational Church in Quincy.

CHAPTER THREE
☆ ☆ ☆

THOMAS JEFFERSON

1743–1826

3rd President of the United States

☆ ☆ ☆

SECTION ONE

BORN

April 13, 1743, at Shadwell Plantation, Goochland County, Virginia.

TERMS SERVED AS PRESIDENT

1801–1805
1805–1809

POLITICAL PARTY

Democratic-Republican

PUBLIC LIFE BEFORE PRESIDENCY

Virginia House of Burgesses

In 1769 he began six years of service as a representative in the Virginia House of Burgesses, in which he became involved in the growing opposition to British rule. It was at that time he began construction of his estate, Monticello, which he designed in every detail and continued to work on and refine for years.

In 1774 he wrote *A Summary View of the Rights of British America,* in which he stated that "The God who gave us life, gave us liberty at the same time: the hand of force may destroy, but cannot disjoin them." Reaction to the pamphlet placed him in the forefront of the revolutionary movement.

Declaration of Independence

At the Second Continental Congress in Philadelphia, Jefferson was drafted on June 11, 1776, to head a committee of five in preparing the Declaration of Independence. The choice of Jefferson as head was based on the response to his pamphlet. Although he was the Declaration's primary author, the final draft was finished in consultation with Benjamin Franklin and John Adams and finally by Congress. The Declaration of Independence made Jefferson internationally famous and fueled the competition between him and Adams.

Virginia Lawmaker

Jefferson returned to Virginia and served until 1779 in the House of Delegates, in which he worked to liberalize the body of law and take control from the powerful and conservative planters. In 1779 a bill he introduced to provide religious freedom touched off a firestorm that raged for more than eight years.

In June 1779, Jefferson was elected governor of Virginia, but ceaseless attacks on his performance during the war led him to retire in 1781, somewhat embittered by his time as a public servant.

Continental Congressman

Despite the resistance of his political enemies he became a member of the Continental Congress in 1783, and in 1784 he helped establish the decimal system and laid the groundwork for adopting the dollar instead of the pound as the basic monetary unit in 1792. Jefferson also introduced radical proposals for the governing of newly opened western territories, which included the banning of slavery.

Commissioner to France

From 1784 to 1789 Jefferson was stationed in Paris to help negotiate commercial treaties. It was a difficult task since most European countries, with the exception of Prussia, had little interest in American economics. In 1785 he succeeded Benjamin Franklin as minister to France.

Secretary of State

On what he expected to be a short return to the United States in 1789, he learned that Congress confirmed his appointment as secretary of state in the first Washington administration. Jefferson accepted largely because of Washington's insistence. Although he had confidence in the symbol of the Revolution, he was dismayed by Washington's intention to regalize the office of president, and he was distrustful of Secretary of the Treasury Hamilton's fiscal proposals. To Jefferson, who firmly believed in the concept of states' rights, Hamilton's policies, done with Washington's approval, were creating the kind of strong central government to which he was very much opposed.

The more Washington sided with Hamilton on important issues of policy, the more Jefferson became frustrated and angry. He resigned on December 31, 1793.

For the next three years Jefferson continued to work on Monticello, experimenting and inventing but still keeping a wary eye on the political scene. Although he strongly disagreed with Washington's policies and the Federalists' positions on almost everything, he knew that the president was too popular a figure to oppose directly.

Vice President

When Washington declined to run for a third term, Jefferson was the undisputed presidential nominee of the Democratic-Republican party and became vice president after losing the election by four votes.

Jefferson took advantage of his time in the "useless" job to write rules of parliamentary procedure and plan for the election of 1800.

CAMPAIGNS

First Election—1800

The level of the political debate in the campaign that pitted John Adams and his running mate Charles Cotesworth Pinckney against Thomas Jefferson and his running mate Aaron Burr may have been the lowest of any presidential election in history. The language was brutal and the accusations that flew back and forth were inflammatory and, at best, half-truths.

By the time the electors cast their votes, a split in Federalist ranks guaranteed a Democratic-Republican party victory. But although Jefferson had been the party's nominee for the top spot, the voting procedure resulted in a tie with Burr, which sent the election into the House of Representatives.

The Federalists controlled the House. Some preferred Burr to the hated Jefferson, but there was also a scheme to keep the House deadlocked past March 4, the date on which the Constitution required that a new president be sworn in. By interpretation of the law they argued, the Federalist president pro tem of the Senate could be the chief executive. The House voted thirty-five times over seven days without Jefferson receiving the support of the required nine states. Finally, Jefferson was named president on the thirty-sixth ballot, and Burr became vice president.

One of the first orders of business was the approval of the Twelfth Amendment to the Constitution, which required that the Electoral College vote separately for president and vice president and was ratified by 1804.

Electoral Votes:
Jefferson 73
Burr 73
Adams 65
Pinckney 64

Second Election—1804

Jefferson was the unanimous nominee for reelection by the Republican party, and the Federalist candidate, Charles Pinckney, was no match. The outcome of the election was never in doubt. Burr returned as vice president, but differences with Jefferson led to his disfavor and he was replaced by George Clinton in 1805.

Electoral Votes:
Jefferson 162
Pinckney 14

VICE PRESIDENTS

Aaron Burr (1756–1836) New York. Lawyer.
George Clinton (1739–1812) New York. Lawyer.

THE CABINET

Secretary of State:
  James Madison (1801–1809)

Secretary of the Treasury:
  Samuel Dexter (1801)
  Albert Gallatin (1801–1814)

Secretary of War:
  Henry Dearborn (1801–1809)

Attorney General:
  Levi Lincoln (1801–1820)
  John Breckinridge (1805–1806)
  Caesar A. Rodney (1807–1811)

Secretary of the Navy:
  Robert Smith (1801–1809)

SIGNIFICANT EVENTS THAT OCCURRED DURING OFFICE——MARCH 4, 1801–MARCH 3, 1809

The Louisiana Purchase

The Louisiana Purchase in 1803, which doubled the size of the United States for the cost of about three cents an acre, was perhaps his greatest achievement. The purchase from France was so important to him that Jefferson had to bend some of his own strongly held constitutional beliefs by taking over the territory without benefit of a constitutional amendment. Following the purchase he sent Lewis and Clark to explore the territory. In 1806 the Lewis and Clark Expedition returned after crossing the continent and bringing back awe-inspiring reports of riches and wealth.

Tripolitan War

Jefferson brought the Tripolitan War (1801–1805), fought over issues of piracy in the Mediterranean, to a successful conclusion. The new navy fought its first successful engagements.

The Embargo Act

One of the most important issues faced by the Jefferson administration was the continued violation of American sovereignty by the British and French. In order to force recognition, Jefferson chose to apply economic pressure with the Embargo Act (December 22, 1807), which prohibited almost all exports and most imports. The effort failed to have much effect on foreign powers, but it caused real hardship on many northern businessmen and was responsible for a resurrection of the dying Federalist party. One of Jefferson's last official acts was the repeal of the embargo.

CONTRIBUTIONS TO AMERICAN HISTORY WHILE PRESIDENT

Jefferson, although hated by the Federalists, proved to be popular with the people because he reduced taxes, cut the military budget, allowed the Alien and Sedition Acts to lapse, and worked to lessen the public debt. Simplicity and frugality became the hallmarks of Jefferson's administration.

☆ ☆ ☆

SECTION TWO

PERSONAL PROFILE

Reddish-haired, with hazel eyes and strong features, Jefferson was well over six feet tall and quite thin, a true reflection of his English heritage. Angular and gawky, he slouched, and walked with an irregular, loping gait. Even as president, he insisted on wearing comfortable, casual clothing, receiving heads of state without benefit of formal dress.

He was known to have an even temperament, was an engaging conversationalist in small groups, and approachable yet somehow reserved. Like Washington, he was uncomfortable with public speaking.

One of Jefferson's major attributes was his insatiable curiosity and genuine interest in the nature of things.

FAMILY BACKGROUND

Ancestors

Descended from King Edward III of England (1312–1377) through his paternal grandmother, Mildred Warner Washington.

Immediate Family

FATHER: Colonel Peter Jefferson (1708–1757) Like Washington's father, Colonel Jefferson was a successful planter, landowner, public servant, and surveyor, whose map of Virginia, done with one Joshua Fry in 1751, was, for many years, the standard reference for the colony.

MOTHER: Jane Randolph Jefferson (1720–1776) Jefferson's mother, born in London and from one of Virginia's first families, seems to have had little effect on his life and is rarely mentioned. She died of a stroke.

BROTHERS AND SISTERS: Jane Jefferson; Mary Jefferson Bolling; Elizabeth Jefferson; Martha Jefferson Carr; Lucy Jefferson Lewis; Anna Jefferson Scott Marks; Randolph Jefferson (twin of Anna).

CHILDHOOD AND EARLY YEARS

Jefferson's early years are not well documented. What is known is that he enjoyed reading, hiking, and the study of nature and science.

EDUCATION

Jefferson was sent to boarding school from ages nine to fourteen at St. James Parish. He received a classical education and enjoyed his studies but was unhappy with his teacher and the distance from home. At fourteen he was sent to school in Fredericksville, which was much closer to home, where he thrived and expanded his knowledge of languages, including French, and all manner of literature and poetry.

He attended the College of William and Mary from 1760 to 1762 where he studied science, philosophy, and mathematics, and expanded his knowledge of the classics and foreign language. After college he studied law with George Wythe and was admitted to the Virginia bar in 1767.

MILITARY SERVICE

None

RELIGION

Deism

FAMILY LIFE

Marriage:

Jefferson married Martha Wayles Skelton a twenty-three-year-old widow on January 1, 1772, at her father's estate in Charles County, Virginia. They were by all accounts a very happy couple. When she died on September 6, 1782, Jefferson was grief-stricken and vowed never to remarry. However, there would be other important relationships in his life—Maria Cosway, whom he met in France, and possibly with Sally Hemings, a slave on his estate who was half sister to his wife by her father, John Wayles.

Children:

Martha Jefferson (1772–1836); Mary Jefferson (1778–1804)

HOBBIES

Thomas Jefferson was truly a Renaissance man. His range of interest and exploration included: architecture, collecting, botany, animal husbandry, meteorology, mechanical engineering, music, reading, landscaping, fine wines, and food. He invented the swivel chair, an adjustable drafting table, a plow, and a handwriting duplicator—among other things.

POST PRESIDENCY

Jefferson spent the last fourteen years of his life in correspondence with friends, designing buildings, and founding the University of Virginia. He sold his vast collection of books to the Library of Congress to help replace what had been lost when British forces burned the Capitol Building in 1815.

DIED

July 4, 1826, 12:50 P.M. at Monticello of complications resulting from chronic rheumatism, diarrhea, and an enlarged prostate. Jefferson spent his last months in considerable discomfort and was forced to take strong doses of laudanum to counteract the pain. Both he and John Adams died the same day. He was buried on the grounds of his beloved Monticello in a private ceremony. The inscription on the simple tombstone he himself designed read: "Here was buried Thomas Jefferson, Author of the Declaration of Independence, of the Statute of Virginia for Religious Freedom, and Father of the University of Virginia."

CHAPTER FOUR
☆ ☆ ☆

JAMES MADISON

1751–1836

4th President of the United States
"The Father of the Constitution"

SECTION ONE

BORN

March 16, 1751, in his mother's parents' home at Point Conway, King George County, Virginia.

TERMS SERVED AS PRESIDENT

1809–1813
1813–1817

POLITICAL PARTY

Democratic-Republican

PUBLIC LIFE BEFORE PRESIDENCY

Virginia Convention—1776

Madison was elected to the Virginia convention that voted for independence and drafted a constitution for the new state. During the convention he proved to be an articulate spokesman. He took his seat as a member of the House of Delegates, in which he became a friend and supporter of Thomas Jefferson but was defeated for re-election.

Continental Congress—1780

Madison became a leader of the group advocating a strong central government. He was regarded as an effective legislator and debater.

Virginia House of Delegates—1784–1786

His term in the House of Delegates convinced him that the Articles of Confederation were too loosely structured to allow the nation to succeed, and in 1786 he became a vocal supporter of the need to draft a new constitution.

Constitutional Convention—1787

Madison took the lead and was a persuasive advocate for a constitution that supported a strong central government. He was responsible for drafting much of the document, and his influence and ideas gained him the nickname "Father of the Constitution." He worked tirelessly with Alexander Hamilton and other supporters to win its ratification. As the representative from Virginia, Madison sponsored the Bill of Rights and became one of the chief advisors to George Washington.

A Change of Party—1790

Madison disagreed with Hamilton's fiscal policies and left Washington's administration to oppose them. He turned to Jefferson and his supporters, who would become the Democratic-Republicans, and argued against economic dependence on Britain. The infighting caused Madison to leave Congress in 1797.

Virginia Resolutions—1798

As a private citizen, Madison drafted the Virginia Resolution to protest the Alien and Sedition Acts made into law by John Adams.

Secretary of State—1801–1809

In 1801, Madison was appointed secretary of state by Jefferson and served both terms in the office. He was responsible for the negotiations that led to the Louisiana Purchase in 1803 and supported the Tripolitan War as well as the Embargo Act. He was Jefferson's choice to succeed him as president.

CAMPAIGNS

First Election—1808

The major issue in the campaign of 1808 was the embargo instituted by Jefferson to protect American ships from the British and French and enforce American neutrality. Not only had it failed but had severely affected the economy of the northern states and caused a revival of the almost dormant Federalist party. Madison needed the help of Jefferson and his influence in the South and West to gain the necessary votes.

Electoral Votes:
Madison 122
Pinckney 47
Clinton 6

Second Election—1812

The War of 1812 drove the campaign. The debate was centered on what Madison's opponents considered mishandling of the war effort that resulted in a string of early victories by the British. The major opposition, who felt Madison had forced the country into an unnecessary war, was centered in the North but Madison again carried the South and West and was reelected easily.

Electoral Votes:
Madison 128
Clinton 89

VICE PRESIDENTS

George Clinton (1739–1812) New York. Lawyer.
Elbridge Gerry (1744–1814) Massachusetts. Former governor of Massachusetts.

THE CABINET

Secretary of State:
  Robert Smith (1809–1811)
  James Monroe (1811–1817)

Secretary of the Treasury:
  Albert Gallatin (1809–1814)
  George W. Campbell (1814)
  Alexander J. Dallas (1814–1816)
  William H. Crawford (1816–1817)

Secretary of War:
  William Eustis (1809–1812)
  John Armstrong (1813–1814)
  James Monroe (1814–1815)
  William H. Crawford (1815–1816)

Attorney General:
  Caesar A. Rodney (1809–1811)
  William Pinkney (1812–1814)
  Richard Rush (1814–1817)

Secretary of the Navy:
  Paul Hamilton (1809–1812)
  William Jones (1813–1814)
  Benjamin W. Crowninshield (1815–1817)

SIGNIFICANT EVENTS THAT OCCURRED DURING
OFFICE——MARCH 4, 1809—MARCH 4, 1817

The War of 1812

Madison inherited a troubled presidency. The unsuccessful embargo against the British and French continued to take center stage and made execution of his policies and plans in other areas of administration difficult. His attempts at diplomatic solutions failed, and, three years after taking office, he bowed to pressure from a group of congressmen, Henry Clay, John C. Calhoun, and Richard M. Johnson. In June of 1812 he asked for a declaration of war on Britain. The decision caused strife within his party and strong opposition from the Federalists and would affect the remainder of his time in office.

Unable to find adequate civilian and military leaders, Madison suffered a string of defeats at Detroit and Niagara, and the intended conquest of Canada failed. Stunning naval victories were not enough to raise American morale, and the defeat of Napoleon in 1814 freed thousands of British troops for the campaign. While American troops fought well, Washington was captured by the British and burned. Madison was forced to abandon the capital and watched the flames from the other side of the Potomac. The burning of the capital would prove a turning point, however, and soon afterward the British were defeated in Baltimore Harbor and at Lake Champlain, New York.

Madison was unaware that these defeats convinced the British to seek peace. He was facing serious internal problems: the likelihood of national bankruptcy; the possibility of secession in New England; and reports of an impending British offensive at New Orleans. In February 1815 news of Andrew Jackson's victory at the Battle of New Orleans along with confirmation that the Treaty of

Ghent had been signed on December 24, 1814, reached Washington. American recognition as a viable foreign power was secured.

Domestic Policy

Madison turned his attention to problems at home and proposed a broad range of domestic reform in December 1815: recharter of the Bank of the United States, a tariff to protect young industries, creation of a national university, and advocated a constitutional amendment to provide federal support for infrastructure, including roads and canals. Although Congress accepted only part of this program, these moves made Madison very popular with the general public, and he left office a loved and respected statesman.

CONTRIBUTIONS TO AMERICAN HISTORY WHILE

PRESIDENT

While not the most effective administrator, Madison was a genius as a statesman and writer of clear and far-reaching legislation. His greatest contribution to American history and the presidency lies in the work he did to frame the Constitution.

☆ ☆ ☆

SECTION TWO

PERSONAL PROFILE

At 5´4˝ in height and 100 pounds in weight, the blue-eyed, brown-haired Madison was our smallest president. He dressed neatly and took care with his appearance. Weak and of nervous disposition, Madison worked against a tendency toward illness his entire life. He exercised regularly to maintain his health.

Although an excellent debater and original thinker, Madison was known to be shy and extremely reserved among strangers. He was deliberate in his decision making, weighing both sides of an argument carefully before committing himself, a trait which gave the mistaken impression of indecisiveness.

FAMILY BACKGROUND

Ancestors

Descended from a long line of English planters and farmers. The first Madison settled in Orange County, Virginia, in 1640.

Immediate Family

FATHER: James Madison, Sr. (1723–1801) James, Sr., built the family estate inherited from his father into the largest and most successful in Orange County. He served the community as sheriff, justice of the peace, and was a vestryman. During the Revolution he was a county lieutenant.

MOTHER: Eleanor Rose Conway Madison (1731–1829) Daughter of an influential Orange County tobacco planter.

BROTHERS AND SISTERS: Francis Madison; Ambrose Madison; Mrs. Nelly; William Madison; Mrs. Sara Macon; Mrs. Frances Rose.

CHILDHOOD AND EARLY YEARS

Madison grew up on his large family estate. During his childhood, Montpelier, the house that would be his permanent residence, was built. The estate produced grains and tobacco, and the land was worked by slaves. His dependence on the institution of slavery would always be at odds with his belief that it should be abolished.

Education

Madison's early education came from tutors, from whom he learned the classics, languages, mathematics, and geography—as well as a lifelong love of reading. Instead of choosing the College of William and Mary, as did most of Virginia's young men, Madison enrolled at the College of New Jersey at Princeton in 1771. He pushed himself and graduated in two years. He was known to be a skilled debater. Madison studied law but was never admitted to the bar.

MILITARY SERVICE

Orange County Militia (1775)
RANK: Colonel (Saw no action)

RELIGION

Episcopalian

FAMILY LIFE

Marriage:

On September 15, 1794, at age forty-three, Madison married Dolley Payne Todd, twenty-six, a widow, at her sister's estate in West Virginia. She was destined to become perhaps the most famous first lady in history. A great supporter of Madison, her legendary charm and wit provided strong counterpoint to his quiet and reserve. She died on July 12, 1849.

Children:

None

HOBBIES

Chess, reading (especially the classics), horseback riding, and nature walks.

POST PRESIDENCY

Madison returned to Virginia and took over the business of running Montpelier. He worked with Jefferson to help found the University of Virginia and served as a member of its board of regents. He remained involved in political life, serving Monroe as an advisor on policy. Although a slaveholder, he believed that the institution would eventually destroy the union and advised a gradual abolition and resettlement of freed slaves.

He strongly resisted the Nullification movement of 1830–1833, denying that he and Jefferson had advocated the states' rights to make federal laws unconstitutional in the Kentucky and Virginia Resolutions of 1798, and fought for the continued union of the United States.

DIED

Madison died peacefully of heart failure on June 28, 1836, after being bedridden for more than six months. He was buried on the grounds of his estate. Found in his papers after his death was yet another plea for the solidarity of the Union.

CHAPTER FIVE
☆ ☆ ☆

JAMES MONROE

1758-1831

5th President of the United States

☆ ☆ ☆

SECTION ONE

BORN

Monroe was born on April 28, 1758, on his parents' plantation in Westmoreland County, Virginia.

TERMS SERVED AS PRESIDENT

1817–1821
1821–1825

POLITICAL PARTY

Democratic-Republican

PUBLIC LIFE BEFORE PRESIDENCY

Monroe's friendships with Jefferson, that grew out of his study of law, and later with James Madison were bonds that lasted for almost fifty years and served him well both personally and politically. His star rose steadily and by 1800 he was among the national leaders of the Democratic-Republican party.

Virginia Assembly—1782

Monroe was a member of the Council of State.

Continental Congress—1783–1786

In his three terms, Monroe was an advocate of the rights of western states and territories.

Virginia Ratifying Convention—1788

Monroe opposed adoption of the new federal Constitution.

U.S. Senator from Virginia—1790–1794

A strong supporter of Jefferson, Monroe was vocal in his anti-Federalist positions and a champion for states' rights. He often found himself at odds with Washington and the administration, and their relationship deteriorated.

Minister to France—1794–1796

Monroe negotiated with French officials for the release of Thomas Paine. He was recalled by Washington when he would not actively support Jay's Treaty.

Governor of Virginia—1799–1802

In his single term, Monroe quelled a slave rebellion, raised the standards of education, and continued to be a strong Jeffersonian.

Special Envoy—1803

Jefferson sent Monroe to help Robert R. Livingston negotiate the purchase of New Orleans from the French. The diplomats were somewhat surprised when Napoleon I offered to sell the entire Louisiana Territory, which they quickly negotiated to purchase.

Secretary of State—1811–1817

Although Monroe might have preferred a military command, he remained as Madison's secretary of state throughout the War of 1812. After the British sacked Washington in August 1814 he also became secretary of war. His skillful direction of the war effort in conjunction with his duties as secretary of state allowed him a share of both the military and diplomatic triumphs that ended the war in 1815.

CAMPAIGNS

First Election—1816

The fact that Monroe was Jefferson's clear choice to succeed Madison, coupled with his war record, loyalty, and public popularity, made the selection inevitable. He had some stiff competition from William Crawford, but, in the end, the Republican caucus nominated him by a vote of 65–64. The Federalists, in serious decline resulting from their opposition to the War of 1812, chose a

Maine man named Rufus King to oppose him, but the northern lawyer was never a significant threat and in fact was not even officially nominated until 1816.

Electoral Votes:
Monroe 183
King 34

Second Election—1820

Only Washington before him had enjoyed such wide-based popular support, and Monroe breezed into a second term by an almost unanimous vote. He ran unopposed.

Electoral Votes:
Monroe 231
John Quincy Adams 1

VICE PRESIDENT

Daniel D. Tompkins (1774–1825) New York. Lawyer and New York Supreme Court justice. (Served both terms)

THE CABINET

Secretary of State:
John Quincy Adams (1817–1825)

Secretary of the Treasury:
William H. Crawford (1816–1825)

Secretary of War:
John C. Calhoun (1817–1825)

Attorney General:
Richard Rush (1817)
William Wirt (1817–1825)

Secretary of the Navy:
Benjamin W. Crowninshield (1817–1818)
Smith Thompson (1819–1823)
Samuel L. Southard (1823–1825)

Postmaster General:
Return Meigs (1817–1823)
John McLean (1823–1825)

SIGNIFICANT EVENTS THAT OCCURRED DURING
OFFICE—MARCH 4, 1817–MARCH 3, 1825

First Seminole War—1817–1818

When bands of runaway slaves and Seminole Indians organized themselves into raiding parties in the Florida swamps and forayed into Georgia the government asked Spain to control them. When that proved futile Monroe sent Andrew Jackson in to settle the issue. Jackson exceeded his directive, crushing the Seminole parties and unseating the Spanish governor. Members of Monroe's cabinet felt that Jackson needed to be punished, but no action was taken, and the war ultimately led to the sale of Florida to the United States by Spain.

Rush-Bagot Agreement—1818

Monroe approved the Rush-Bagot Agreement, which demilitarized the boundary with Canada along the Great Lakes.

Convention of 1818

This treaty formalized the boundary between Canada from Minnesota to the Rocky Mountains.

The Adams-Onis Treaty—1819

The Adams-Onis Treaty detailed the purchase of Florida from Spain and marked the U.S. boundary with Spanish territories across the Rocky Mountains to the Pacific Ocean.

Panic of 1819

Suspect banking practices, unchecked land speculation in the West, and a glut of European imports resulted in the first major economic depression, which lasted until 1821.

Missouri Compromise—1820

The Missouri Compromise attempted to strike a balance between slave and free states by allowing Missouri to hold slaves and admitting Maine as a free state. It also set a middle boundary line at latitude 36°30′ in the Louisiana Territory, north of which was free and south of which was slave.

Monroe Doctrine—1823

Fearful that Spain might attempt to regain former territories in Latin America and that Russia might strengthen its position in Alaska, Oregon, and the Northwest, Monroe addressed the Congress and therefore the world. He stated firmly that foreign powers must stay out of the Western Hemisphere. The Doctrine effectively outlined the nature of both U.S. westward expansion and relations with the rest of the world throughout the remainder of the nineteenth century.

CONTRIBUTIONS TO AMERICAN HISTORY WHILE

PRESIDENT

On the surface, the Monroe presidency seemed to be the "Era of Good Feelings," as it was designated by a Boston newspaper in 1817. But issues were boiling beneath that surface that continued to divide the nation—most notably slavery and protectionism—that would lead eventually to the Civil War. What domestic policy may have lacked under the Monroe administration, however, was more than made up for in the brilliance of its efforts abroad to firmly establish the United States as a part of international politics.

SECTION TWO

PERSONAL PROFILE

Sturdy and tall with prominent features and prematurely grey hair, Monroe was an imposing figure who had the gift of setting people at ease with his frankness and honesty. Jefferson said that he valued Monroe for his persistence, patriotism, and devotion to republican principles.

FAMILY BACKGROUND

Ancestors

Monroe, of Scottish heritage, was descended from King Edward III on the side of his paternal grandfather. His great-grandfather, Andrew Monroe, was exiled to Virginia after taking part in the Battle of Preston under Charles I in 1648.

Immediate Family

FATHER: Spence Monroe (d. 1774) A moderately successful planter and carpenter, Spence Monroe was one of many Virginia planters who were actively involved in opposition to British rule.

MOTHER: Elizabeth Jones Monroe (d. 1774)

BROTHERS AND SISTERS: Mrs. Elizabeth Bruckner; Spence Monroe; Andrew Monroe; Joseph Jones Monroe, who became Monroe's private secretary while he was president.

CHILDHOOD AND EARLY YEARS

Orphaned at age sixteen, Monroe inherited his father's house and lands as well as the care of his younger siblings. His wealthy uncle, Joseph Jones, was named his guardian. Jones was a member of the Continental Congress and influenced Monroe's decision to join the Continental Army and introduced him to law and politics.

EDUCATION

As a young man, Monroe pursued a classical education at Campbelltown Academy in Washington Parish. In 1774, at sixteen, he entered the College of William and Mary, but revolution was in the air and Monroe left school in March 1776 to fight in the Continental Army. In 1779, Monroe began to study law under Thomas Jefferson, who was then governor of Virginia. He passed the Virginia bar in 1786.

MILITARY SERVICE

Third Virginia Regiment (1776–1778)

RANK: Rose from lieutenant to major. Later appointed military commander of Virginia by Governor Thomas Jefferson. (1780)

FOUGHT AT: The Battle of New York, Battle of Trenton. Wintered at Valley Forge. His courageous service led Washington to praise him as "a brave, active, and sensible officer."

RELIGION

Episcopalian

FAMILY LIFE

Marriage:

Monroe married Elizabeth Kortright on February 16, 1786, in New York City. He was twenty-seven and she was seventeen. Her father, Laurence Kortright, was a British officer during the Revolutionary War. Described as a beautiful woman, she possessed charm and social graces but was subject to an unidentified illness that forced her out of the public eye and made her an unpopular first lady—especially when compared with her predecessor, Dolley Madison.

Children:

Eliza Monroe (1786–1835), Martha Hester Monroe (1803–1850)

HOBBIES

Horseback riding and hunting.

POST PRESIDENCY

Monroe and his wife, who was very ill, returned to Oak Hill estate in Virginia. The home had been designed by Thomas Jefferson. He served as a member of the board of regents at the University of Virginia. When his wife died in 1830 he found himself unable to remain at Oak Hill and moved to New York City to live with his daughter and son-in-law.

DIED

James Monroe died peacefully in the late afternoon of July 4, 1831, at his home in New York City, from heart failure.

★ ★ ★

CHAPTER SIX

JOHN QUINCY ADAMS

1767–1848

6th President of the United States
"Old Man Eloquent"

☆ ☆ ☆

SECTION ONE

BORN

Adams was born in Braintree (now Quincy), Massachusetts, on July 11, 1767.

TERM SERVED AS PRESIDENT

1825–1829

POLITICAL PARTIES

Federalist; Democratic-Republican; Whig

PUBLIC LIFE BEFORE PRESIDENCY

Adams began to practice law in Boston after being admitted to the bar in 1790. But he did not attract clients and began to focus on writing political commentary in the local newspapers. His attacks on Thomas Paine's *The Rights of Man* drew attention from the Washington administration and soon he received an assignment abroad.

Minister to the Netherlands—1794–1797

Because he was fluent in Dutch, Adams was sent to Holland to monitor payment of the debts on Dutch loans to the United States.

Minister to Prussia—1797–1801

Adams's letters to American officials contained useful insights concerning European affairs, especially Napoleon's rise to power.

U.S. Senator—1803–1808

Although elected as a Federalist, his sympathies lay more with Thomas Jefferson, and he resigned his seat in 1808.

Minister to Russia—1809–1814

President Madison appointed Adams minister to Russia, and he served there for four years, gaining the confidence of Russian officials, who began negotiations leading to the end of the War of 1812.

Treaty of Ghent—1814

Adams signed the Treaty of Ghent on Christmas Eve 1814, ending the War of 1812, although confirmation of the signing did not reach Madison until February 1815 after the American victory at New Orleans.

Minister to Britain—1815–1817

In sometimes difficult postwar atmosphere, Adams began negotiations for the demilitarization of the Western Hemisphere.

Secretary of State—1817–1825

As secretary of state Adams took a leading policy role and was perhaps the most successful secretary of state in American history. He concluded negotiations with England to stabilize the border with Canada, brokered the purchase of Florida, defined the border with Mexico that recognized American claims extending to the Pacific Ocean, and defined the principles of the independence of the Western Hemisphere, which became known as the Monroe Doctrine.

CAMPAIGN

Election—1825

Four men vied for the presidency in 1825: Andrew Jackson, William H. Crawford, Henry Clay, and John Quincy Adams. The campaign was fought on regional and sectional issues which mirrored the backgrounds and personalities of the candidates. Jackson of Tennessee was down-home southern to the core; Crawford of Virginia, a southern gentleman; Clay of Kentucky, self-educated and a man of the people; and Adams of Massachusetts, formal and seemingly aloof.

Jackson won the popular vote by a plurality (42%), but since none of the candidates received a majority of electoral votes, the election was thrown into the House of Representatives as specified in the Twelfth Amendment. The House was instructed to select from the top three, so Clay was out immediately and threw his support to Adams. Clay's support was just enough to allow Adams a victory on the first ballot.

Electoral Votes:
Jackson 99
Adams 84
Crawford 41
Clay 37

VICE PRESIDENT

John C. Calhoun (1782–1850) South Carolina. Lawyer.

THE CABINET

Secretary of State:
  Henry Clay (1825–1829)

Secretary of the Treasury:
  Richard Rush (1825–1829)

Secretary of War:
  James Barbour (1825–1828)
  Peter B. Porter (1828)

Attorney General:
  William Wirt (1825–1829)

Secretary of the Navy:
  Samuel L. Southard (1825–1829)

Postmaster General:
  John McLean (1825–1829)

SIGNIFICANT EVENTS THAT OCCURRED DURING

OFFICE——MARCH 4, 1825–MARCH 3, 1829

The Panama Congress—1826

Southern politicians refused to confirm the delegates in time to attend this conference, conceived to foster good relations between Pan-American countries, fearing it might become a forum to denounce slavery, to which Adams was vehemently opposed.

Tariff of Abominations—1828

In order to protect northern industry, Adams requested a bill imposing a high tariff on imported goods. Andrew Jackson and other southern congressmen were opposed to the bill and added a high tariff on imported raw materials, thinking it would kill the legislation. To the surprise of all the bill was voted into law and, although quickly rolled back, it accelerated tensions between North and South.

CONTRIBUTIONS TO AMERICAN HISTORY WHILE PRESIDENT

Although inaugurated as a president without benefit of the popular vote, he submitted a far-reaching domestic program to a Congress increasingly factionalized and driven by sectional interests. He asked for federally sponsored internal improvements, including: an integrated network of roads and canals, a national university, support for scientific exploration, and an observatory with a full-time astronomer. Congress, however, ignored most of his agenda, approving only an extension of the Cumberland Road into Ohio and the Chesapeake and Ohio canal.

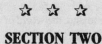

☆　☆　☆

SECTION TWO

PERSONAL PROFILE

John Quincy Adams was average in height and weight, about 5′7″ and weighing around 175 pounds. In his diaries he complained constantly of poor health and indicated that he suffered from bouts of severe depression. A product of his New England upbringing, Adams was at times reserved, rigid, demanding, self-righteous, and often cool and distant. "I never was and never shall be what is commonly termed a popular man . . ." he once wrote to his wife. But, at the same time, his personal integrity, strong will, and high principles made him, for over seventy years of public service, one of the most dominant figures in American politics.

FAMILY BACKGROUND

Ancestors

Adams was descended from King Edward III.

Immediate Family

FATHER: John Adams (1735–1826), the second president of the United States. He was the only president whose son followed him into office.

MOTHER: Abigail Smith Adams (1744–1818) She is the only woman to be the wife of one president and the mother of another.

BROTHERS AND SISTERS: Mrs. Abigail Smith; Charles Adams; Thomas Boylston Adams, secretary to John Quincy Adams during his stations abroad.

CHILDHOOD AND EARLY YEARS

Adams was the quintessential child of the American Revolution. His father, John Adams, a founding father, was at the center of the whirlwind, and it would have been difficult if not impossible not to be caught up in these extraordinary times. When he was eight years old, he watched the Battle of Bunker Hill with his mother, and by age ten he was traveling with his father in Europe, meeting heads of state, and learning, firsthand, the world of politics and diplomacy.

EDUCATION

The Revolution suspended school in Braintree, and Adams's early education came from tutors and family. In 1778, at the age of eleven, he went to Europe as his father's secretary during a diplomatic mission to France. From that point on he pursued his education on the road, studying wherever his father was stationed. When he entered Harvard College in 1785, he was fluent in at least five modern languages as well as Latin and Greek and had traveled throughout Europe.

Adams graduated from Harvard in 1787 and two years later finished his legal apprenticeship.

MILITARY SERVICE

None

RELIGION

Unitarian

FAMILY LIFE

Marriage:

Adams married Louisa Catherine Johnson (1775–1852) on July 26, 1797, at All Hallows Barking parish in London. Daughter of an American businessman, Joshua Johnson, and an Englishwoman, Catherine Nuth Johnson, she grew up in England and France. They met in France when she was four and he, at twelve, was abroad with his father. Their marriage was stable but not happy, and Louisa was reclusive, subject to depression and severe headaches.

Children:

George Washington Adams (1801–1829); John Adams II (1803–1834); Charles Francis Adams (1807–1886)

HOBBIES

Billiards, reading, horticulture, walking, horseback riding, skinny-dipping, the theater, food, and wine.

POST PRESIDENCY

Adams's retirement was to be short-lived; he was elected to the House of Representatives in 1830 and served nine consecutive terms. He used his seat as a "Bully Pulpit" to remind the nation of its responsibility to its citizens. His nickname, "Old Man Eloquent," was well deserved as he spoke relentlessly and passionately against the institution of slavery.

DIED

Adams collapsed at his desk on the floor of Congress of a massive stroke on February 21, 1848, shortly after voting against a resolution thanking the American generals of the Mexican War, which he had opposed. He died on February 23 at the age of eighty.

CHAPTER SEVEN
☆ ☆ ☆

ANDREW JACKSON
1767–1845

7th President of the United States
"Old Hickory"

☆ ☆ ☆

SECTION ONE

BORN

Jackson was born on March 15, 1767, in the Waxhaw area, which straddles the border between North and South Carolina. The exact location is unknown and both states make claims as the birthplace of "Old Hickory."

TERMS SERVED AS PRESIDENT

1829–1833
1833–1837

POLITICAL PARTY

Democrat

PUBLIC LIFE BEFORE PRESIDENCY

Jackson practiced law in Martinsville and Jonesboro, North Carolina, and Nashville, Tennessee, where he was a public prosecutor. He served as a delegate to the Tennessee constitutional convention in 1796 and as congressman from Tennessee (1796–1797).

U.S. Senator—1797–1798

Financial problems forced his resignation and return to Tennessee in less than a year.

Tennessee Superior Court Judge— 1798–1804

Jackson left the bench to pursue business ventures and tend to his plantation, the Hermitage, near Nashville. His political career seemed to be over.

U.S. Senator—1823–1825

In 1822 the Tennessee legislature nominated Jackson for the presidency, then elected him to the Senate. After his bitter defeat by Adams, he resigned from the Senate to prepare for the campaign of 1828 and with the help of powerful supporters developed a "common man" strategy that would ensure his election.

CAMPAIGNS

First Election—1828

The election of 1828 was a grudge match between Jackson, who won the popular vote in 1824 and Adams, who had won the presidency by vote of Congress. Jackson was the first candidate of what was to become the modern Democratic party, and Adams's camp called themselves National Republicans.

Since both candidates favored similar domestic policies, the campaign focused more on personalities than on issues. Once again it was a battle of the common man (Jackson) versus the elite northeastern intellectual (Adams), but the rhetoric from both sides was full of implications of infidelity, extortion, and even murder.

Electoral Votes:
Jackson 178
Adams 83

Second Election—1832

In July, 1832, Jackson stunned the nation's financial community by vetoing a bill renewing the charter of the Bank of the United States, proclaiming that the bank only benefited the rich and powerful at the expense of "the humble members of society—the farmers, merchants, and laborers." His action became the major issue of the campaign.

For the first time, presidential candidates were selected by national nominating conventions. The Anti-Masonic party, formed simply to oppose Jackson, held the first convention, selecting former U.S. Attorney General William Wirt. The National Republicans selected Henry Clay, a fervent bank supporter. Jackson picked Martin Van Buren of New York as his running mate. South Carolina's Nullification party supported John Lloyd.

Clay's supporters spent an unprecedented amount of money to defeat Jackson, but the organization he had built in 1828 easily overcame his opponent's deep pockets.

Electoral Votes:
Jackson 219
Clay 49
Lloyd 14
Wirt 7

VICE PRESIDENTS

John C. Calhoun (1782–1850) South Carolina. Lawyer.
Martin Van Buren (1782–1862) New York. Lawyer.

THE CABINET

Secretary of State:
Martin Van Buren (1829–1831)
Edward Livingston (1831–1833)
Louis McLane (1833–1834)
John Forsyth (1834–1837)

Secretary of the Treasury:
Samuel D. Ingham (1829–1831)
Louis McLane (1831–1833)
William J. Duane (1833)
Roger B. Taney (1833–1834)
Levi Woodbury (1834–1837)

Secretary of War:
John H. Eaton (1829–1831)
Lewis Cass (1831–1836)

Attorney General:
John M. Berrien (1829–1831)
Roger B. Taney (1831–1833)
Benjamin F. Butler (1833–1837)

Postmaster General:
William T. Barry (1829–1835)
Amos Kendall (1835–1837)

Secretary of the Navy:
John Branch (1829–1831)
Levi Woodbury (1831–1834)
Mahlon Dickerson (1834–1837)

SIGNIFICANT EVENTS THAT OCCURRED DURING OFFICE——MARCH 4, 1829—MARCH 3, 1837

Kitchen Cabinet

Jackson, who was unhappy with the members of his cabinet, relied heavily on a group of unofficial advisors. Dubbed the Kitchen Cabinet, the group included journalists Amos Kendall and Francis P. Blair; nephew, Andrew Jackson Donelson; William B. Lewis, a friend; Secretary of State Martin Van Buren, and Secretary of War John H. Eaton.

Internal Improvements

In 1830, for political reasons, Jackson vetoed a bill appropriating funds to construct a road between Maysville and Lexington entirely within Kentucky, the state of his rival Henry Clay. But since much of Jackson's support in the West favored internal improvements at federal expense, his administration actually increased federal spending for road, canal, and harbor construction.

Trail of Tears

Despite two Supreme Court decisions (1831 and 1832) upholding the rights of the Cherokee Nation against the state of Georgia, Jackson refused to intervene on behalf of the Indians. Many tribes were resettled west of the Mississippi while he was in office.

Tariff and Nullification

Southerners, generally opposed to a protective tariff, had supported Jackson, believing that he would significantly lower duties established in 1828. But Jackson approved only modest reductions. In November of 1832, South Carolina declared the federal tariff laws of 1828 and 1832 null and void and prohibited the collection of tariffs in the state after February 1, 1833. Jackson said he would enforce the law but also seek reductions. Other southern states failed to rally to the support of South Carolina, which accepted the new tariff, and the threat of secession was postponed.

The Bank of the United States

In July 1832, President of the Bank of the United States Nicholas Biddle, pushed a bill through Congress granting recharter. Jackson, who considered the bank an elitist and aristocratic institution, quickly vetoed the bill.

The Lone Star State

Although sympathetic to the Texans' rebellion against Mexico, Jackson did not actively support Texan independence. He did not want to split the Democratic party in a battle over the expansion of slavery, nor did he want war with Mexico. Jackson left the issue of annexation to the next president by not recognizing Texas until the day before he left office.

CONTRIBUTIONS TO AMERICAN HISTORY WHILE PRESIDENT

Jackson saw himself as, and was, the president of the common man. A strong supporter of states' rights, he believed that the rights of individuals should, for the most part, supersede the needs of government. Jackson formally instituted a system he called "rotation in office," proclaiming that officeholding was not a right but a privilege. He vowed to protect the public from corruption by removing long-term officeholders at the president's discretion. Although only a minority of federal officials were actually replaced by Jackson, opponents called "rotation in office" the "spoils system" and argued that it was merely a means of rewarding friends for political favors.

ATTEMPTED ASSASSINATION—JANUARY 30, 1835

A housepainter, Richard Lawrence, approached Jackson as he left the Capitol Building and fired a derringer pistol at almost point-blank range. When it misfired, he pulled another, but it misfired as well. Lawrence was found not guilty by reason of insanity and spent the rest of his life in a mental institution.

☆　☆　☆

SECTION TWO

PERSONAL PROFILE

Jackson, at six feet and 140 pounds, was as wiry and tough as the hickory trees from which he got his nickname. Red-haired and blue-eyed, he was a man of the frontier, self-made and determined, with a wild streak and temper that made him a dangerous opponent on the battlefield or on the floor of Congress. He was at ease in any situation and a witty conversationalist.

As he grew older, he was subject to coughing fits, headaches, and other ailments that might have slowed another man, but his innate toughness allowed him to remain a force in the political arena for many years.

Jackson truly believed that government was for the people and that it took a strong and powerful president to ensure that their voice would be heard.

FAMILY BACKGROUND

Ancestors

Jackson was descended from Scotsmen who emigrated to Ireland in the late seventeenth century. The family trades were farming, weaving, and storekeeping.

Immediate Family

FATHER: Andrew Jackson (d. 1767) Jackson's father emigrated from Ireland to start a farm near the North Carolina/South Carolina border. He died in a logging accident before his son was born.

MOTHER: Elizabeth Hutchinson Jackson (d. 1781) Jackson's mother took over the raising of her three sons. She was a fiercely independent, anti-British woman who believed in the Revolution. Elizabeth died of cholera while nursing wounded sailors in Charleston when Andrew was fourteen.

BROTHERS AND SISTERS: Hugh Jackson; Robert Jackson. Both of Jackson's older brothers died in service of the Continental Army during the Revolution.

CHILDHOOD AND EARLY YEARS

Orphaned at fourteen, Jackson grew up to be a young man with a quick temper, always ready for a fight. On his own, he lived for a while with two of his uncles. At fifteen, he received an inheritance from his grandfather in Ireland but spent it quickly on gambling and women.

EDUCATION

Jackson's mother wished him to be a minister, so she did her best to give him an education. He learned to read and was exposed to the classics but was never a committed student. After reading law and gaining admission to the bar in North Carolina in 1787, he moved to Nashville.

MILITARY SERVICE

American Revolution

Jackson joined the Continental Army in 1779, at age thirteen, and served as an orderly and messenger. He and his brother were captured and held by the British in 1781, making him the only president also to be a prisoner of war.

The War of 1812

In 1814, Major General Jackson, of the Tennessee militia, crushed Creek resistance at Horseshoe Bend (March 1814). He was then ordered to command the defense of New Orleans. "Old Hickory" soundly defeated the British invaders on January 8, 1815, bringing to a conclusion a war that had actually ended with the signing of the Treaty of Ghent on December 24, 1814, in Belgium. The Battle of New Orleans made Andrew Jackson a national hero.

First Seminole War—1817–1818

At the request of President Monroe, Jackson led an army into Spanish Florida to pursue raiding parties of Seminole Indians and runaway slaves that had been wreaking havoc in southern Georgia. He apparently exceeded his instructions by overthrowing the Spanish authorities and executing two British subjects, but efforts to censure him failed. His campaign paved the way to the purchase of Spanish Florida in 1819.

Jackson resigned his commission in 1821 and served briefly as a provisional territorial governor of Florida in the same year.

RELIGION

Presbyterian

FAMILY LIFE

Marriage:

In August of 1791, Jackson married Rachel Donelson Robards, daughter of Colonel John Donelson, a surveyor and member of the House of Burgesses, in Natchez, Mississippi. At the time they both believed that she and her first husband had received a legal divorce. They legally remarried on January 17, 1794, in Nashville. But the issue and charges of adultery would follow them for the rest of their lives and was constant political fodder for Jackson's opponents.

In 1806, he challenged a man named Charles Dickinson to a duel over the issue. The men met at Harrison's Mills, Kentucky. Jackson took a bullet so close to his heart that it was impossible to remove and then killed Dickinson.

Rachel's sudden death on December 22, 1828, was attributed in part to the endless scandal surrounding the illegal marriage.

Children:

None

HOBBIES

Breeding and racing horses, fighting birds, practical jokes, reading, and tobacco.

POST PRESIDENCY

Jackson retired to the Hermitage immediately after he left office but remained a force in the Democratic party. His support of James K. Polk, who won the Democratic nomination and subsequently the presidency in 1844, was essential in strengthening Polk's bid for office.

DIED

Jackson's rough-and-tumble life caught up with him in his later years, and he suffered from a variety of painful ailments including tuberculosis and dropsy. He died on June 8, 1845, at the Hermitage outside of Nashville, Tennessee.

CHAPTER EIGHT
☆ ☆ ☆

MARTIN VAN BUREN

1782–1862

8th President of the United States
"The Little Magician"

☆ ☆ ☆

SECTION ONE

BORN

Martin Van Buren was born on December 5, 1782, in Kinderhook, New York.

TERM SERVED AS PRESIDENT

1837–1841

POLITICAL PARTY

Democrat

PUBLIC LIFE BEFORE PRESIDENCY

New York State Senator—1812–1820

A strong opponent of Governor DeWitt Clinton, Van Buren helped develop and led the Albany Regency, a political machine that was a major factor in state politics for many years. Van Buren also served as attorney general of New York (1816–1819).

U.S. Senator—1821–1828

He led Senate opposition to the Adams administration and was instrumental in organizing the political coalition that elected Andrew Jackson president in 1828. His efforts for Jackson ensured the new president's loyalty and Van Buren's place in the administration.

Governor of New York—January–March 1829

Van Buren resigned shortly after his election, when he was appointed Jackson's secretary of state.

Secretary of State—1829–1831

Van Buren became a close companion and advisor to Jackson and a trusted member of the Kitchen Cabinet. To enable Jackson to remove the pro-Calhoun element from his cabinet, Van Buren agreed to resign so that Jackson could call for a general resignation of all other members. As a reward, Jackson appointed Van Buren minister to Great Britain, but the Senate refused to confirm him. Jackson, angered by this blatant display of partisan politics, supported Van Buren for the vice presidency, then chose him as his successor.

CAMPAIGN

Election—1836

Martin Van Buren was Jackson's clear choice to succeed him as president. For partisan political reasons the choice was not a popular one. But the Democratic organization that Van Buren had been so instrumental in developing began the process of convincing Southerners alienated by Jackson's position on tariffs that Van Buren was the right man for the party.

In 1834, a number of Southerners joined together with the Anti-Masons and the national bank supporters to form a new party. They called themselves Whigs, after the English party that was formed to bring down the monarchy. Their strategy was to run three different candidates, each of whom had strong appeal in different areas of the country, split the party, and throw the election into the House of Representatives where they stood a better chance of defeating Van Buren.

The Whigs viciously attacked Van Buren as an aristocratic dandy who had such a difficult time making up his mind that for a time the word "vanburenish" entered the language, meaning "evasive." Van Buren's supporters countered with rallies and parades in the Jackson style, and although the election was close, the strong Democratic machine overcame the disorganized Whig opposition.

Electoral Votes:
Van Buren 170
Harrison 73
White 26
Webster 14
Mangum 11

VICE PRESIDENT

Richard Mentor Johnson (1780–1850) Kentucky. Lawyer.

THE CABINET

Secretary of State:
John Forsyth (1834–1841)

Secretary of the Treasury:
Levi Woodbury (1834–1841)

Secretary of War:
Joel R. Poinsett (1834–1841)

Attorney General:
Benjamin F. Butler (1837–1838)
Felix Grundy (1838–1839)
Henry D. Gilpin (1840–1841)

Postmaster General:
Amos Kendall (1837–1840)
John M. Niles (1840–1841)

Secretary of the Navy:
Mahlon Dickerson (1837–1838)
James K. Paulding (1838–1841)

SIGNIFICANT EVENTS THAT OCCURRED DURING
OFFICE——MARCH 4, 1837–MARCH 3, 1841

Panic of 1837

In May of 1837, banks in New York City stopped converting paper money into silver and gold on demand. The action, brought on by trade imbalances, crop failures, and high tariffs with their roots in the Jackson administration, set off a frenzy that resulted in banks closing throughout the country. Committed to the concept of limited federal intervention in the business of states, he refused to yield to pressure to relieve economic problems with federal funds. The United States fell into a depression that lasted until 1843 and probably cost Van Buren reelection.

Aroostook War—1839

A potential war between the United States and Canada over the definition of the border of northern Maine and New Brunswick was averted when Van Buren sent General Winfield Scott to arrange a truce. The opposing militias gathered on the border agreed to fall back and wait for a diplomatic resolution to the issue, which finally came with the Webster-Ashburton Treaty in 1842.

The Problem of Texas

Jackson had left office with the Texas question still up in the air. When the Republic applied for statehood in 1836 there was a strong negative reaction from Northerners opposed to allowing another slave state into the Union. Van Buren sided with the North, fearing it would inflame that already volatile issue, and Texas did not achieve statehood until 1845.

Second Seminole War

Van Buren inherited Jackson's policy of moving the Seminole Indians from Florida to the western territories. Although the policy was unpopular in the North because Florida would likely become a slave state on admission to the Union, he continued conducting the protracted and costly war until 1842.

CONTRIBUTIONS TO AMERICAN HISTORY WHILE

PRESIDENT

As president, Van Buren sought to hold southern Democrats in the party by adhering to a strict states' rights policy on slavery. He firmly believed that the federal government should not interfere with any internal matter, including slavery, in the states.

SECTION TWO

PERSONAL PROFILE

Van Buren had the square and sturdy build that bespoke his Dutch heritage. At 5´ 6˝ he was short and fair of complexion, with a large nose and penetrating eyes. He wore the fashionable side-whiskers of the period and dressed fashionably. His style of dress often drew criticism from his opponents, who referred to him as a dandy and a fop.

A witty and gifted conversationalist, he had all the charm and skill necessary to develop and nurture the machinery of politics.

FAMILY BACKGROUND

Ancestors

Van Buren's family emigrated as indentured servants from the Gelderland province of the Netherlands in the early sixteenth century and became citizens after working off their indenture.

Immediate Family

FATHER: Abraham Van Buren (1737–1817) A Dutch farmer and tavern owner living in Kinderhook, New York, the elder Van Buren owned slaves. Abraham Van Buren was an American citizen, making Martin the first president who was not formerly a British subject.

MOTHER: Maria Hoes Van Alen Van Buren (1747–1818) After Maria's first husband died, she married Abraham in 1776.

BROTHERS AND SISTERS: Lawrence Van Buren; Abraham Van Buren; Miss Hanna Van Buren; Miss Derike Van Buren. There were two half brothers and one half sister from Maria's first marriage.

CHILDHOOD AND EARLY YEARS

By virtue of helping his father in the family tavern, Van Buren was exposed to the practical side of politics early in life. The tavern was a gathering place for many politicians, including Aaron Burr and Alexander Hamilton. Young Van Buren enjoyed listening to insiders debate the important issues of the day. The draw of politics was so strong that by his eighteenth birthday he had formed strong anti-Federalist views, campaigned for Thomas Jefferson, and served as a delegate to the Republican caucus in Troy, New York.

EDUCATION

Van Buren had a typical lower-class education at the small school in Kinderhook. He began to study law at age fourteen as an apprentice to a local lawyer and was admitted to the bar in New York in 1803. He was twenty-one years old.

MILITARY SERVICE

None

RELIGION

Dutch Reform and sometimes Episcopalian

FAMILY LIFE

Marriage:

Van Buren married Hannah Hoes on February 21, 1807, at the home of Hannah's sister in Catskill, New York. He was twenty-four, she twenty-three. Hannah was a farmer's daughter raised in the traditional Dutch fashion. She died of tuberculosis on February 5, 1819. Van Buren never remarried.

Children:

Abraham Van Buren (1807–1873); John Van Buren (1810–1866); Martin Van Buren (1812–1855); Smith Thompson Van Buren (1817–1876)

HOBBIES

Gambling, fine wines, opera and theater, and fishing.

POST PRESIDENCY

In 1844, three years after leaving office, Van Buren again sought the Democratic nomination. Although he entered the convention with the support of a majority of the delegates, his refusal to support the annexation of Texas cost him the support of the South and, ultimately, the nomination.

He tried again in 1848, under the banner of the Barnburners, a faction of northern Democrats opposed to the extension of slavery, but finished third.

Van Buren retired to his estate in Kinderhook, where he fished and raised potatoes in his garden while keeping track of the ebb and flow of politics.

DIED

Van Buren died of heart failure at Kinderhook on July 24, 1862, after a bout with bronchial asthma.

CHAPTER NINE
☆ ☆ ☆

WILLIAM HENRY HARRISON

1773–1841

9th President of the United States
"Granny"

☆ ☆ ☆

SECTION ONE

BORN

Harrison was born on February 9, 1773, at Berkeley Plantation in Charles City County, Virginia.

TERM SERVED AS PRESIDENT

1841– (Died in office April 4, 1841.)

POLITICAL PARTY

Whig

PUBLIC LIFE BEFORE PRESIDENCY

Secretary for the Northwest Territory— 1798

Harrison served for a year until he was elected to Congress in 1799.

Northwest Territorial Delegate— 1799–1800

As a delegate Harrison could introduce legislation and debate but could not vote. He was active, however, and helped win passage of the Land Act of 1800, which provided credit and support to small frontier settlers.

Governor of the Indiana Territory— 1800–1812

After the Northwest Territory was divided into the Ohio and Indiana Territories, Harrison was appointed governor by Thomas Jefferson.

As governor, Harrison negotiated a series of treaties with Indians that made millions of acres of land available to white settlement. Indian factions led by Shawnee warriors, Tecumseh and his brother, the Shawnee Prophet, created a tribal confederacy to resist further loss of land.

The Battle of Tippicanoe

In November 1811, conflict became open war, and Harrison was directed by the Jefferson administration to lead an army into Indian territory and settle the issue. At Tippicanoe Creek, Harrison was surprised by an early-morning Indian attack, and lost nearly two hundred men in the intense and brutal skirmish. But he rallied his troops and drove off the attackers, burning a nearby Indian village to the ground in revenge. The Battle of Tippicanoe ended the Indian Wars in the Northwest Territory, and the victory earned Harrison the nickname "Old Tip" and made him a national hero. He resigned the governorship to serve in the War of 1812.

Harrison left the army in May 1814 and returned to North Bend, where he reentered the political arena. He served in public offices for the next twenty-five years.

U.S. Representative—1816–1819

Ohio State Senator—1819–1821

U.S. Senator—1825–1828

U.S. Minister to Colombia—1828–1829

Recalled from Colombia by President Jackson, he became clerk of the local court of common pleas in Hamilton County, Ohio. After being defeated by Van Buren in 1836 he continued clerking and was still serving in that capacity when he campaigned for and was elected president in 1840.

CAMPAIGN

Election—1840

In the fragmented election of 1836, Harrison carried seven states and proved his widespread appeal as a military hero without a damaging political history. He was the first candidate to campaign actively for office and, for the next three years, ran not on the issues but on his popularity and war record.

Harrison's Democratic critics attacked him as "General Mum." An opposition newspaper suggested that sixty-seven-year-old "Granny" Harrison would be happy to retire to his "log cabin" if someone gave him a "pension and a barrel of hard cider." In return, the Whigs trumpeted Harrison as the "log cabin and hard cider candidate"—a real man of the people as opposed to the snobbish and aristocratic Van Buren, who was defined as politically corrupt, elitist, and responsible for the Panic of 1837. In the end, the most famous campaign slogan in American political history—"Tippicanoe and Tyler, too" carried the day.

The 1840 campaign was the first to make use of extensive ballyhoo, publicity stunts, and memorabilia designed to sell the image rather than the substance of the candidates. It seemed to work, with a turnout of over a million more voters than in the election of 1836.

Electoral Votes:
Harrison 234
Van Buren 60

VICE PRESIDENT

John Tyler (1790–1862) Virginia. Lawyer. (Succeeded Harrison.)

THE CABINET

Secretary of State:
Daniel Webster*

Secretary of the Treasury:
Thomas Ewing*

Secretary of War:
John Bell*

Attorney General:
John J. Crittenden*

Postmaster General:
Francis Granger*

Secretary of the Navy:
George E. Badger*

*Served in Tyler's administration.

SIGNIFICANT EVENTS THAT OCCURRED DURING
OFFICE——MARCH 4,—APRIL 4, 1841

Harrison was taken ill during his inaugural address and his condition steadily worsened until he died after less than a month in office. He spent his thirty odd days in office avoiding the Whigs, who petitioned him endlessly for jobs that they deemed their right under Jackson's spoils system, which, ironically, he wished to end.

SECTION TWO

PERSONAL PROFILE

Although born into the Virginia aristocracy, Harrison was more a reflection of his life as a frontier soldier. Average in height and weight, he was considered plainspoken, unpretentious, simple, and straightforward, with a ready sense of humor. His experience as an officer and his military bearing gave him a commanding presence.

FAMILY BACKGROUND

Ancestors

Descended from King Henry III (1207–1272) on his father's side. Five generations of Harrisons, dating from 1632, settled and lived in Virginia. They were all named Benjamin. All were politically active, primarily in the House of Burgesses.

Immediate Family

FATHER: Benjamin Harrison V (1726–1791) An active and vocal opponent of British rule, he served in the House of Burgesses, the Continental Congress, as governor of Virginia, and signed the Declaration of Independence. The Harrisons were a family of great wealth, holding large amounts of land and owning several plantations.

MOTHER: Elizabeth Bassett Harrison (1730–1792) She died while Ensign Harrison was stationed at Fort Washington in the Ohio territory.

BROTHERS AND SISTERS: Mrs. Elizabeth Rickman Edmondson; Mrs. Anna Coupland; Benjamin Harrison VI; Mrs. Lucy Randolph Singleton; Carter Basset Harrison; Mrs. Sarah Minge.

CHILDHOOD AND EARLY YEARS

In 1781, when Harrison was eight years old, troops under the command of loyalist Benedict Arnold sacked Berkeley Plantation. The family fled to Richmond and lived there while Harrison's father served as governor.

EDUCATION

Harrison and his brothers and sisters studied with hired tutors at Berkeley. Deciding to become a doctor, Harrison went to Hampden-Sydney College and registered in premedicine. At college he studied the classics, language, mathematics, and military history. In 1791 he journeyed to Philadelphia to continue his medical studies at the University of Pennsylvania Medical School. But, when his father died later that same year, he left university and joined the army.

MILITARY SERVICE

United States Army: First Infantry Regiment (1791–1798)
RANK: Ensign promoted to captain.
Kentucky Militia-Regular U.S. Army (1812–1814)
RANK: Brigadier general promoted to major general.

Northwest Territory

Commissioned as an ensign in the infantry, he recruited a company of fellow soldiers and, in 1793, at age eighteen, became aide-de-camp to General "Mad" Anthony Wayne, joining the battle against Indian forces under the leadership of Tecumseh and the Shawnee Prophet. He was commended for bravery at the Battle of Fallen Timbers in 1794. Harrison rose to the rank of captain before he resigned from the army in 1798.

War of 1812 (Northwest frontier)

In August 1812, Harrison was made commander of all the troops in the Northwest Territories. He recaptured Detroit on September 29, 1813, caught up the retreating British and Indians, and defeated them in the Battle of the Thames River in Ontario on October 5. The battle, in which the legendary Indian leader Tecumseh died, meant the end of fighting in the Northwest and the withdrawal of British forces into Canada. The victory made Harrison a national hero and ripe for politics.

RELIGION

Episcopalian. Harrison was a devout Christian with a strong faith and remained a student and reader of the Bible throughout his entire life.

FAMILY LIFE

Marriage:

Harrison married Anna Tuthill Symmes (1775–1864) at North Bend, Ohio. Anna's father, John Cleves Symmes, owned vast property in southwestern Ohio and disapproved of the whirlwind courtship and "secret" marriage of his daughter to a mere ensign and was not supportive of the marriage until Harrison became a war hero. Anna remained in Ohio while Harrison journeyed to Washington for the inauguration, intending to join him later in the year, but he died before she could arrive. She died on February 25, 1864.

Children:

Elizabeth Bassett Harrison (1796–1846); John Cleves Symmes Harrison (1798–1830); Lucy Singleton Harrison (1800–1826); William Henry Harrison (1802–1838); John Scott Harrison (1806–1840); Mary Symmes Harrison (1809–1842); Carter Bassett Harrison (1811–1839); Anna Tuthill Harrison (1813–1865); James Findlay Harrison (1814–1817).

HOBBIES

Walking, Bible study, and horseback riding.

DIED

Harrison was given to lengthy speeches and his inaugural address was no exception—at over an hour and forty minutes it was the longest in history. The incumbent president spoke in the bitter cold March air without hat, coat, or gloves and, shortly afterward, caught a cold which grew steadily worse. Harrison died on April 4, 1841, of pneumonia.

CHAPTER TEN
☆ ☆ ☆

JOHN TYLER

1790–1862

10th President of the United States
"The Accidental President"

☆ ☆ ☆

SECTION ONE

BORN

Tyler was born on March 29, 1790, at Greenway, the family estate in Charles City County, Virginia.

TERM SERVED AS PRESIDENT

1841–1845 (Succeeded Harrison.)

POLITICAL PARTY

Democrat; Whig

PUBLIC LIFE BEFORE PRESIDENCY

Virginia House of Delegates—1811–1816

When Virginia's U.S. Senators went against instructions and voted for the Bank of the United States, Tyler spearheaded the movement to censure them.

U.S. House of Representatives— 1817–1821

Tyler was a vocal opponent of the economic programs of Clay and Calhoun, voting against tariffs, federal aid for internal improvements, and the successful bill to charter a second Bank of the United States. Tyler also opposed the Missouri Compromise of 1820 as unconstitutional.

Governor of Virginia—1825–1827

After two uneventful years, Tyler was elected to the Senate and resigned.

U.S. Senator—1827–1836

As a senator, Tyler continued to maintain a strict states' rights stance and fundamentalist interpretation of the Constitution, opposing tariffs, internal improvements, and anything else that was at odds with his beliefs. He supported Jackson's presidential bid and many of his policies until Jackson requested troops to collect unpaid tariffs in South Carolina in 1833. In 1834 he censured the president's removal of federal funds from the National Bank. In February 1836 the Virginia legislature instructed Tyler to vote to expunge the Senate censure resolution. He refused, resigned his seat, and ended his Democratic career.

Virginia House of Delegates—1838–1840

Tyler joined the Whig party, was elected to the house, and served as Speaker from January of 1839.

Vice President—March–April 1841

Tyler was chosen in 1836 as the vice presidential candidate on a Whig sectional ticket. In 1839 when the Whig national convention chose William Henry Harrison as their presidential candidate, they picked Tyler to balance the ticket. When Harrison died, Tyler assumed the presidency in April of 1841.

CAMPAIGN

Because he succeeded to office on the death of President Harrison, he did not campaign. He chose not to run for reelection.

VICE PRESIDENT

None

THE CABINET

Secretary of State:
Daniel Webster (1841–1843)
Abel P. Upshur (1843–1844)
John C. Calhoun (1844–1845)

Secretary of the Treasury:
Thomas Ewing (1841)
Walter Forward (1841–1843)

John C. Spencer (1843–1844)
George M. Bibb (1844–1845)

Secretary of War:
John Bell (1841)
John C. Spencer (1841–1843)
James M. Porter (1843–1844)
William Wilkins (1844–1845)

Attorney General:
John J. Crittenden (1841)
Hugh S. Legaré (1841–1843)
John Nelson (1843–1845)

Postmaster General:
Francis Granger (1841)
Charles A. Wickliffe (1841–1845)

Secretary of the Navy:
George E. Badger (1841)
Abel P. Upshur (1841–1843)
David Henshaw (1843–1844)
Thomas W. Gilmer (1844)
John Y. Mason (1844–1845)

SIGNIFICANT EVENTS THAT OCCURRED DURING OFFICE——APRIL 6, 1831–MARCH 3, 1845

Veto of the Third National Bank—1841

When Tyler vetoed two Whig-sponsored bills to create a new national bank, his entire cabinet, except Secretary of State Daniel Webster, resigned in September 1841. The Whigs then expelled him from the party. He ultimately vetoed more legislation than Jackson and Tyler and in 1845 became the first president to have Congress override his veto.

Preemption Act—1841

This act recognized the rights of squatters to occupy public lands and set a price of $1.25 per acre as a first-purchase right for 160 acres of property.

Webster-Ashburton Treaty—1842

Tyler signed the treaty that settled the Maine boundary dispute with Great Britain and called for efforts to suppress the slave trade.

Treaty of Wanghia—1844

This treaty opened the first American trade mission to China.

Annexation of Texas—1845

Tyler vigorously pursued the annexation of the Republic of Texas. Annexation had been a political football since the Jackson administration because of the slavery issue. Tyler, having no political ties after his expulsion from the Whig party, negotiated a treaty, but the Senate rejected it in June 1844. Democrat James K. Polk won the presidency on a pro-annexation platform, and in March 1845, just before leaving office, Tyler signed a joint resolution of Congress annexing the Lone Star State.

CONTRIBUTIONS TO AMERICAN HISTORY WHILE PRESIDENT

After some controversy over the Constitution's somewhat ambiguous terms for succession, Tyler forced a resolution of Congress that affirmed that he had full powers of office and not merely those of an acting president. With this action he strengthened the presidency by protecting the office from power struggles during the process of succession.

☆   ☆   ☆

SECTION TWO

PERSONAL PROFILE

A classic nineteenth-century southern aristocrat, Tyler, tall, thin, and always well dressed, was very much at ease in society, extremely well mannered, and very polite. He appears to have been quite class-conscious and most comfortable with people of his own social circle.

FAMILY BACKGROUND

Ancestors

Tyler's family emigrated from England.

Immediate Family

FATHER: John Tyler (1747–1812) Planter and plantation owner. Tyler, Sr., was a friend of Jefferson's and served as governor of Virginia from 1809–1811 and then as a circuit judge.

MOTHER: Mary Arimistead Tyler (1761–1797) Died when Tyler was a child of seven.

BROTHERS AND SISTERS: Mrs. Anne Contesse Semple; Mrs. Elizabeth Armistead Pryor; Mrs. Martha Jefferson Waggaman; Mrs. Maria Henry Seawell; Dr. Watt Henry Tyler; William Tyler; Mrs. Christiana Booth Curtis.

CHILDHOOD AND EARLY YEARS

After the death of their mother, Tyler and his brothers and sisters were raised by their father at Greenwood. Active in the Revolutionary War, Tyler, Sr., took care to pass along the lessons learned by the young country.

EDUCATION

Tyler was sent to prep school at the College of William and Mary and continued his college education there, graduating in 1807. His favorite subject was economics. He returned to Greenwood, studied law, and was admitted to the Virginia bar in 1809.

MILITARY SERVICE

War of 1812: Charles City Rifles
RANK: Captain
Assigned to defend Richmond, the unit saw no action.

RELIGION

Episcopalian

FAMILY LIFE

Marriage:

On March 29, 1813, the twenty-three-year-old Tyler was married to Letitia Christian (1790–1842) at Cedar Grove in New Kent County, Virginia, she was twenty-two. Daughter of a wealthy planter, Colonel Robert Christian, she met Tyler while he was a law student. They were engaged for five years. John and Letitia were married for twenty-nine years. In 1839 she was paralyzed by a stroke and remained an invalid throughout the remaining years of her life. She died on September 10, 1842, of complications from a second stroke two days before.

On June 26, 1844, Tyler, at fifty-four, remarried. His twenty-four-year-old bride, was named Julia Gardiner (1820–1889), daughter David Gardiner, a wealthy landowner and New York State senator. Julia died of a stroke on July 10, 1889. Her age caused some friction in the Tyler family.

Children:

By Letitia: Mary Tyler (1815–1848); Robert Tyler (1816–1877); John Tyler (1819–1896); Letitia Tyler (1821–1907); Elizabeth Tyler (1823–1850); Anne Contesse Tyler (1825); Alice Tyler (1827–1854); Tazewell Tyler (1830–1874).

By Julia: David Gardiner Tyler (1846–1927); John Alexander Tyler (1848–1883); Julia Gardiner Tyler (1849–1871); Lachlan Tyler (1851–1902); Lyon Gardiner Tyler (1853–1935); Robert Fitzwalter Tyler (1856–1927); Pearl Tyler (1860–1947)

HOBBIES

Music (Tyler was an accomplished violinist), hunting, target shooting, fox hunting, and raising animals.

POST PRESIDENCY

In 1845 Tyler retired to Sherwood Forest, his Virginia plantation, where he began his second family. He served as chancellor of the College of William and Mary and returned to the Democratic party. In February 1861, he was a delegate from Virginia to the Washington peace convention, a last-ditch attempt to avoid civil war. When the Senate rejected his plan, Tyler urged Virginia's immediate secession. He served in the provisional Confederate Congress in 1861, and was elected to the Confederate House of Representatives. He died before he could take office.

DIED

Tyler died on January 18, 1862, at the Exchange Hotel in Richmond, Virginia, where he was about to take his seat in the newly formed Confederate House of Representatives. The cause was listed as complications of bronchitis. He was seventy-one.

CHAPTER ELEVEN
☆ ☆ ☆

JAMES KNOX POLK

1795–1849

11th President of the United States
"Fifty-four Forty or Fight"

☆ ☆ ☆

SECTION ONE

BORN

Polk was born on November 2, 1795, at his family farm in Mecklenburg County, North Carolina.

TERM SERVED AS PRESIDENT

1845–1849

POLITICAL PARTY

Democrat

PUBLIC LIFE BEFORE PRESIDENCY

Tennessee House of Representatives— 1823–1825

Polk, an admirer of Jackson, worked on legislation to protect and benefit the common man.

U.S. House of Representatives— 1825–1839

While serving his seven consecutive terms, Polk was a loyal supporter of Jackson and became a leader of the Democratic party, serving as Speaker of the House from 1835 to 1839.

Governor of Tennessee—1839–1841

As a political move, Polk ran for governor in order to strengthen his position as a presidential or vice presidential candidate. He served only one term and was defeated in 1841 and 1843 by a Whig, James C. Jones. In spite of the defeats, he was still considered a strong vice presidential candidate in 1844 on a ticket to be headed by former president Van Buren. But Van Buren's stance on the annexation issue lost him the support of the South.

Polk, who was on record as backing claims to Texas and Oregon, was the party's choice on the ninth ballot and won not only the presidency but the distinction of becoming the first "dark horse" as well.

CAMPAIGN

Election—1844

The campaign of 1844 was centered on one of the major American political and social issues of the mid-nineteenth century—Manifest Destiny. Many Americans believed that God willed the expansion of the United States from coast to coast. The concept was appealing not only philosophically but economically and politically as well—especially to Southerners who saw the annexation of Texas as the addition of another slave state to the Union.

Martin Van Buren had been the odds-on favorite to win the Democratic nomination, but his opposition to annexation denied him a majority vote in the nominating convention. Polk's clear pro-annexation platform won him the bid.

Polk's Whig opponent, Henry Clay, who had been against annexation, was unable to convince southern voters that he altered his stance. In a tight election, the relatively unknown Polk defeated the more nationally known Clay to become the eleventh president.

Electoral Votes:
Polk 170
Clay 105

VICE PRESIDENT

George Mifflin Dallas (1792–1864) Pennsylvania. Lawyer.

THE CABINET

Secretary of State:
James Buchanan (1845–1849)

Secretary of the Treasury:
Robert J. Walker (1845–1849)

Secretary of War:
William L. Marcy (1845–1849)

Attorney General:
  John Y. Mason (1845–1846)
  Nathan Clifford (1846–1848)
  Isaac Toucey (1848–1849)

Postmaster General:
  Cave Johnson (1845–1849)

Secretary of the Navy:
  George Bancroft (1845–1846)
  John Y. Mason (1846–1849)

SIGNIFICANT EVENTS THAT OCCURRED DURING OFFICE——MARCH 4, 1845–MARCH 3, 1849

Oregon Treaty of 1846—"Fifty-four Forty or Fight"

British or American ownership of the Oregon territory (a vast expanse of land west of the Rocky Mountains between 42° and 54°40′ latitude) was an ongoing and potentially dangerous dispute.

Polk publicly vowed not to compromise, giving birth to one of America's greatest battlecries—"Fifty-four Forty or Fight." But in the back rooms a diplomatic compromise was achieved, and he offered the Senate a British plan to divide the territory along the forty-ninth parallel. The Senate accepted the compromise, but many Westerners felt Polk had betrayed them.

Mexican War—1846–1848

After the annexation of Texas, Mexico had broken off diplomatic relations with the United States. When the Mexican government refused to receive an American emissary to negotiate claims, Polk made plans to ask for a declaration of war. But, in the meantime, a Mexican force was alleged to have crossed the Rio Grande and attacked U.S. soldiers under the command of General Zachary Taylor. In May of 1846, Congress declared war and, after two years of bloody fighting, a peace was negotiated.

The Treaty of Guadalupe Hidalgo, finished in February 1848, recognized the U.S. claim to Texas and provided for the cession of California and New Mexico and bolstered the dream of Manifest Destiny. But the issues of slavery that arose from the Mexican War would lead inevitably to the Civil War.

Walker Tariff—1846

The Walker Tariff instituted a substantial reduction of tariffs which continued to accelerate tension between the North and South.

The Independent Treasury Act—1846

The Independent Treasury Act required that all federal funds be placed in treasuries not tied to private banks to reduce federal expenditures for internal improvements. It also provided that all debt to the government had to be repaid in gold, silver, or federal treasury notes.

CONTRIBUTIONS TO AMERICAN HISTORY WHILE

PRESIDENT

The Polk administration placed more square miles of territory within U.S. boundaries than any other since Jefferson. That he was able to meet his legislative agendas and conduct a war under the burden of illness that plagued him throughout his life is a testament to his personal strength and commitment to the office of president.

SECTION TWO

PERSONAL PROFILE

Average in height, but strongly built, Polk's physical bearing, belied his generally poor health. Although a hard worker, he was subject to exhaustion and pushed himself ruthlessly.

In his teens, Polk discovered a burning desire to be in politics and overcame his introverted nature to achieve his goal. Once he began his career, there was room for little else in his life.

FAMILY BACKGROUND

Ancestors

Descended from John Knox, founder of Scottish Presbyterianism. Family emigrated from Ireland in the early 1720s and settled in Maryland, moving eventually to North Carolina.

Immediate Family

FATHER: Samuel Polk (1772–1827) Planter, surveyor, and land speculator. Samuel Polk moved to Tennessee in 1806, where he eventually owned a great deal of land.

MOTHER: Jane Knox Polk (1776–1852) Religious and determined, she stressed the importance of faith and education.

BROTHERS AND SISTERS: Mrs. Jane Maria Walker; Mrs. Lydia Eliza Caldwell; Franklin Ezekiel Polk; Marshall Tate Polk; John Lee Polk; Mrs. Naomi Tate Harris; Mrs. Ophelia Clarissa Hays; William Hawkins Polk; Samuel Polk.

CHILDHOOD AND EARLY YEARS

When Polk was ten years old the family moved from North Carolina to Tennessee. Because of his poor health, life on the frontier proved difficult, and he suffered so much from gallstones that he underwent a risky but successful operation in Kentucky to remove them.

EDUCATION

He began his formal education in Columbia, Tennessee, and after studying the classics at a private school in Murfreesboro he enrolled at the University of North Carolina, where he excelled in debate and mathematics. While in college he decided on a political career. He began to study law, in which he had little interest, knowing it was the conventional first step to elected office. While he studied law he worked as a clerk of the state senate and was admitted to the North Carolina bar in 1820.

MILITARY SERVICE

Although he never saw active duty, Polk rose to the rank of colonel in a local militia after enlisting in 1820.

RELIGION

Presbyterian

FAMILY LIFE

Marriage:

On January 1, 1824, Polk, twenty-eight, was married to Sarah Childress (1803–1891), age twenty at her home near Murfreesboro, Tennessee. Daughter of Joel Childress, a wealthy plantation owner and merchant, Sarah was well educated, with strong opinions. She was well suited to life with a man dedicated to politics.

Children:

None

HOBBIES

Polk had few other interests in life except politics.

POST PRESIDENCY

From the beginning Polk had made it clear that he intended to retire at the end of a single term. He left office and took an extended tour of the southern states. While on tour he became ill and returned to Polk Place, a home he had recently purchased in Nashville, and began the task of remodeling and renovation. But his condition worsened and he died three months after leaving office.

DIED

Polk died of complications from a series of stomach ailments on June 15, 1849, at Polk Place in Nashville, Tennessee.

CHAPTER TWELVE

☆ ☆ ☆

ZACHARY TAYLOR

1784–1850

12th President of the United States
"Old Rough and Ready"

☆ ☆ ☆

SECTION ONE

BORN

Taylor was born at the home of one of his mother's relatives in Orange County, Virginia, on November 24, 1784, while the family was moving to the Louisville port area of Kentucky.

TERM SERVED AS PRESIDENT

1849–1850 (Died in office.)

POLITICAL PARTY

Whig

PUBLIC LIFE BEFORE PRESIDENCY

Taylor was a career military officer, serving in the U.S. Army until his nomination for president in 1848.

CAMPAIGN

Election—1848

The Whigs attempted to regain the White House by doing what worked for them eight years before—they nominated a war hero. Although a popular figure because of his success during the Mexican War, Taylor was a political outsider with no experience, which was a source of irritation to professional politicians in the party. But the Democratic opposition was in chaos and the holdouts, including Daniel Webster, finally agreed to unite behind him. His Democratic opponent was Michigan Senator Lewis Cass.

Slavery in new states entering the Union was the major issue in American politics. Although Cass himself felt that settlers of new territories should decide the question of slavery by popular vote, the party avoided the issue by leaving it off the platform. Antislavery Democrats formed the new Free Soil party, which split the party and promised "Free Soil, Free Speech, Free Labor, and Free Men." The Free-Soilers nominated Martin Van Buren and Charles Frances Adams (John Quincy's son).

Like Harrison, Taylor campaigned on his war record and not the issues. The campaign attacks from both sides centered on personalities and character. Taylor won, but it was close, and the Free Soil split probably cost Cass the presidency. The election is also notable for being the first one in which all voting took place on the first Tuesday in November.

In 1845, Congress had passed a law requiring that all presidential voting take place on the first Tuesday in November.

Electoral Votes:
Taylor 163
Cass 127

VICE PRESIDENT

Millard Fillmore (1800–1874) New York. Lawyer. (Succeeded Taylor.)

THE CABINET

All members served only the length of Taylor's term of office.

Secretary of State:
John M. Clayton.

Secretary of the Treasury:
William M. Meredith.

Secretary of War:
George W. Crawford.

Attorney General:
Reverdy Johnson.

Postmaster General:
Jacob Collamer.

Secretary of the Navy:
William B. Preston.

Secretary of the Interior:
  Thomas Ewing.

SIGNIFICANT EVENTS THAT OCCURRED DURING
OFFICE——MARCH 5, 1849–JULY 9, 1850

Clayton-Bulwer Treaty—1850

Both Britain and the United States were concerned that a canal built through Central America to connect the Atlantic and Pacific remain neutral. The Clayton-Bulwer Treaty stated this and also put vague restrictions on the colonization of Central America.

Galphin Claim

A Georgia family, the Galphins, was suing for interest on a prior settlement in the amount of almost two hundred thousand dollars. The amount was paid in full. Then it was discovered that Secretary of War George W. Crawford had been representing the family and stood to collect half the settlement. Congress was enraged by the apparent conflict of interest and threatened impeachment. Taylor was about to shuffle his cabinet when he died.

CONTRIBUTIONS TO AMERICAN HISTORY WHILE
PRESIDENT

Although a slave owner himself, Taylor favored both New Mexico and California applying for admission to the Union as free states. He angered Southerners by ignoring the claims of Texas—a slave state—to territory assigned to New Mexico. His threat to veto the Compromise of 1850 was the only issue that postponed southern secession.

SECTION TWO

PERSONAL PROFILE

Of average height and large of frame, Taylor was a product of the frontier—tough, plainspoken, but very warm and friendly. He dressed in so sloppy and careless a fashion that his intelligence, charm, and sophistication often took people, especially his critics, by surprise.

FAMILY BACKGROUND

Ancestors

A descendant of William Brewster, leader of the Pilgrims on the *Mayflower*. Taylor's family settled in Virginia and eventually became large landowners.

Immediate Family

FATHER: Richard Taylor (1744–1829) Successful planter, large landowner, local official and veteran of the Revolution, Taylor moved the family to Kentucky in 1774, when Zachary was eight months old.

MOTHER: Sarah Dabney Strother Taylor (1760–1822) Raised in Virginia, Sarah was refined and received a good education but adapted well to the rough life on the Kentucky frontier, where she raised eight children.

BROTHERS AND SISTERS: Hancock Taylor; William Dabney Strother Taylor; George Taylor; Mrs. Elizabeth Lee Taylor; Joseph Pannill Taylor; Mrs. Sarah Baily Gray; Mrs. Emily Richard Allison.

CHILDHOOD AND EARLY YEARS

In the late eighteenth century, Kentucky was still real frontier country, combining a difficult and dangerous life with the threat of Indian attacks still an everyday reality. The life shaped him as a man of action and prepared him for the military career that occupied the majority of his life.

EDUCATION

Education was almost a secondary pursuit in the wilds of Kentucky. Considered a good student, however, Taylor had very little formal education. Although he read and studied the classics, he was poor with grammar and spelling.

MILITARY SERVICE

U.S. Army (1808–1848)

RANK: Rose from first lieutenant to major general.

An able commander and gifted at organization, he quickly caught the eye of his superiors and was promoted to captain in 1810.

War of 1812

His defense of Fort Harrison against the Indians and his part in the action at Credit Hill eventually won him the rank of major (at captain's pay), and he finally received the full promotion, but at the end of the war he was reduced to captain. He left the army for one year.

Service—1816–1832

In 1816, he reentered the army as a major and for sixteen years served at a variety of frontier outposts and eastern garrisons.

Black Hawk Wars—1832

Promoted to colonel, he commanded the First Infantry Regiment in the Black Hawk War against the Sac and Fox Indians and participated in the Battle of Bad Axe, the final conflict.

Second Seminole War—1837–1840

Taylor defeated the Seminoles in the Battle of Okeechobee. He was promoted, again without pay, to brigadier general and given command of the entire army in Florida. In Florida, he was nicknamed "Old Rough and Ready" by his troops.

Service—1841–1845

After three years as commander at Fort Smith, Arkansas, Taylor was sent to Fort Jesup in Baton Rouge, Louisiana, and then to the Republic of Texas in 1845, where he occupied territory on the bank of the Nueces River.

Mexican War—1846–1848

As hostilities increased, Taylor moved his army south, to the banks of the Rio Grande River, under orders from President Polk in March of 1846. The war began on April 25, after Mexican troops crossed the Rio Grande and allegedly attacked an American detachment.

Shortly after the formal declaration on May 13, Taylor was promoted to major general, received a service medal, and began to gain national recognition. After some initial successes, the remainder of the war did not go well, and he was severely criticized by Polk for his poor judgment and lack of success. However in 1847, at Buena Vista, Taylor overcame a vicious attack by Santa Anna, winning a surprise victory which made him a hero and catapulted him into prominence and the nomination for president.

RELIGION

Episcopalian

FAMILY LIFE

Marriage:

Taylor, twenty-five, was married on June 21, 1810, to twenty-one-year-old, Margaret Mackall Smith (1788–1852) in her sister's home near Louisville. The daughter of Walter Smith, a successful planter in Maryland and veteran of the Revolution, Margaret was raised in wealth and comfort. The soldier's dangerous life and the hardship of raising children at a variety of military bases were difficult and quite different from her childhood. Her health declined after the death of her husband, and she died in August of 1852.

Children:

Ann Mackall Taylor (1811–1875); Sarah Knox Taylor (1814–1835); Octavia P. Taylor (1816–1820); Margaret Smith Taylor (1819–1820); Mary Elizabeth Taylor (1824–1909); Richard Taylor (1826–79)

HOBBIES

Taylor's main diversion was spending time in the company of his friends.

POST PRESIDENCY

Died in office.

DIED

Taylor died on July 9, 1850, at the White House in Washington, D.C., of cholera, probably contracted from eating raw fruit.

CHAPTER THIRTEEN
☆ ☆ ☆

MILLARD FILLMORE

1732–1799

13th President of the United States

☆ ☆ ☆

SECTION ONE

BORN

Fillmore was born in a log cabin near Locke Township, Cayuga County, New York, on January 7, 1800.

TERM SERVED AS PRESIDENT

1850–1853

POLITICAL PARTY

Whig

PUBLIC LIFE BEFORE PRESIDENCY

Fillmore began to practice law in East Aurora, New York, in 1823. He was introduced to politics in the Anti-Masonic movement.

New York State Assemblyman— 1829–1831

Fillmore successfully sponsored a bill to end imprisonment for debt.

U.S. Representative—1833–1835, 1837–1843

Although he went to Congress as an Anti-Mason, he switched to the Whigs because he supported their opposition to Andrew Jackson. He was a strong advocate of internal improvements and of the protective tariff. In 1840 he was named chairman of the powerful House Ways and Means Committee. Although opposed to slavery, his conservative views were at odds with the antislavery movement, and his opposition to the abolitionists probably helped cost him election as governor of New York in 1844.

In 1847 he was elected comptroller of the state of New York and then vice president in 1849.

CAMPAIGN

Election—1849

Fillmore was selected by a group of northern Whigs as a candidate to be Taylor's running mate, and he was nominated on the second ballot. Taylor and Fillmore had never met and weren't formally introduced until after the election. Because there was no real friendship and connection, Fillmore was generally ignored by Taylor and his administration. He felt no particular loyalty to the president as evidenced by his willingness, as president pro tem, to cast the tiebreaking vote in favor of the Compromise of 1850, which Taylor opposed.

He was sworn into office on July 10, 1850, the day after Taylor died.

VICE PRESIDENT

None

THE CABINET

Secretary of State:
John M. Clayton (1850)
Daniel Webster (1850–1852)
Edward Everett (1852–1853)

Secretary of the Treasury:
William M. Meredith (1850)
Thomas Corwin (1850–1853)

Secretary of War:
George W. Crawford (1850)
Charles M. Conrad (1850–1853)

Attorney General:
Reverdy Johnson (1850)
John J. Crittenden (1850–1853)

Postmaster General:
Jacob Collamer (1850)
Nathan K. Hall (1850–1852)
Samuel D. Hubbard (1852–1853)

Secretary of the Navy:
  William B. Preston (1850)
  William A. Graham (1850–1852)
  John P. Kennedy (1852–1853)

Secretary of the Interior:
  Thomas Ewing (1850)
  Thomas M. T. McKennan (1850)
  Alexander H. H. Stuart (1850–1853)

SIGNIFICANT EVENTS THAT OCCURRED DURING OFFICE——JULY 10, 1850–MARCH 3, 1853

The Compromise of 1850

Fillmore signed the five acts of the Compromise of 1850 into law as quickly as Congress passed them. California was admitted as a free state and the states created from Mexican territories were allowed to choose their status by vote. The borders of Texas were defined, the territories of New Mexico and Utah were established, and slavery was abolished in the District of Columbia.

The most controversial act of the Compromise was the Fugitive Slave Law, which forced Northerners to help return escaped slaves to their southern owners. Many free blacks were claimed by white Southerners as runaways. Fillmore's support for the law made him popular in the South, but criticism in the North cost him the support to gain renomination.

The Opening of Japan—1852–1854

Fillmore sent Commodore Matthew C. Perry and four ships of war to Japan to open trade. The mission opened two Japanese ports to foreigners for taking on supplies and purposes of trade.

CONTRIBUTIONS TO AMERICAN HISTORY WHILE PRESIDENT

On taking office, Fillmore began to try to resolve the widening division between North and South by negotiation and compromise. He accepted the resignations of Taylor's troubled cabinet and appointed Daniel Webster secretary of state. He filled the remaining posts with men favorable to compromise. His efforts would put off the Civil War for another decade.

☆ ☆ ☆

SECTION TWO

PERSONAL PROFILE

Fillmore was an imposing figure, well built and handsome. He dressed carefully and in fashion. The hard years of his youth and his experience on the land gave him a practical and determined character. Self-taught and proud of his struggle to better himself, he was a passionate advocate of education and personal growth.

FAMILY BACKGROUND

Ancestors

Of English descent on both sides of his family, Fillmore's grandfather was a veteran of the Revolution.

Immediate Family

FATHER: Nathaniel Fillmore (1771–1863) A poor farmer who moved to New York from Vermont after purchasing land which turned out to have a faulty title. The family was forced off the property and spent the next years moving west in an attempt to find workable land, finally settling near Buffalo, New York.

MOTHER: Phoebe Millard Fillmore (1780–1831) From Pittsfield, Massachusetts, she died while Millard was a New York State legislator.

BROTHERS AND SISTERS: Mrs. Olive Armstrong Johnson; Cyrus Fillmore; Almon Hopkins Fillmore; Calvin Turner Fillmore; Mrs. Julia Harris; Darius Ingrahm Fillmore; Charles DeWitt Fillmore; Phoebe Maria Fillmore.

CHILDHOOD AND EARLY YEARS

The Fillmore family farmed small acreages in the wilderness of New York, and Fillmore grew up used to hard work and difficult conditions. At age fourteen, his father indentured him as an apprentice to a series of clothesmakers.

EDUCATION

While he was working in the mills, Fillmore began to expand his rudimentary education by reading library books and studying a dictionary. When he finally went to school he was a motivated and eager student, eventually marrying his teacher, Abigail Powers. In Montville, New York, he began the study of law in the office of Judge Walter Wood, who helped him pay off his indenture so he could clerk and study full-time. After a disagreement with Wood he left the firm, taught school, and was finally admitted to the bar in 1823.

MILITARY SERVICE

At the beginning of the Civil War, Fillmore, then a former president, organized an honorary home guard called the Union Continentals and took the rank of major. The unit performed ceremonial functions in Buffalo.

RELIGION

Unitarian

FAMILY LIFE

Marriage:

On February 5, 1826, Fillmore, age twenty-six, married Abigail Powers, twenty-seven, at the home of the bride's brother in Moravia, New York. The daughter of a Baptist minister, Abigail became the teacher of the local academy in New Hope, New York, where she taught the nineteen-year-old Fillmore. The shared love of books and knowledge led to a long courtship and a happy marriage. She died of pneumonia on March 30, 1853.

On February 10, 1858, in Albany, New York, Fillmore remarried. The bride was Caroline Carmichael McIntosh, a wealthy widow. They settled in a large home in an affluent section of Buffalo. She died on August 11, 1881.

Children:

Millard Powers Fillmore (1828–1889); Mary Abigail Fillmore (1832–1854)

HOBBIES

Fillmore's passion was his personal library, which he filled with more than four thousand books over the course of his life. He was always active in civic affairs and used his influence to establish organizations and associations to further good works in his community.

POST PRESIDENCY

Fillmore returned to Buffalo after leaving the White House but remained active in politics, running again in 1856 under the banner of the Know-Nothing party and also winning the nomination of the southern Whigs. He ran a poor third.

Although he felt the conflict could have been avoided, Fillmore supported the Union during the Civil War. He was a vocal critic of the Lincoln administration, endorsing George B. McClellan in the election of 1864. After retiring from politics, he remarried and was heavily involved in Buffalo's civic affairs.

DIED

Fillmore, who was healthy for the majority of his life, suffered a succession of strokes that eventually left him unable to take food. He died in Buffalo at age seventy-four on March 8, 1874.

CHAPTER FOURTEEN
☆ ☆ ☆

FRANKLIN PIERCE

1732–1799

14th President of the United States
"The Dark Horse"

SECTION ONE

BORN

Franklin Pierce was born on November 23, 1804, in a log cabin on the Contoocook River at Hillsborough, New Hampshire.

TERM SERVED AS PRESIDENT

1853–1857

POLITICAL PARTY

Democrat

PUBLIC LIFE BEFORE PRESIDENCY

New Hampshire Legislature—1829–1833

Pierce served as Speaker in 1831–1832 and was an active supporter of education. Pierce was a Jackson Democrat and became a leader in state politics.

U.S. House of Representatives—1833–1837

Pierce was an unqualified partisan politician, supporting the Jackson administration without question.

U.S. Senator—1837–1842

As the youngest member of the Senate, Pierce continued to support the Democratic party and campaigned for Van Buren. He was strongly opposed to the abolitionist movement.

In all, Pierce was a popular but undistinguished legislator and resigned his office in 1842 at the insistence of his wife Jane, who hated the Washington social scene. They returned to Concord,

New Hampshire, where Pierce resumed his law practice, campaigned for Polk, and was given an appointment as U.S. district attorney.

After the Mexican War, Pierce returned to New Hampshire and civilian life but remained active in politics, supporting the Compromise of 1850, which gained him recognition in the South and helped make him a compromise candidate for the presidency in 1852.

CAMPAIGN

Election—1852

Both political parties wanted the Compromise of 1850 to work, and neither wanted to risk supporting a seasoned politician whose views might at some time have alienated electors. The Whigs went to the fifty-third ballot before naming General Winfield Scott. The Democrats named Pierce on the forty-ninth ballot. Since both candidates were war heroes of a sort, and both supported the Compromise of 1850, there was really little to debate.

With everyone sidestepping the major issue, the campaign was waged on personality. What eventually swayed the election, however, was the disintegration of the Whig party. Pierce handily won both the popular and electoral vote.

Electoral Votes:
Pierce 254
Scott 42

VICE PRESIDENT

William Rufus De Vane King (1786–1853) North Carolina. Lawyer.

THE CABINET

Secretary of State:
William L. Marcy (1853–1857)

Secretary of the Treasury:
James Guthrie (1853–1857)

Secretary of War:
Jefferson Davis (1853–1857)

Attorney General:
   Caleb Cushing (1853–1857)

Postmaster General:
   James Campbell (1853–1857)

Secretary of the Navy:
   James C. Dobbin (1853–1857)

Secretary of the Interior:
   Robert McClelland (1853–1857)

SIGNIFICANT EVENTS THAT OCCURRED DURING
OFFICE——MARCH 4, 1853–MARCH 3, 1857

Gadsden Purchase—1853

The United States acquired land that is now southern Arizona and New Mexico from Mexico, land necessary to complete a southern railroad route to the Pacific.

Kansas-Nebraska Act—1854

Presented as a bill to help settle the western territories and help in the construction of the proposed transcontinental railroad, it actually overrode the Missouri Compromise because it allowed settlers in Kansas and Nebraska to decide the slavery issue for themselves. The North was opposed to the bill, but Pierce supported it. Nebraska would become a free state, but Kansas was divided on the issue and violent confrontations brought the territory to the brink of civil war. More than two hundred people were killed in the conflict remembered as Bleeding Kansas.

Ostend Manifesto—1854

Manifest Destiny in the extreme, the Ostend Manifesto was an attempt to purchase Cuba from Spain or take it by force if they refused to sell. When the contents of the manifesto were leaked to the press the scandal embarrassed the president and aroused further controversy over the extension of slavery.

CONTRIBUTIONS TO AMERICAN HISTORY WHILE
PRESIDENT

Pierce did his best to defuse the growing tensions between the North and South over the issue of slavery.

☆ ☆ ☆

SECTION TWO

PERSONAL PROFILE

Pierce was a handsome and charming man who made friends easily but suffered from chronic alcoholism and depression. His steady drinking caused stomach problems that troubled him most of his life.

FAMILY BACKGROUND

Ancestors

Pierce's family emigrated from England around 1634 and settled in Massachusetts.

Immediate Family

FATHER: Benjamin Pierce (1757–1839) A farmer until the Revolutionary War, Pierce served from the beginning until 1784, rising to the rank of brigadier general. His first wife died during the war. He spent the rest of his life in politics, serving in the New Hampshire legislature and later as governor. He supported Jefferson and was a Democrat.

MOTHER: Anna Kendrick Pierce (1768–1838) A vibrant and loving woman who suffered from alcoholism and depression, she died while Franklin was a U.S. Senator.

BROTHERS AND SISTERS: Half sister—Mrs. Elizabeth McNeil; Full brothers and sisters—Benjamin Kendrick Pierce; Mrs. Nancy McNeil; John Sullivan Pierce; Mrs. Harriet Jameson; Charles Pierce; Henry Pierce.

CHILDHOOD AND EARLY YEARS

When he was a young man the family moved from their cabin into a large house in town. Pierce grew up listening to stories of his older brother's exploits during the War of 1812. He was an active and popular young man.

EDUCATION

Pierce received his early education in a traditional New England brick schoolhouse. He was an excellent student. In 1820 he enrolled at Bowdoin College in Brunswick, Maine, where he became friends with budding author Nathaniel Hawthorne. After a rough start, he graduated near the top of his class in 1824. Pierce was politically active on campus, debating and supporting various causes. Following college, he studied law and was admitted to the bar in New Hampshire in 1827.

MILITARY SERVICE

Concord Volunteers—U.S. Army: Mexican War (1846–1848)

RANK: Enlisted as a private in the Concord Volunteers. Rose from colonel to brigadier general in the regular army.

When the Mexican War broke out, Pierce volunteered to serve. Commissioned as a colonel and then a brigadier general, Pierce, with his brigade of twenty-five hundred men, was part of General Winfield Scott's campaign against Mexico City in 1847. Injuries and illness prevented him from taking much active part in the fighting.

RELIGION

Episcopalian. By the time he was in college, Pierce was a devout and practicing Christian, but he did not publicly profess his faith until his son was killed in a train accident.

FAMILY LIFE

Marriage:

On November 19, 1834, at the age of twenty-nine, Pierce married Jane Means Appleton, twenty-eight, at the home of the bride's grandparents in Amherst, New Hampshire. She was not a happy woman and suffered from bouts of depression. The couple's marriage was troubled, and she blamed the death of their son on Pierce's political ambitions. She was a reluctant first lady, leaving the duties of hostess to others. She died of tuberculosis on December 2, 1863.

Children:

The Pierces' only child, Benjamin (1841–1853) died when the railway car they were traveling in disconnected from the train and rolled down an embankment. He was the only fatality. The accident happened two months before Pierce took office.

HOBBIES

Fishing.

POST PRESIDENCY

Pierce retired to Concord and a secure but unhappy life. His wife had fallen into severe depression over the death of their son and remained reclusive and distant. An opponent of Lincoln, he spoke out against the coming Civil War and generally supported southern rights to slavery. He was careful, however, to support the Union and speak against secession. But, the slaughter on both sides appalled him and he began to express antiwar sentiments. He was branded a traitor and abandoned by friends and supporters. His tendency to heavy drinking became steadily worse, and his last years were spent in an alcoholic haze.

DIED

Pierce died on October 8, 1869, at his home in Concord, of complications from chronic stomach problems and dropsy (an old term for edema).

CHAPTER FIFTEEN
☆ ☆ ☆

JAMES BUCHANAN

1791–1868

15th President of the United States

☆ ☆ ☆

SECTION ONE

BORN

Buchanan was born on April 23, 1791, in a log cabin at Cove Gap near Mercersburg, Pennsylvania.

TERM SERVED AS PRESIDENT

1857–1861

POLITICAL PARTY

Democrat

PUBLIC LIFE BEFORE PRESIDENCY

Pennsylvania House of Representatives—1814–1816

Buchanan served two terms. He opposed conscription for the War of 1812, arguing that the burden of defending the country fell too much on the poor.

U.S. House of Representatives— 1821–1831

Entering the House as a Federalist, he served three terms and in the process switched his support to Jackson and the Democrats. He retired from Congress in 1831.

U.S. Minister to Russia—1832–1834

Jackson offered Buchanan the Russian ministry, which he accepted against his mother's wishes. He served in St. Petersburg from 1832 to 1834, where he concluded a commercial treaty. Buchanan's mother died during his Russian service.

U.S. Senator—1834–1845

During his three terms, Buchanan continued to support Jackson's policies, campaigned for Martin Van Buren and James K. Polk, and supported the annexation of Texas.

Secretary of State—1845–1849

More an assistant to Polk, who handled his own foreign policy, than a policy maker himself, Buchanan handled the details and refined issues surrounding the annexation of Texas, the Oregon Treaty, and the Mexican War. He retired from office at the end of the Polk administration in 1849.

Minister to Great Britain—1853–1856

Buchanan lost the Democratic nomination in 1852 to Franklin Pierce. He campaigned for the nominee, who named him minister to Great Britain to bolster his political résumé. The fact that he was in London during the controversy over the Kansas-Nebraska Act and the Ostend Manifesto allowed him to stay above the fray and protect his political reputation.

CAMPAIGN

Election—1856

Buchanan won the Democratic nomination on the seventeenth ballot and began his campaign against Republican, John C. Frémont. Almost a throwback to earlier times, the campaign battles were fought by party representatives while the candidates remained above the fray. While there were issues of personality and the usual accusations of corruption and attempts at character assassination, the ever-widening division between the North and South on the matter of slavery was at the center of the campaign.

Electoral Votes:
Buchanan 174
Frémont 114
Fillmore 8

VICE PRESIDENT

John Cabell Breckinridge (1821–1875) Kentucky. Lawyer.

THE CABINET

Secretary of State:
  Lewis Cass (1857–1860)
  Jeremiah S. Black (1860–1861)

Secretary of the Treasury:
  Howell Cobb (1857–1860)
  Philip F. Thomas (1860–1861)
  John A. Dix (1861)

Secretary of War:
  John B. Floyd (1857–1860)
  Joseph Holt (1861)

Attorney General:
  Jeremiah S. Black (1857–1860)
  Edwin M. Stanton (1860–1861)

Postmaster General:
  Aaron V. Brown (1857–1859)
  Joseph Holt (1859–1861)
  Horatio King (1861)

Secretary of the Navy:
  Isaac Toucey (1857–1861)

Secretary of the Interior:
  Jacob Thompson (1857–1861)

SIGNIFICANT EVENTS THAT OCCURRED DURING
OFFICE——MARCH 4, 1857–MARCH 3, 1861

Kansas—Slave or Free

The Dred Scott decision by the Supreme Court stated firmly that Congress had no right to legislate or control slavery in the new western territories because the Constitution clearly placed the decision in the hands of the states. Buchanan, a constitutionalist, shared this view even though he personally was opposed to slavery. He said that Kansas should legally be admitted as a slave state. To his mind, the Supreme Court's ruling put an end to the matter. But Republicans and many northern Democrats refused to accept the Court's opinion.

Buchanan urged Congress to recognize the proslavery Lecompton Constitution, even though it had been drawn up in an illegal convention and had not been submitted for popular vote. Illinois Democrat Stephen A. Douglas forced the issue, and the citizens of Kansas rejected the constitution by popular vote. Kansas became a free state in 1861.

Panic of 1857

The failure of the Ohio Life Insurance Company in August 1857 set off a run on banks around the country and plunged the country into a depression that lasted until the beginning of the Civil War.

Lame Duck

When Lincoln was elected in November of 1860, seven southern states seceded immediately and formed the Confederate States of America.

Buchanan, with five months left in his administration, was caught in the middle, criticized both by secessionists for calling their actions illegal and by supporters of the Union because he was convinced that the president did not have the constitutional authority to interfere in state issues. In his last months in office he struggled to find compromises that would keep the Union intact. But his efforts failed, and finally the issues of states' rights and slavery would force the nation into civil war. Feeling that sectional differences were too great to be resolved, he decided not to run for a second term.

CONTRIBUTIONS TO AMERICAN HISTORY WHILE
PRESIDENT

Buchanan hoped his administration would run an active foreign policy. He sought to extend American influence in the Caribbean, but the coming war and other internal problems continued to take up his time. Ultimately, even the president of the United States would be unable to stop the move to war.

☆ ☆ ☆

SECTION TWO

PERSONAL PROFILE

Buchanan was over six feet tall, well built, and considered handsome. He suffered from an eye disorder that left him nearsighted in one eye and farsighted in the other. The left eye was also set higher in its socket, so he cocked his head and closed one eye or the other depending on what he was looking at. Honest and straightforward, he was considered to be a loyal, generous, and forgiving friend. While in Washington he bought slaves and freed them in Pennsylvania.

FAMILY BACKGROUND

Ancestors

Scotch-Irish. Buchanan's father was first in his family to emigrate to America.

Immediate Family

FATHER: James Buchanan, Sr., (1761–1821) Born in Ireland, Buchanan, Sr., emigrated to America in 1783. He became a successful storekeeper and farmer in Mercersburg, where he served as justice of the peace.

MOTHER: Elizabeth Speer Buchanan (1767–1833) Elizabeth was self-educated and well-read. She insisted that her children go to school, and Buchanan considered her a source of inspiration throughout his life.

BROTHERS AND SISTERS: Mrs. Jane Lane; Mrs. Maria Magaw Yeats Johnson; Mrs. Sara Huston; Mrs. Harriet Henry; William Speer Buchanan; George Washington Buchanan; Edward Young Buchanan.

CHILDHOOD AND EARLY YEARS

Buchanan's early years were spent in the family's log cabin near Cove Gap. When he was five years old, the Buchanans moved into a comfortable house in Mercersburg.

EDUCATION

Buchanan had a basic education at local schools. He studied the classics at Old Stone Academy in Mercersburg and entered Dickinson College in 1807 as a junior. Although a bright student, the record shows that he was a disciplinary problem in college and needed his father's influence to stay in school. After graduation in 1809 he studied law in Lancaster and was admitted to the bar in 1812.

MILITARY SERVICE

War of 1812: Buchanan volunteered for a company of Lancaster dragoons. Under the banner of the First Cavalry, the unit served in Baltimore.

RELIGION

Presbyterian

FAMILY LIFE

Marriage:

Buchanan never married. In 1819 he was engaged to Anne C. Coleman, daughter of a wealthy manufacturer in Lancaster, but she broke off the engagement after an argument later that year and died suddenly on December 9, 1819, perhaps a victim of suicide.

Children:

None

HOBBIES

Cards, reading, and private entertaining.

POST PRESIDENCY

Following the inauguration of Abraham Lincoln Buchanan returned to Lancaster, where he spent his last five years living a very private life at Wheatland, the estate he purchased while secretary of state. He supported the Union and Lincoln's administration during the course of the long war, corresponded with friends, and wrote a book defending his administration. Buchanan served on the board of trustees of Franklin and Marshall College.

DIED

Buchanan died at Wheatland on June 1, 1868, of pneumonia and heart problems.

CHAPTER SIXTEEN
☆ ☆ ☆

ABRAHAM LINCOLN
1809–1865

16th President of the United States
"The Great Emancipator"

☆ ☆ ☆

SECTION ONE

BORN

Lincoln was born on February 12, 1809, in a one-room log cabin near Hodgenville in Hardin County, Kentucky.

TERMS SERVED AS PRESIDENT

1861–1864
1865– (Assassinated while in office April 15, 1865.)

POLITICAL PARTY

Republican

PUBLIC LIFE BEFORE PRESIDENCY

Illinois Legislature—1834–1842

Lincoln made an unsuccessful bid for the Illinois legislature in 1832 and the following year he was appointed postmaster of New Salem, Illinois, by Andrew Jackson, a post he held until 1836. In 1834 he was elected as a Whig to the lower house for the first of four successive terms.

He supported the Second Bank of the United States, the Illinois State Bank, federal funds for internal improvements such as roads, canals, railroads, and harbors, and protective tariffs. Lincoln stated his political opposition to slavery as early as 1837.

While in the legislature, Lincoln studied law and was admitted to the bar in 1836. After the legislature, he practiced law in Springfield with a succession of partners and built a successful practice.

U.S. Representative—1847–1849

Lincoln was against the Mexican War, viewing it as unnecessary and unconstitutional. Like many Whigs, Lincoln felt Polk had exceeded his authority, but he voted provisions to keep troops supplied. He opposed any expansion that would allow slavery into new areas and supported the Wilmot Proviso, which would have barred slavery from any territory gained as a result of the Mexican War.

He returned to Springfield at the end of his term and rejoined his law practice.

Slavery and the Lincoln-Douglas Debates—1858

Lincoln opposed the Kansas-Nebraska Act, which was passed by Congress in 1854. He saw this act, which had been sponsored by Democratic Senator Stephen A. Douglas, as an attempt to alter the intentions of the Constitution in regard to the expansion of slavery.

In 1856 he joined the newly formed Republican party, and two years later he campaigned for the Senate against Douglas. Accepting the senatorial nomination, he predicted that the country would become either all slave or all free, quoting from the Bible—"A house divided against itself cannot stand."

Lincoln challenged his opponent for the Senate seat, Stephen A. Douglas, to a series of seven debates in city centers throughout Illinois—Ottawa, Freeport, Jonesboro, Charleston, Galesburg, Quincy, and Alton—on the issue of slavery. Lincoln brilliantly used the debates to underscore the difference between Republican opposition to slavery as a moral wrong and the moral indifference of the Democrats and their position of popular sovereignty. Lincoln's success in the debates made him a national figure, but the legislature was controlled by the Democrats, and Douglas won the seat.

Lincoln continued his practice of law until the presidential nomination in 1860.

CAMPAIGNS

First Election—1860

The Republican platform focused on the absolute solidarity of the Union, internal reform and improvements, and statehood for Kansas. Pragmatically, they upheld the rights of southern states to hold slaves but wanted an end to slavery in the territories. William H. Seward came into the convention as the probable choice for the Republican nomination, but he ran into difficulties in critical swing states—Pennsylvania, Indiana, Illinois, and New Jersey. Lincoln won as a compromise nominee on the third ballot. Seward campaigned for Lincoln and would become his secretary of state.

Once again the Democratic party split itself over the issue of slavery in the territories. Nominee Stephen A. Douglas attempted to walk a fine line by opposing the Lecompton Constitution in Kansas but supporting the right of the South to hold slaves (Popular Sovereignty). Southern Democrats abandoned the convention in outrage and formed the National Democrats, nominating John C. Breckinridge.

John Bell represented the Constitutional Union party, a mix of remnant Whigs and Know-Nothings.

With the exception of Douglas, none of the candidates campaigned personally, and the split in the Democratic party resulted in Lincoln's election.

Electoral Votes:
Lincoln 150
Breckinridge 72
Bell 39
Douglas 12

Second Election—1864

Republican party leaders opposed the renomination of Lincoln because they felt he could not win the war, but he was still popular with the rank and file, and there was no formal opposition to his run for a second term. Lincoln replaced Vice President Hamlin with Andrew Johnson, a pro-Union Tennessee Democrat. The basis of the Republican platform was a quick end to the war, a constitutional amendment banning slavery, and exacting punishment of rebel leaders.

General George B. McClellan, former general of the Union Army, who had been replaced by Lincoln, easily won the Democratic nomination and campaigned on a platform espousing the Civil War as a failure and calling for a quick negotiated settlement.

McClellan, an extremely popular figure to the war-weary nation, was considered the likely winner. But during the campaign, Union victories proved that the tide was turning and his "stop the war" campaign floundered. Although the popular vote was close, Lincoln won in the electoral college by a landslide.

Electoral Votes:
Lincoln 212
McClellan 21

VICE PRESIDENTS

Hannibal Hamlin (1861–1865) Maine. Lawyer.
Andrew Johnson (1865) Tennessee. Tailor. (Succeeded Lincoln.)

THE CABINET

Secretary of State:
  William H. Seward (1861–1865)

Secretary of the Treasury:
  Salmon P. Chase (1861–1864)
  William P. Fessenden (1864–1865)
  Hugh McCulloch (1865)

Secretary of War:
  Simon Cameron (1861–1862)
  Edwin M. Stanton (1862–1865)

Attorney General:
  Edward Bates (1861–1864)
  James Speed (1864–1865)

Postmaster General:
  Montgomery Blair (1861–1864)
  William Dennison (1864–1865)

Secretary of the Navy:
  Gideon Welles (1861–1865)

Secretary of the Interior:
  Caleb B. Smith (1861–63)
  John P. Usher (1863–65)

SIGNIFICANT EVENTS THAT OCCURRED DURING

OFFICE——MARCH 4, 1861–APRIL 15, 1865

The Civil War—1861–1865

By Lincoln's inauguration, seven states had seceded from the Union, and four more would soon follow. He used his inaugural address as a last attempt to avert the coming war. But the lines were firmly drawn, and on April 12, 1861, South Carolina fired on Fort Sumter, and the Civil War began.

This brutal conflict over slavery and states' rights, which cost the lives of more than a million men, was the dominant issue of the Lincoln administration.

As a commander in chief Lincoln was active, involved, and practical, sometimes at odds with the Constitution and often at odds with his advisors. He believed that once the battle was joined, it must be fought to win—whatever the cost—and he shuffled his military commanders throughout the war until he placed Ulysses S. Grant at the head of the army and found a winning combination.

Lincoln came to believe that as commander in chief in time of war, the president could abolish slavery as a military necessity, something that the Constitution would not allow in peacetime. On January 1, 1863, the Emancipation Proclamation took effect, freeing all slaves in states that had joined the Confederacy. In November of that same year he gave what is perhaps the most eloquent speech in presidential history—the Gettysburg Address, in which he reminded the nation of the ideals set forth in the Declaration of Independence.

While running the government and the war with a firm hand, Lincoln tolerated brutal criticism from the press and politicians and remained, to the end, fair and just in his balancing of the complex issues. All the while, he continued to maintain the nation's confidence that the conflict would eventually end.

The Civil War ended with the surrender of Robert E. Lee at Appomattox on April 9, 1865.

Homestead Act—1862

Granting ownership of 160 acres of public land to squatters after they had worked it for five years, the Homestead Act was the beginning of the settling of the West.

Morrill Act—1862

Each state was given public lands to sell for the purpose of establishing agricultural colleges.

CONTRIBUTIONS TO AMERICAN HISTORY WHILE PRESIDENT

For guiding his country through the Civil War, Abraham Lincoln is considered perhaps the greatest president in American history.

☆ ☆ ☆

SECTION TWO

PERSONAL PROFILE

Gangly and loose-limbed, Lincoln was considered by many and, by himself as well, homely at best, indescribable, and perhaps even ugly. He was the tallest president, at 6´ 4˝, and weighed around 180 pounds. Tough and wiry from his years as a boatman and railsplitter, Lincoln was comfortable with himself and even joked about his appearance and sloppy dress.

Lincoln loved good conversation and especially jokes. His quick wit and sense of humor is evident in personal anecdotes as well as in his speeches and writing.

He did, however, suffer from severe bouts of depression throughout his life which were compounded by the pressures of waging the Civil War. As much as he loved a joke he was, by his own admission, not a happy man.

FAMILY BACKGROUND

Ancestors

Lincoln's family emigrated from England, settled in Massachusetts in the early seventeenth century, and began moving west for cheap land and opportunities.

Immediate Family

FATHER: Thomas Lincoln (1778–1851) Carpenter and farmer. He could not read or write. Lincoln did not speak much of him and did not attend his funeral.

MOTHER: Nancy Hanks Lincoln (1784–1818) Since Nancy and Thomas were not registered as married until 1808, the sixteenth president was likely illegitimate. Lincoln, who wrote of her kindness, was very close to her and helped his father build her coffin when she died. He was nine years old.

BROTHERS AND SISTERS: Mrs. Sarah Grigsby.

CHILDHOOD AND EARLY YEARS

Lincoln's family struggled to make a living, and he grew up essentially in poverty. From childhood he worked the land with his father. When the elder Lincoln remarried, their tiny cabin was home to eight people. His stepmother, Sarah Bush Johnston, was a good woman, and it was because of her that he gained the confidence to learn to read and write. In order to bring in extra income, Lincoln was hired out to neighbors and he gained a reputation as handy with an ax and a good railsplitter. At nineteen, he built a flatboat and began to haul goods back and forth on the Mississippi River. When he was twenty-one the family moved upriver to Coles County, but Lincoln stayed behind with his boat and was on his own.

EDUCATION

With little more than a year of formal education, Lincoln was truly self-taught. Once he learned to read it became the passion of his life and one of his few pleasures.

MILITARY SERVICE

Black Hawk War: Illinois volunteers. (1832)

RANK: Captain. Although he saw no real action, Lincoln was extremely proud of his service.

RELIGION

Although his family were Baptist, Lincoln, who did believe in a Creator, was not formally religious.

FAMILY LIFE

Marriage:

Lincoln, thirty-three, married Mary Todd, twenty-three, on November 4, 1842, at the home of the bride's sister in Springfield, Illinois. She was the daughter of a successful banker, Robert Smith Todd. Abe and Mary came from different worlds. She was raised in affluence and comfort, and he was a river man and farmer who grew up in poverty, but in the beginning they were content. Unfortunately, Mary suffered from mental illness that became more pronounced as she grew older. By the time Lincoln was elected president, she was clearly unstable and his assassination, as well as the death of son Will, pushed her over the edge. She was briefly committed to a mental institution by her son Robert. She died on July 16, 1882.

Children:

Robert Todd Lincoln (1843–1926); Edward Baker Lincoln (1846–1850); William Wallace Lincoln (1850–1862); Thomas Lincoln (1853–1871)

HOBBIES

Lincoln was so consumed with his work that he found little time for diversions. He enjoyed reading, chess, joke-telling, and the theater.

ASSASSINATION

On April 14, 1865, five days after Robert E. Lee's surrender to Grant at Appomattox Court House, the Lincolns attended a performance of *Our American Cousin* at Ford's Theater in Washington. During the third act, John Wilkes Booth, an actor and southern sympathizer, made his way to the presidential box and shot Lincoln once in the head with a .44 caliber, single-shot derringer. Lincoln was moved to the Peterson Boardinghouse across the street, where he died the next morning without regaining consciousness. Booth was captured on April 26, 1865, and died of a gunshot wound. Four co-conspirators were eventually hanged for their part in the plot.

CHAPTER SEVENTEEN
☆ ☆ ☆

ANDREW JOHNSON

1808–1875

17th President of the United States
"He was not a coward."

☆ ☆ ☆

SECTION ONE

BORN

Andrew Johnson was born into poverty on December 29, 1808, in Raleigh, North Carolina.

TERM SERVED AS PRESIDENT

1865–1869 (Succeeded Lincoln.)

POLITICAL PARTY

Democrat

PUBLIC LIFE BEFORE PRESIDENCY

Greeneville Alderman—1829–1830

Johnson, a Jackson Democrat, was suspicious of those in power and used his position as alderman to promote small businessmen and farmers.

Mayor of Greeneville—1831–1833

He broadened his political base and became a voice in the Democratic party in Tennessee.

Tennessee State Representative— 1835–1837, 1839–1841

Johnson served two terms and campaigned for Martin Van Buren.

Tennessee State Senator—1841–1842

As a state senator, Johnson continued to represent free labor and opposed a law that gave more political power to slaveholders than nonslaveholders.

U.S. Representative—1843–1853

In the House, Johnson's belief in central government over states' rights began to separate him from his southern colleagues.

Governor of Tennessee—1853–1857

As governor, he started the public school system, founded a library, and supported advances in agricultural technology.

U.S. Senator—1857–1862

While he defended slavery, Johnson took a strong stand against secession and supported the Union. He argued against Tennessee's secession and became the only southern senator to denounce the Confederacy and not resign his seat. Although his life was threatened, he supported the Lincoln administration and was considered a traitor in the South. The North regarded him as a national hero.

Military Governor of Tennessee— 1862–1864

Union forces occupied significant areas of Tennessee by 1862, and Lincoln appointed Johnson military governor, charging him with restoring order.

Vice President—1864–1865

Seeing the need to balance the ticket with a pro-Union southern Democrat for the 1864 election, Lincoln convinced the party to dump Vice President Hamlin and choose Johnson as his running mate.

CAMPAIGN

None (Succeeded Lincoln.)

VICE PRESIDENT

None

THE CABINET

Secretary of State:
William H. Seward (1865–1869)

Secretary of the Treasury:
  Hugh McCulloch (1865–1869)

Secretary of War:
  Edwin M. Stanton (1865–1868)
  John M. Schofield (1868–1869)

Attorney General:
  James Speed (1865–1866)
  Henry Stanbery (1866–1868)
  William M. Evarts (1868–1869)

Postmaster General:
  William Dennison (1865–1866)
  Alexander W. Randall (1866–1869)

Secretary of the Navy:
  Gideon Welles (1865–1869)

Secretary of the Interior:
  John P. Usher (1865)
  James Harlan (1865–1866)
  Orville Browning (1866–1869)

SIGNIFICANT EVENTS THAT OCCURRED DURING OFFICE——APRIL 15, 1865–MARCH 3, 1869

Thirteenth Amendment—1865

The amendment abolishing slavery was added to the Constitution in 1865.

Seward's Folly—1867

The territory of Alaska was purchased from Russia in 1867 for a little over $7 million. Negotiated by Secretary of State William H. Seward, the purchase was believed by critics to be a huge waste of money.

Impeachment

Johnson exercised his veto power over twenty-nine times in an attempt to soften some of the more punitive measures legislated by northern congressmen. Many were overridden, and tension between Johnson and Congress boiled over into political war. Johnson defied the Tenure of Office Act, passed over his veto in 1867, and fired Secretary of War Edwin M. Stanton. He was impeached by Congress for "high crimes and misdemeanors" and forced into a trial by the Senate. Although the Senate found him not guilty, lacking one vote of the majority necessary for conviction, Johnson's administration was ruined, and he spent the last part of his term without political power.

CONTRIBUTIONS TO AMERICAN HISTORY WHILE PRESIDENT

In his final inaugural address, Lincoln had advocated healing the country's wounds "with malice towards none and charity towards all." After taking office Johnson pledged to follow Lincoln's plan for Reconstruction. He pardoned nearly all Southerners for their parts in the conflict, argued that they should be allowed to reorganize their local and state governments, abolished slavery, and asked Congress to allow representatives who could pass loyalty tests to retake their old seats in the House.

Divisions between the North and South, however, were still too great for real reconciliation. The South had no intention of accepting blacks into society as freemen, and the North, bent on revenge, set up military districts rather than allow local governments to handle affairs during the reorganization and process of readmission to the Union. The bitterness that rose out of the period of Reconstruction would haunt both domestic and political life for generations, giving rise to the Ku Klux Klan in the South and northern "carpetbaggers" who took advantage of the South's powerlessness to conduct its own affairs.

☆ ☆ ☆

SECTION TWO

PERSONAL PROFILE

Johnson had the mark of the common man. He was of dark complexion, square-jawed, and, although congenial, polite, and well-spoken, he projected a sober and determined demeanor. Because of his early poverty, he had genuine sympathy for small laborers and businessmen and fought for their rights throughout his public life. He avoided society and remained loyal to his friends. He loved oratory and was a skilled speaker.

FAMILY BACKGROUND

Ancestors

Johnson was of mixed Anglo-Saxon origin.

Immediate Family

FATHER: Jacob Johnson (1778–1812) A porter at a local inn in Raleigh, North Carolina, Jacob was poor but respected and active in local affairs. He died when Andrew was three years old from complications resulting from his rescue of two drowning men from a frigid pond near Raleigh in December 1811.

MOTHER: Mary McDonough Johnson (1783–1856)

BROTHERS AND SISTERS: William Johnson.

CHILDHOOD AND EARLY YEARS

Johnson grew up in poverty, and he and his brother were indentured to a Raleigh tailor by his mother at age fourteen. After two years he and William ran away. The tailor placed a price on his head, and Johnson was forced into hiding. Later he returned to Raleigh for his mother and stepfather and the family escaped to Greeneville, Tennessee. There Johnson opened a tailor shop.

EDUCATION

Johnson had no formal education and taught himself to read with a collection of the world's greatest oratory given to him while an indentured servant. His wife Eliza, would continue his education, teaching him mathematics and spelling as well as improving his reading skills.

MILITARY SERVICE

Civil War appointment as brigadier general by President Lincoln as military governor of Tennessee. (1862–1865)

RELIGION

No formal religious beliefs.

FAMILY LIFE

Marriage:

Johnson, eighteen, married Eliza McCardle, sixteen, at the home of her parents on May 17, 1827. She was the daughter of a local shoemaker and well educated for the time. Eliza became consumptive in her later years and died on January 15, 1876.

Children:

Martha Johnson (1828–1901); Charles Johnson (1830–1863); Mary Johnson (1832–1883); Robert Johnson (1834–1869); Andrew Johnson (1852–1879).

HOBBIES

Gardening and checkers.

POST PRESIDENCY

When his term ended in 1869, Johnson returned to Greeneville, where he was welcomed as a patriot in the town where he had only recently been branded a traitor. He remained active in politics, rebuilding his Democratic organization. After two unsuccessful runs for office he became the only former president to serve in the Senate, when he was elected in 1875.

DIED

Johnson contracted cholera during the epidemic of 1873 and never fully recovered. Shortly after taking his Senate office, he suffered a series of strokes and died on July 31, 1875.

CHAPTER EIGHTEEN
☆ ☆ ☆

ULYSSES S. GRANT

1822–1885

18th President of the United States
"Old Three Stars"

☆ ☆ ☆

SECTION ONE

BORN

Grant was born in a log cabin in Point Pleasant, Ohio, on April 27, 1822.

TERMS SERVED AS PRESIDENT

1869–1873
1873–1877

POLITICAL PARTY

Republican

PUBLIC LIFE BEFORE PRESIDENCY

With the exception of a seven-year period from 1854 to 1861, when he farmed and sold real estate unsuccessfully near St. Louis and worked in his father's leather goods store in Galena, Illinois, Grant was a professional soldier until he was elected to the presidency.

CAMPAIGNS

First Election—1868

Grant, the general who saved the Union, was nominated on the first ballot at the Chicago Republican convention in 1868. The platform supported suffrage for blacks in the South, called for increased immigration and full rights for naturalized citizens and tough Reconstruction policies in the South.

With Johnson rendered powerless in the aftermath of his impeachment, the Democrats struggled to settle on a candidate and finally nominated Horatio Seymour (1810–1886), a New York politician.

Grant did not campaign and said little beyond a call for peace and harmony. The Republicans were more than content to let his war record speak for itself. The Democrats tried to mount an attack but were damaged in the North by the strongly pro-southern speeches of vice presidential candidate Francis P. Blair, which Seymour did his best to undo. Because of strong southern support, Seymour did well in the popular vote but was swamped in the Electoral College.

Electoral Votes:
Grant 214
Seymour 80

Second Election—1872

There was no doubt that Grant would be renominated at the Philadelphia convention but Colfax, his vice president, could not overcome the aftermath of the Crédit Mobilier scandal, and Senator Henry Wilson of Massachusetts replaced him. The platform called for an end to racial and religious discrimination, took positions on hard currency, furthering women's rights and the expansion of foreign trade.

The Democrats nominated a liberal Republican, Horace Greeley (1811–1872) of New York. Greeley was the founder of the *New York Tribune,* a liberal and influential newspaper.

Once again Grant refused to campaign, leaving others the difficult task of explaining away the series of scandals that shadowed his administration. Greeley, though long opposed to slavery, garnered the very reluctant support of southern voters who saw him as the only alternative to four more years of Radical Reconstruction. Grant's war record and his ability to stay clear of the tainted paintbrush was enough to bring him an even more convincing electoral landslide.

Electoral Votes:
Grant 286
Greeley 0

VICE PRESIDENTS

Schuyler Colfax (1823–1885) New York. Journalist.
Henry Wilson (1812–1875) Massachusetts. Shoe manufacturer. (Died in office.)

THE CABINET

Secretary of State:
  Elihu B. Washburne (1869)
  Hamilton Fish (1869–1877)

Secretary of the Treasury:
  George S. Boutwell (1869–1873)
  William A. Richardson (1873–1874)
  Benjamin H. Bristow (1874–1876)
  Lot M. Morrill (1876–1877)

Secretary of War:
  John A. Rawlins (1869)
  William T. Sherman (1869)
  William W. Belknap (1869–1876)
  Alphonso Taft (1876)
  James D. Cameron (1876–1877)

Attorney General:
  Ebenezer R. Hoar (1869–1870)
  Amos T. Akerman (1870–1871)
  George H. Williams (1871–1875)
  Edwards Pierrepont (1875–1876)
  Alphonso Taft (1876–1877)

Postmaster General:
  John A. J. Creswell (1869–1874)
  James W. Marshall (1874)
  Marshall Jewell (1874–1876)
  James N. Tyner (1876–1877)

Secretary of the Navy:
  Adolph E. Borie (1869)
  George M. Robeson (1869–1877)

Secretary of the Interior:
  Jacob D. Cox, Jr. (1869–1870)
  Columbus Delano (1870–1875)
  Zachariah Chandler (1875–1877

**SIGNIFICANT EVENTS THAT OCCURRED DURING
OFFICE——MARCH 3, 1869–MARCH 3, 1877**

Treaty of Washington—1871

Great Britain agreed to settle in excess of $15 million for damages to American ships by vessels of the Confederate Navy that were constructed in British shipyards.

Radical Reconstruction

Grant remained committed to the policies of Radical Reconstruction and authorized mass arrests of suspected members of the Klu Klux Klan in South Carolina. He signed the Civil Rights Act of 1875 that guaranteed blacks full rights under the law. The law was repealed as unconstitutional in 1883.

Panic of 1873

The Black Friday scandal was the catalyst for a depression that lasted over five years.

Resumption of Specie Act—1875

This law directed the secretary of the treasury to gather and hold gold reserves equal to the amount of greenbacks tendered after January 1, 1879.

**CONTRIBUTIONS TO AMERICAN HISTORY WHILE
PRESIDENT**

Grant's term in office was marked by a series of continuing scandals and, although he was never personally involved in any of the schemes, his slowness to react, and often seeming indifference, allowed graft and corruption to flourish. Black Friday, a gold speculation scheme masterminded by financiers James Fish and Jay Gould, which caused the ruin of many businesses and investors by driving up the price of gold; Crédit Mobilier, in which members of the holding company skimmed large amounts of money from the federally subsidized construction of the Union Pacific Railroad; kickbacks to federal officials on the collection of delinquent taxes; the Whiskey Ring, a scheme to pocket millions of tax dollars on liquor, in which Grant's private secretary was implicated, and The Belknap Bribery Conspiracy, in which Secretary of War W. W.

Belknap was impeached but resigned before conviction of taking kickbacks from traders at Indian posts.

SECTION TWO

PERSONAL PROFILE

A legacy from his hardworking youth, Grant was small, but well built and strong. An unlikely candidate for a soldier's life, he did not hunt and was uncomfortable at the sight of blood. As a young man he was shy and retiring, but extremely disciplined and determined, qualities that would serve him well in his military career. He had a weakness for alcohol that would plague him throughout his life.

FAMILY BACKGROUND

Ancestors

Members of his family emigrated from England to Massachusetts and then to Connecticut in 1630. The military tradition in Grant's family began in the French and Indian War, in which his great-grandfather was killed in action.

Immediate Family

FATHER: Jesse Root Grant (1794–1873), Grant's father, was a wealthy merchant who owned tanneries and leather goods stores throughout Ohio and the surrounding states and territories. He was not afraid to take unpopular positions, speaking out against slavery, and served as a postmaster and as mayor of Bethel, Ohio.

MOTHER: Hanna Simpson Grant (1798–1833) Deeply religious, she was known as quiet and somewhat withdrawn. Grant was much closer to her than his father.

BROTHERS AND SISTERS: Simpson Grant; Clara Grant; Mrs. Virginia P. Corbin; Orvil L. Grant; Mrs. Mary F. Cramer.

CHILDHOOD AND EARLY YEARS

From childhood, Grant much preferred the outdoor life to the gruesome work in his father's tanneries. He became an adept horseman and worked as a farmer which he decided would be his profession.

EDUCATION

A bright and disciplined student, Grant excelled in mathematics. While Grant was studying at the Presbyterian Academy in Ripley, Ohio, his father submitted his name to U.S. Representative Thomas L. Hamer, who gained him admission to West Point.

Grant was not consulted in the decision and was unsure whether or not he was cut out to be a soldier. This uncertainty seemed to be reflected in the fact that he graduated twenty-first in a class of thirty-nine. Because of his skills as a horseman, he requested assignment to a cavalry unit, but his poor record landed him a position as second lieutenant.

MILITARY SERVICE

In 1845 his commission was made permanent, and he served with honor under Zachary Taylor at Monterey and then with General Winfield Scott during the campaign for Mexico City. While he served with honor and was promoted, he privately opposed the war, believing that the United States—and not Mexico—had started the conflict.

Garrison Duty

After the war Grant was assigned to posts around the Great Lakes region, where he was allowed to have his family live with him. However, in 1852, he was sent alone to Humbolt Bay, California. Heavy drinking evidently affected the performance of his duties and he was either forced to resign or quit the army in 1854.

Civil War

After the outbreak of the Civil War, Grant requested a commission but was never contacted by the army. He then organized a company of volunteers in Illinois and his early successes quickly brought him appointment as a brigadier general of volunteers. In 1862, he captured Fort Henry and Fort Donelson on the Tennessee and Cumberland rivers, the first major Union victory, and he was catapulted into national prominence and won a promotion to major general.

After a major defeat at Shiloh, Grant lost support of the commanders and languished until 1863 and his victory in the forty-seven-day siege of Vicksburg.

By this time, his determination and courage had caught Lincoln's eye, and in 1864 he was promoted to lieutenant general and named general in chief of all the federal armies, replacing McClellan. Grant's tactical and administrative skills served him well. Over the next year, Union armies continued to pressure the Confederate Army until General Robert E. Lee was forced to surrender at Appomattox Court House on April 9, 1865. In victory Grant was generous and fair, treating his former enemies with honor and respect.

Interim Secretary of War—1867

After the war, Grant, a national hero, was promoted to full general and served briefly, as interim secretary of war after President Johnson fired Edwin M. Stanton.

RELIGION

Methodist

FAMILY LIFE

Marriage:

On August 22, 1848, Grant, age twenty-six, married Julia Boggs Dent, twenty-two, at her home in St. Louis, Missouri. Daughter of Colonel Fredrick Dent, a wealthy planter and slaveholder, she grew up in luxury and contentment. Both families disapproved of the marriage—Dent senior because of the uncertainty of a soldier's life and Grant senior because his prospective in-law held slaves.

Julia was a very active first lady, entertaining often and involved in Washington social life. She died on December 14, 1902.

Children:

Frederick Dent Grant (1850–1912); Ulysses Simpson Grant (1852–1929); Ellen Wrenshall Grant (1855–1922); Jesse Root Grant (1858–1934)

HOBBIES

Grant had a passion for tobacco, especially cigars. Throughout his life he enjoyed fast horses.

POST PRESIDENCY

After leaving office, Grant took an extended world cruise, traveling for two years. He tried and failed for a third-term nomination. After repeated business failures resulting in bankruptcy he wrote his memoirs, which were extremely successful. Suffering from throat cancer, he hurried to complete the two-volume set before he died and the sales, along with congressional reinstatement of his general's pay, guaranteed his family's financial security.

DIED

Grant died of throat cancer at Mount McGregor, New York, on July 23, 1885.

CHAPTER NINETEEN
☆ ☆ ☆

RUTHERFORD B. HAYES

1822-1893

19th President of the United States

☆ ☆ ☆

SECTION ONE

BORN

Hayes was born on October 4, 1822, in Delaware, Ohio, within weeks of the death of his father.

TERM SERVED AS PRESIDENT

1877–1881

POLITICAL PARTY

Republican

PUBLIC LIFE BEFORE PRESIDENCY

Cincinnati City Solicitor—1858–1861

Appointed to fill the post after the incumbent's death, Hayes was reelected once and then defeated.

U.S. Representative—1865–1867

Elected to Congress in 1864 while still serving in the Civil War, he took his seat in December 1865 and was reelected in 1866. He supported a tough Reconstruction policy for the South.

Governor of Ohio—1868–1872, 1876–1877

He served two terms as governor of Ohio, retired, and then was elected to a third term in 1875. He was nominated for president at the Republican National Convention in 1876.

CAMPAIGN

Election—1876

Maine's James G. Blaine was considered the man likely to emerge from the Cincinnati convention as presidential nominee for the Republican party, but five ballots later, Rutherford B. Hayes took the nomination by only six votes. The Republicans remained committed to tough Reconstruction measures in the South, hard money, and civic reform.

The Democrats put up Samuel J. Tilden, a lawyer and political activist, and promised to replace corruption with honest politics, soften the harsh measures taken against the South, protect the rights of naturalized citizens, and encourage trade with tariff reform.

The battle for the presidency was over corruption and graft. The Grant administration was the focus, and each party attempted to convince the voters that they would not be tainted by past sins in office. Hayes and the Republicans were hurt by the stigma of scandal. As election day approached and passed it seemed that Tilden would be the next president.

But there was confusion in the Electoral College, and a fifteen-man electoral commission was established to sort it out. Unfortunately for Tilden, the commission held eight Republicans and seven Democrats, and after it voted, strictly along party lines, Hayes was elected. The Democrats were incensed, and only Tilden's restraint and good influence stopped open rebellion over the dispute. Hayes also acted in good faith, promising to ease the burden of Reconstruction and end military occupation of the South. He promised not to run for a second term.

Electoral Votes:
Hayes 185
Tilden 184

Electoral Commission:
Hayes 8
Tilden 7

VICE PRESIDENT

William Almon Wheeler (1819–1887) New York. Banker and lawyer.

THE CABINET

Secretary of State:
  William M. Evarts (1877–1881)

Secretary of the Treasury:
  John Sherman (1877–1881)

Secretary of War:
  George W. McCrary (1877–1879)
  Alexander Ramsey (1879–1881)

Attorney General:
  Charles Devens (1877–1881)

Postmaster General:
  David M. Key (1877–1880)
  Horace Maynard (1880–1881)

Secretary of the Navy:
  Richard W. Thompson (1877–1880)
  Nathan Goff, Jr. (1881)

Secretary of the Interior:
  Carl Schurz (1877–1881)

SIGNIFICANT EVENTS THAT OCCURRED DURING
OFFICE——MARCH 4, 1877—MARCH 3, 1881

Following the Compromise of 1877

Hayes kept his promise and withdrew federal troops from southern states, ending Reconstruction and returning them to local government. He placed southern Democrat David M. Key from Tennessee on his cabinet as postmaster general.

Bland-Allison Act—1878

To relieve the pressure on working-class Americans, Congress overrode Hayes's veto and passed a law requiring the government to purchase a fixed amount of silver each month for coinage.

Resumption of Specie Act—1879

Hayes pushed for enforcement of the Resumption of Specie Act from the Grant administration, which required the treasury to hold gold to buy paper currency.

Civil Service Reform

Hayes felt that government jobs should be given on merit, not on patronage, and sought to establish tests and standards of qualification for those seeking them.

Panama Canal

Knowing that the French were attempting to build a canal across Central America connecting the Atlantic and Pacific Oceans, Hayes evoked tenets of the Monroe Doctrine stating that European powers had no business in the Western Hemisphere.

CONTRIBUTIONS TO AMERICAN HISTORY WHILE PRESIDENT

Hayes came to office under the difficult circumstances of the disputed election of 1876. He was a skilled executive who restored the morale of his party and the dignity of his office after the scandals, excesses, and corruption of the Grant presidency.

☆ ☆ ☆

SECTION TWO

PERSONAL PROFILE

A powerful and confident man of average height and weight, Hayes projected a sense of openness and confidence that won him friends and made him a good officer and public servant. Secure in his opinions, he listened to criticism and was willing to change his mind if a convincing argument was made. He was gracious and respectful of his opponents and fair in his decision making.

FAMILY BACKGROUND

Ancestors

Hayes's heritage was a mix of English and Irish. His great-grandfather emigrated from Scotland in the late seventeenth century and settled in Connecticut. Both sides of his family fought in the American Revolution.

Immediate Family

FATHER: Rutherford Hayes (1787–1822) A successful merchant, he left a partnership in Vermont to open his own store in Delaware, Ohio. He died of a fever eleven weeks before the birth of his son.

MOTHER: Sophia Brichard Hayes (1792–1866) She rented land and, with the help of her brother, farmed it to support her family.

BROTHERS AND SISTERS: Mrs. Fanny A. Platt, to whom he was very close.

CHILDHOOD AND EARLY YEARS

Hayes helped on the family farm doing chores. From childhood he dreamed of being a lawyer.

EDUCATION

After a basic education in Ohio and prep school in Connecticut, Hayes enrolled at Kenyon College and graduated in 1842 as valedictorian. He entered Harvard in 1843 to study law and graduated in 1845. Later that year he was admitted to the bar in Ohio.

MILITARY SERVICE

Civil War: 23rd Ohio Volunteers (1861–1865)

RANK: Rose from major to major general.

Hayes fought in many battles during the course of the war, and ended the war serving under General Philip Sheridan in the Shenandoah Valley. He seemed to find a way to be in the center of the conflict and was wounded several times.

RELIGION

Presbyterian

FAMILY LIFE

Marriage:

On December 30, 1852, Hayes, thirty, married Lucy Ware Webb, twenty-one, in Cincinnati, Ohio. Lucy was the daughter of

Dr. James Webb, a prominent physician who had died when she was a child. She was the first wife of a president to graduate from college. She died of a stroke on June 25, 1889.

Children:

Birchard Austin Hayes (1853–1926); James Webb Cook Hayes (1856–1934); Rutherford Platt Hayes (1858–1927); Joseph Thompson Hayes (1861–1863); George Crook Hayes (1864–1866); Fanny Hayes (1867–1950); Scott Russell Hayes (1871–1923); Manning Force Hayes (1873–1874)

HOBBIES

Hunting, fishing, chess, and reading.

POST PRESIDENCY

Hayes retired to his estate, Spiegel Grove, in Fremont, Ohio. For the next thirteen years, he remained involved in public affairs, speaking out for prison reform and education for blacks. He was a trustee of Ohio State University.

DIED

Hayes died on January 17, 1893, at his estate in Fremont, Ohio, of a heart attack he suffered at the train station in Cleveland, Ohio.

CHAPTER TWENTY
☆ ☆ ☆

JAMES ABRAM GARFIELD

1831–1881

20th President of the United States

☆ ☆ ☆

SECTION ONE

BORN

On November 19, 1831, Garfield was born in a log cabin in Orange, Cuyahoga County, Ohio.

TERM SERVED AS PRESIDENT

1881–(Assassinated July 2, 1881. Died September 19, 1881.)

POLITICAL PARTY

Republican

PUBLIC LIFE BEFORE PRESIDENCY

After a stint as a teacher of classical languages at the Eclectic Institute, he served as its president for two years. Deciding that the academic life was not for him, he took up the study of law and was admitted to the Ohio bar in 1860.

Ohio State Senator—1859–1863

Garfield was adamantly against slavery and campaigned for Lincoln in 1860. When the Civil War broke out he joined the army.

U.S. Representative—1863–1880

Still in the army when he was elected to Congress in 1862, Garfield resigned his commission and took his seat in December 1863. During his eight terms he focused on economic and financial issues as a member of both the Appropriations and Ways and Means Committees. He reluctantly voted for Radical Reconstruction only after failing to soften the harsh measures. He lost faith in Lincoln's ability to end the war and did not campaign for his reelection in 1864.

In 1873 he went before a congressional investigating committee to explain his involvement with the Crédit Mobilier company and a small loan that he had taken from officials there.

U.S. Senate—1880

Garfield was elected to the Senate but was elected president and did not accept his seat.

CAMPAIGN

Election—1880

The brief period of nearly equal rights southern blacks had enjoyed during Reconstruction ended abruptly when Hayes removed federal troops from southern states. Civil rights would cease to be a political issue for seventy-five years. Corruption in the civil service became the major issue of the campaign.

Both major parties nominated candidates who supported civil service reform. Because so many leading Republicans had been touched by scandal, it took the party convention thirty-six ballots to settle on a man with an acceptable record, Ohio congressman James Garfield. The Democrats went for a Civil War hero—General Winfield Scott Hancock.

Garfield's assets were his simple country origins, folksy manner, and an astute political mind. Hancock had a distinguished military career highlighted by his major contribution to the critical Union victory at Gettysburg. Since both parties agreed on the major issue, the campaign became one of personalities, with Hancock portrayed as an overrated military man with no understanding of politics and Garfield, who had received a small amount of money from the Crédit Mobilier holding company, which he insisted he had paid back, as just another corrupt politico.

Electoral Votes:
Garfield 214
Hancock 155

VICE PRESIDENT

Chester A. Arthur (1829–1886) New York. Lawyer. (Succeeded Garfield.)

THE CABINET

Secretary of State:
James G. Blaine (March–December, 1881)

Secretary of the Treasury:
William Windom (March–November, 1881)

Secretary of War:
Robert Todd Lincoln (1881–1885)

Attorney General:
I. Wayne MacVeagh (March–October, 1881)

Postmaster General:
Thomas L. James (March–December, 1881)

Secretary of the Navy:
William H. Hunt (1881–1882)

Secretary of the Interior:
Samuel J. Kirkwood (1881–1882)

SIGNIFICANT EVENTS THAT OCCURRED DURING OFFICE——MARCH 4–SEPTEMBER 19, 1881

Port of New York

Garfield was able to appoint his choice, William H. Robertson, as collector of the Port of New York over the wishes of party boss Senator Roscoe Conkling of New York. His victory in this bitter struggle over patronage broke Conkling's stranglehold on political appointments in New York.

Star Route Scandal

Garfield's postmaster general investigated claims that some influential Republicans, and possibly cabinet members, were involved in a kickbacks for mail contracts awarded illegally. The investigation produced no convictions but accelerated the demand for civil service reform.

CONTRIBUTIONS TO AMERICAN HISTORY WHILE PRESIDENT

Garfield's presidency was too short to confirm the kind of leader he had the potential to become, but it is likely that he would have remained a moderate politician and served the country well.

SECTION TWO

PERSONAL PROFILE

Garfield was tall, well built, and considered handsome. He wore a heavy beard in the style of the day and dressed fashionably. He was considered well-read and had an outgoing and friendly nature. Known as a strong and able speaker, he was skillful and convincing in his oratory.

FAMILY BACKGROUND

Ancestors

English and French Huguenot. The Garfields arrived from England in the early sixteenth century and settled in Massachusetts and, later, New York.

Immediate Family

FATHER: Abram Garfield (1799–1833) Farmer and sometime construction supervisor, Abram was a powerful and robust man who died of complications from a cold caught while fighting a forest fire. James was eighteen months old.

MOTHER: Eliza Ballou Garfield (1810–1888) After the death of her husband, Eliza worked hard to support her family. She briefly remarried in 1842, but it was a difficult marriage and she was divorced in 1848. Later in life Garfield talked of how much he disliked his stepfather.

BROTHERS AND SISTERS: Mrs. Mehitabel Trowbridge; Thomas Garfield; Mrs. Mary Larabee.

CHILDHOOD AND EARLY YEARS

Garfield, who learned to read at an early age, grew up in rural poverty and dreamed of making a life as a sailor. At sixteen he went to Cleveland and roamed the docks, looking for a ship that would take him on. Eventually, his cousin put him to work on a canal boat, but Garfield fell overboard several times and returned home to continue his education.

EDUCATION

Garfield was a gifted student and studied hard. He worked to put himself through school from the time he was a child. He enrolled at Williams College in Williamstown, Massachusetts, and excelled, graduating with honors in 1856. After considering the ministry, he chose teaching as a profession.

MILITARY SERVICE

Civil War: 42nd Ohio Volunteer Infantry (1861–1863)
RANK: Rose to major general.
Garfield helped recruit the 42nd Ohio Volunteer Infantry. He fought at Shiloh and Chickamauga, rose to major general. His organizational skills landed him the post of chief of staff of the Army of the Cumberland.

RELIGION

Disciples of Christ

FAMILY LIFE

Marriage:

Garfield, twenty-six, married Lucretia Rudolph, also twenty-six, on November 11, 1858, at her home in Hiram, Ohio. The daughter of Zebulon Rudolph, who was a farmer and cofounder of the Eclectic Institute in Hiram, which Garfield attended from 1851 to 1854, she contracted malaria in 1881 while Garfield was president and became quite ill. Garfield was on his way to visit her when he was assassinated.

Children:

Eliza A. Garfield (1860–1863); Harry A. Garfield (1863–1942); James R. Garfield (1865–1950); Mary Garfield (1867–1947); Irvin M. Garfield (1870–1951); Abram Garfield (1872–1958); Edward Garfield (1874–1876)

HOBBIES

Hunting, fishing, cards, chess, and reading.

ASSASSINATION

On July 2, 1881, Garfield was in the waiting room of Washington's railroad station preparing to visit his wife in New Jersey. Charles J. Guiteau, a man who had supported Garfield and had requested and been refused a government position, shot him twice, in the arm and in the back. Garfield survived for eleven weeks, finally dying in Elberon, New Jersey, on September 19, 1881. Garfield quickly faded from public and historical memory. The fact that a president had been assassinated over a government position led to the passage of the Pendleton Civil Service Act in 1883.

CHAPTER TWENTY-ONE
☆ ☆ ☆

CHESTER ALAN ARTHUR

1829–1886

21st President of the United States
"The Gentleman's Boss"

☆　☆　☆

SECTION ONE

BORN

Arthur was born on October 5, 1829, in his father's parsonage in North Fairfield, Vermont.

TERM SERVED AS PRESIDENT

1881–1885 (Succeeded Garfield.)

POLITICAL PARTY

Republican

PUBLIC LIFE BEFORE PRESIDENCY

Lizzie Jennings Suit—1855

Arthur took on and won a case brought by Jennings, a black woman, against a Brooklyn street car company when she was thrown off a whites-only car. The action led to desegregation of public transportation in New York City.

Senator Roscoe Conkling and the New York Political Machine

Arthur became involved with the powerful and influential Boss Conkling in the mid-1860s and, with his aid, began to move up the Republican political ladder.

Collector of the Port of New York— 1871–1878

Appointed by Grant, Arthur held this important and visible post for six years. When President Hayes created the Jay Commission in 1877 to investigate corruption in the customhouse, they confirmed that kickbacks and influence were rampant in hiring policies. Arthur, not personally implicated in the scandal, was asked to step down but refused, and Hayes suspended him in order to start cleaning house.

Vice President, March–September 1881

After Garfield's nomination, Arthur won the vice presidential nomination on the first ballot as a compromise candidate. Conkling, knowing that Garfield was opposed to the spoils system, urged Arthur to turn down the nomination. But, against the boss's wishes, Arthur accepted.

As president of an evenly divided Senate, Arthur's tiebreaking vote was essential to successful Republican legislation.

He was quickly sworn in on September 20, 1881, in his New York office, after notification that Garfield had died.

CAMPAIGN

None (Succeeded Garfield in office.)

VICE PRESIDENT

None

THE CABINET

Secretary of State:
  James G. Blaine (1881)
  Frederick T. Frelinghuysen (1881–1885)

Secretary of the Treasury:
  William Windom (1881)
  Charles J. Folger (1881–1884)
  Walter Q. Gresham (1884)
  Hugh McCulloch (1884–1885)

Secretary of War:
  Robert Todd Lincoln (1881–1885)

Attorney General:
  I. Wayne MacVeagh (1881)
  Benjamin H. Brewster (1882–1885)

Postmaster General:
  Thomas L. James (1881–1882)
  Timothy O. Howe (1882–1883)
  Walter Q. Gresham (1883–1884)
  Frank Hatton (1884–1885)

Secretary of the Navy:
  William H. Hunt (1881–1882)
  William E. Chandler (1882–1885)

Secretary of the Interior:
  Samuel J. Kirkwood (1881–1882)
  Henry M. Teller (1882–1885)

SIGNIFICANT EVENTS THAT OCCURRED DURING
OFFICE—SEPTEMBER 20, 1881–MARCH 4, 1885

Chinese Exclusion Act—1882

Congress essentially ignored the Treaty of 1880 and placed a ban on Chinese immigration for twenty years. Arthur vetoed the measure but signed a compromise ban of ten years.

River and Harbors Act—1882

Arthur also vetoed this bill, which earmarked almost $20 million of improvements for harbors and rivers. Congress overrode it.

Pendleton Act—1883

The assassination of Garfield by an insane office-seeker prompted Congress to enact legislation to create civil service reform. The Pendleton Act put an end to the spoils system and ensured promotion and assignment on merit as opposed to political influence. The act was the birth of the civil service system. Arthur, who was himself a beneficiary of the spoils system, surprised and angered colleagues, especially ally and party boss Roscoe Conkling, when he supported the measure.

Mongrel Tariff—1883

Intended to examine and fairly reduce a body of stiff tariffs, this bill suffered so many compromises that it was essentially ineffective, and both the protectionist Republicans and free-trade Democrats were unhappy with the result.

CONTRIBUTIONS TO AMERICAN HISTORY WHILE PRESIDENT

Conscientious and hardworking, Arthur had never expected to be president and was quite nervous upon entering office. While his achievements were not inspiring, the office made him presidential, and he showed that an honest man could learn to be a good president.

SECTION TWO

PERSONAL PROFILE

Tall, urbane, sophisticated, well mannered, and outgoing, Arthur wore muttonchop sideburns and dressed in expensive and fashionable clothes. He was a skillful negotiator and administrator.

FAMILY BACKGROUND

Ancestors

Arthur's family emigrated from Ireland, through Quebec, settling in Vermont.

Immediate Family

FATHER: Reverend William Arthur (1796–1875) After teaching school in Canada, Arthur's father became a Baptist minister. He served in at least eleven parishes in the New England area. He was active in the abolition movement and spoke out against slavery.

MOTHER: Malvina Stone Arthur (1802–1869) Born in Vermont, she met William Arthur while living in Quebec.

BROTHERS AND SISTERS: Mrs. Regina Caw; Jane Arthur; Mrs. Almeda Masten; Ann Eliza Arthur; Mrs. Malvina Haynesworth; William Arthur, Jr.; Mrs. Mary McElroy.

CHILDHOOD AND EARLY YEARS

Arthur's father was a temperamental, outspoken, and sometimes argumentative preacher. As a result the family moved from parish to parish during Chester's childhood.

EDUCATION

The Arthur children were taught the basics at home by their father. Arthur later studied at the Lyceum in Schenectady and went on to Union College in 1845, where he became a member of Phi Beta Kappa. He began to study law upon graduation in 1848 and, after a stint at teaching, was admitted to the bar in 1853.

MILITARY SERVICE

Civil War: New York State Militia (1858–1862)

RANK: Rose from brigade judge advocate to quartermaster general of New York.

He received commendations for his organizational skills and ability to keep the troops supplied.

RELIGION

Episcopalian

FAMILY LIFE

Marriage:

Arthur, thirty, married Ellen Lewis Herndon, twenty-two, on October 25, 1859, in New York City. Born in Virginia in 1837, Ellen was secretly sympathetic to the Confederate cause, which created some tension in their otherwise happy marriage. She died of pneumonia on January 10, 1880.

Children:

William Lewis Herndon Arthur (1860–1863); Chester Alan Arthur, Jr., (1864–1937); Ellen Herndon Arthur (1871–1915)

HOBBIES

Hunting, fishing, and society life in Washington and New York

POST PRESIDENCY

The split between Arthur and the Republican party officials over the Pendleton Act made him unlikely to receive the nomination in 1884. He was also suffering from Bright's disease (a malfunction of the kidneys) and knew that he would probably not live out a second term. Arthur retired to his law practice in New York City, where his health continued to decline.

DIED

Arthur, already quite ill, died on November 18, 1886, of a paralyzing stroke.

CHAPTER TWENTY-TWO
☆ ☆ ☆

GROVER CLEVELAND

1837–1908

22nd President of the United States
"Grover the Good"

☆ ☆ ☆

SECTION ONE

BORN

Cleveland was born in Caldwell, New Jersey, on March 18, 1837.

FIRST TERM SERVED AS PRESIDENT

1885–1889
Grover Cleveland is the only president to serve nonconsecutive terms. (See Chapter 24)

POLITICAL PARTY

Democrat

PUBLIC LIFE BEFORE PRESIDENCY

Assistant District Attorney, Erie County, New York—1863–1865

Although Cleveland was drafted for service in the Civil War, he purchased a substitute to serve in his place so he could continue to support his family.

Sheriff of Erie County—1871–1873

By stopping graft and ending corruption in the sheriff's office, Cleveland began to earn his reputation as an honest politician. He served one term and returned to his law practice.

Mayor of Buffalo, New York—1882

Winning office on a strict reform ticket, Cleveland started competitive bidding for every city contract and instituted a merit system for gaining city jobs. His reform movement gained him recognition in the Democratic party and he was nominated for governor, running against the Republican party machine. He won the election and began a battle with Tammany Hall boss John Kelly over patronage and the spoils system.

Governor of New York—1883–1885

Taking office in 1883, he maintained his reputation as an independent, incorruptible, and principled public official. He was persistently at odds with the leadership of New York City's Democratic machine (Tammany Hall) and continued to be an irritant to Kelly's powerful party faction.

He received the nomination for president in 1884.

CAMPAIGN

Election—1884

With the Republican party struggling to overcome the scandals of previous administrations, the Democrats sensed the first real opportunity to win since 1856. Cleveland, who as governor of New York had battled against his own party and the Tammany Hall machine during his time in office, seemed the perfect choice. The *New York World* stated that Cleveland had four major assets: "1. He is an honest man. 2. He is an honest man. 3. He is an honest man. 4. He is an honest man."

Ties to corruption and graft on the railroads had prevented James G. Blaine from winning in 1876 and 1880, but in 1884, with Chester Arthur out of the picture, he finally captured the nomination. A group of reform Republicans or "mugwumps," as they came to be called, left the convention in protest to support Cleveland.

The campaign was fought not on public issues but on personal and moral grounds. Blaine was tied once again by a series of letters to railroad kickbacks, and his campaign seemed doomed. But there was a skeleton in Cleveland's closet as well. Although his political record was unblemished, Cleveland had fathered a son out of wedlock and had paid for the child's support, thereby tacitly admitting paternity.

The race hinged on the vote in New York, which Blaine lost by just one thousand votes, and New York's electoral votes gave Cleveland the presidency.

Electoral Votes:
Cleveland 219
Blaine 182

VICE PRESIDENT

Thomas Andrews Hendricks (1819–1885) Indiana. Lawyer.

Hendricks died of a stroke while in office in 1885. The line of presidential succession was broken for almost two weeks until John Sherman was elected president pro tem of the Senate.

THE CABINET

Secretary of State:
  Thomas F. Bayard (1885–1889)

Secretary of the Treasury:
  Daniel Manning (1885–1887)
  Charles S. Fairchild (1887–1889)

Secretary of War:
  William C. Endicott (1885–1889)

Attorney General:
  Augustus H. Garland (1885–1889)

Postmaster General:
  William F. Vilas (1885–1888)
  Donald M. Dickinson (1888–1889)

Secretary of the Navy:
  William C. Whitney (1885–1889)

Secretary of the Interior:
  Lucius Q. C. Lamar (1885–1888)
  William F. Vilas (1888–1889)

Secretary of Agriculture:
  Norman J. Colman (1889)

SIGNIFICANT EVENTS THAT OCCURRED DURING
OFFICE——MARCH 4, 1885–MARCH 3, 1889

Presidential Succession Act—1886

This law, outlining the order of succession in case of the death or incapacity of the president and vice president, stated that the of fice would be assumed by cabinet members in the order of the creation of their posts.

Testing the Merit System

Cleveland gradually gave in to his party's demands for jobs after almost twenty-five years of Republican rule, giving most of the available patronage to loyal party members. He also vetoed a myriad of pension and relief bills that would have awarded benefits to suspect claims.

Interstate Commerce Act—1887

Cleveland signed the law to regulate railroad freight rates and laid the groundwork for the sweeping reforms of Theodore Roosevelt's administration.

Protection vs. Free Trade—1887

In December 1887, Cleveland urged Congress to reduce tariffs, arguing that lower tariffs would save consumers money, reduce the treasury surplus, and end the need to protect favored industries. The Republicans defended the tariff structure and would turn it into a campaign issue.

Defeat for Reelection—1888

Although Cleveland won the popular vote for reelection, he lost to Republican Benjamin Harrison in the Electoral College.

☆   ☆   ☆

SECTION TWO

PERSONAL PROFILE

At more than 250 pounds, Grover Cleveland was the heaviest president to hold office until William Howard Taft. He loved German food and drank large quantities of beer. He took his public responsibilities seriously and was a stern and demanding taskmaster, but he enjoyed himself thoroughly in his off hours, playing cards and joking with friends.

FAMILY BACKGROUND

Ancestors

Cleveland's ancestors emigrated from England and Ireland in the mid-sixteenth century and settled in Massachusetts and Connecticut. He was descended from a long line of ministers.

Immediate Family

FATHER: The Reverend Richard Falley Cleveland (1804–1853) A Presbyterian minister, Cleveland's father served in a number of churches in the New England and Mid-Atlantic states. He died when his son was sixteen.

MOTHER: Ann Neal Cleveland (1806–1882) Daughter of a wealthy publisher in Baltimore, she died in Holland Patent, New York, while Cleveland was mayor of Buffalo.

BROTHERS AND SISTERS: Mrs. Anna N. Hastings; William N. Cleveland; Mrs. Mary A. Hoyt; Richard Cecil Cleveland; Mrs. Margaret L. Bacon; Lewis Cleveland; Mrs. Susan S. Yoemans; Rose E. Cleveland.

CHILDHOOD AND EARLY YEARS

The Cleveland family moved several times during the course of Grover's childhood. He was a hardworking, good-natured young man.

EDUCATION

After studying with his mother and father, Cleveland attended an academy in Fayetteville, New York, and the Clinton Liberal Institute in New York. He had intended to go to college, but his father's death made it necessary for him to go to work. He taught briefly at the Institute for the Blind in New York City and decided to move on to Ohio. An uncle in Buffalo persuaded him to stay there and gave him a job editing a book on raising cattle. The uncle also arranged for Cleveland to study law in a local office, and he was admitted to the New York State bar in 1859.

MILITARY SERVICE

None. Cleveland was drafted for service in the Civil War but purchased a substitute to serve in his place.

RELIGION

Presbyterian

FAMILY LIFE

Marriage:

When Cleveland was forty-nine years old, he married Francis Folsom, twenty-one, on June 2, 1886. She was the daughter of Oscar Folsom, a prominent Buffalo lawyer and close friend of the Clevelands. When Folsom was killed in an accident in 1875, Cleveland was appointed administrator of his estate and he supervised Francis's education and upbringing. Shortly after she graduated from college he proposed, and they held the ceremony a year later in the White House, making Cleveland the only president to be married there.

Children:

Ruth Cleveland (1891–1904); Esther Cleveland (1893–1980); Marion Cleveland (1895–1977); Richard Folsom Cleveland (1897–1974); Francis Grover Cleveland (1903–)

PREMARITAL AFFAIR

While in Buffalo, Cleveland had an affair with a widow named Maria Halpin. She gave birth to a son in 1874 and named Cleveland the father. He accepted the responsibility of raising the child until it was adopted by a family in New York. The affair would become a national scandal when it was disclosed during Cleveland's presidential campaign in 1884.

HOBBIES

Fishing, hunting, poker, cigars, beer, and German food.

POST FIRST TERM

After his defeat by Harrison in 1888, Cleveland practiced law in New York City. During Harrison's administration, he consolidated his position as a conservative Democrat and prepared for the election of 1892.

CHAPTER TWENTY-THREE
☆ ☆ ☆

BENJAMIN HARRISON

1833–1901

23rd President of the United States
"He wore his grandfather's hat"

☆ ☆ ☆

SECTION ONE

BORN

Harrison was born on August 20, 1833, at the home of William Henry Harrison in North Bend, Ohio.

TERM SERVED AS PRESIDENT

1889–1893

POLITICAL PARTY

Republican

PUBLIC LIFE BEFORE PRESIDENCY

Harrison practiced law in Indianapolis where he had moved after passing the bar in 1854. Harrison joined the Republican party and was elected city attorney in 1857. In 1860 and again in 1864, after serving in the Civil War, he was a supreme court reporter for Indiana.

U.S. Senator—1881–1887

After losing a close race for the governor in 1876, he returned to his law practice but remained active in politics and was elected to the Senate in 1880. Harrison chaired the Senate Committee on the Territories, advocated a moderate protective tariff, spoke for civil service reform, and endorsed railroad regulation.

He was defeated for reelection in 1887 and became the Republican nominee for president in 1888.

CAMPAIGN

Election—1888

Cleveland's call to vitalize the economy by lowering tariffs in 1887 gave the Republicans a cause to rally the huge northern industrialists. The party found a strong supporter of high tariffs in Benjamin Harrison and nominated him on the eighth ballot.

Although Cleveland had been an effective and popular president, the tariff issue dominated the campaign, and the Republicans, with almost unlimited resources, played to the fears of working people, arguing that Cleveland's reelection would stagnate the economy and cause huge layoffs.

While the Republicans stumped actively, the Democrats waged an old-fashioned, almost gentlemanly campaign. Cleveland's sense of decorum and morality would not allow him to step into the trenches.

Cleveland actually won the popular vote but lost in the Electoral College when his enemies at Tammany Hall cut deals to cost him northern support—including that of his home state—and Harrison became president.

Electoral Votes:
Harrison 233
Cleveland 168

VICE PRESIDENT

Levi Parsons Morton (1824–1920) New York. Banker.

THE CABINET

Secretary of State:
James G. Blaine (1889–1892)
John W. Foster (1892–1893)

Secretary of the Treasury:
William Windom (1889–1891)
Charles Foster (1891–1893)

Secretary of War:
Redfield Proctor (1889–1891)
Stephen B. Elkins (1891–1893)

Attorney General:
William H. H. Miller (1889–1893)

Postmaster General:
John Wanamaker (1889–1893)

Secretary of the Navy:
  Benjamin F. Tracy (1889–1893)

Secretary of the Interior:
  John W. Noble (1889–1893)

Secretary of Agriculture:
  Jeremiah M. Rusk (1889–1893)

SIGNIFICANT EVENTS THAT OCCURRED DURING OFFICE—MARCH 4, 1889–MARCH 3, 1893

Dependent and Disability Pensions Act—1890

Harrison signed the law that extended benefits to dependents of veterans and to veterans disabled from nonmilitary causes.

Sherman Antitrust Act—1890

This act began attempts by the federal government to stop corporate monopolies from restraining trade.

Sherman Silver Purchase Act—1890

Once signed into law, the treasury was required to purchase over four million ounces of silver each month in notes redeemable in gold or silver. Holders of the notes turned them in for gold and put a serious drain on the federal reserve.

McKinley Tariff Act—1890

The steepest tariff ever introduced actually drove consumer prices up and produced an antiprotectionist backlash among voters, causing huge Republican losses in the 1890 elections and undermining Harrison's bid for reelection.

Foreign Policy

Although Harrison had little success with domestic issues, his foreign policy efforts fared somewhat better. He pursued reciprocal trade agreements with Latin America, arranged the first Pan-American conference in 1889, and fought for the expansion of the navy and merchant marine.

CONTRIBUTIONS TO AMERICAN HISTORY WHILE
PRESIDENT

Talented, hardworking, and aggressive as an administrator, Harrison was unable to understand how politics worked, and the mistakes he made on domestic issues overshadowed his modest successes in foreign policy.

SECTION TWO

PERSONAL PROFILE

Short and stocky, with a full beard and piercing eyes, Harrison was known as a cold and distant man uncomfortable dealing with people on any level other than business. He was respected rather than liked and considered a very fair and decent, although aloof, public figure.

FAMILY BACKGROUND

Ancestors

Benjamin Harrison was grandson to William Henry Harrison, the ninth president of the United States.

Immediate Family

FATHER: John Scott Harrison (1804–1878) A successful farmer, John Scott was the son of William Henry Harrison. He served in the House of Representatives from 1853–1857.

MOTHER: Elizabeth Irwin Harrison (1810–1850) Pennsylvania born, she was John Scott's second wife. She died in childbirth.

BROTHERS AND SISTERS: Half sisters—Mrs. Elizabeth Eaton; Mrs. Sarah Devin. Full brothers and sisters—Colonel Irwin Harrison; Mrs. Mary Jane Morris; Carter Harrison; Mrs. Anna Morris; John Scott Harrison, Jr.

CHILDHOOD AND EARLY YEARS

Harrison grew up on a large farm his grandfather had given to the family. Even though he was raised in a modest state of privilege, Harrison worked the land and was responsible for his share of the chores. He loved the outdoor life and when he wasn't working spent time in the woods and fields, walking, fishing, or hunting.

EDUCATION

Harrison began his education at home and continued through a progression of schools. He was considered an extremely bright student with a particular interest in history. He entered Miami University in Oxford, Ohio, in 1850 and graduated high in his class in 1852. Although interested in the ministry, he decided on law and studied at a firm in Cincinnati. He passed the bar in 1854.

MILITARY SERVICE

Civil War: 70th Indiana Infantry (1862–1865)
RANK: Rose from second lieutenant to brigadier general.
Although he didn't like the military, he was a good soldier and was part of Sherman's march through Georgia. He received the promotion to brigadier for his part in the taking of Atlanta in 1864.

RELIGION

Presbyterian

FAMILY LIFE

First Marriage:

At age twenty, Harrison married Caroline Lavinia Scott, twenty-one, on October 20, 1853, at her home in Oxford, Ohio. She was the daughter of Presbyterian minister John W. Scott. Harrison met her while attending Farmer's college and began courting her while at Miami University. She died of tuberculosis on October 25, 1892, while Harrison was running for a second term.

Children:

Russell Benjamin Harrison (1854–1936); Mary Scott Harrison (1858–1930)

Second Marriage:

Harrison, sixty-two, married Mary Scott Lord Dimmick, age thirty-one, on April 6, 1896, at St. Thomas Episcopal Church in New

York City. Mary was an assistant to Harrison's first wife in the White House. Although they did not announce their engagement until 1895, Harrison's children by his first wife were angry and did not attend the wedding. She died on January 5, 1948.

Children:

Elizabeth Harrison (1897–1955)

HOBBIES

Billiards, hunting, and walking.

POST PRESIDENCY

Harrison returned to Indianapolis and resumed his law practice. He campaign for William McKinley in 1896. As a lawyer he represented Venezuela in the country's action against Britain over the border with British Guiana in 1899. He wrote *This Country of Ours* (1897) and *Views of an Ex-President* (1901).

DIED

Harrison died on March 13, 1901, at his home in Indianapolis, of complications from pneumonia.

CHAPTER TWENTY-FOUR
☆ ☆ ☆

GROVER CLEVELAND

1837–1908

24th President of the United States

☆ ☆ ☆

SECTION ONE

SECOND TERM SERVED AS PRESIDENT

1893–1897

POLITICAL PARTY

Democrat

CAMPAIGN

Second Election—1892

Cleveland, who had stiff opposition from his enemies at Tammany Hall as well as western and southern Democrats who were angered by his stand against free coinage of silver, won the nomination on the first ballot but by a very narrow margin. The incumbent Harrison, although not popular in his party, had an easier time, but neither candidate inspired a great deal of confidence or affection. Dissatisfied farmers from the South and West met in Omaha to form the Populist party and nominated James B. Weaver, an Iowa lawyer. The major issues were protectionism, tariffs, and hard money.

Harrison's wife was very ill and died two weeks before the election. Out of respect, the candidates ceased active campaigning. But events outside the campaign would have an unpredicted effect on the election.

The steelworkers union was engaged in a bitter labor negotiation with Carnegie Steel Corporation. Manager Henry Fricke, under orders from Carnegie, tried to break the union by offering a Contract containing a contract cutting wages by 22 percent. The union rejected the agreement, Fricke locked them out, hired scabs, and the National Guard had to be brought in to stop the war at the picket lines.

The Republican position that tariffs protecting American industries guaranteed higher wages for workers was shattered, and many voters defected to the Democrats. Cleveland was elected, becoming the first and only president to win a second term after being defeated.

Electoral Votes:
Cleveland 277
Harrison 145
Weaver 22

VICE PRESIDENT

Adlai Ewing Stevenson (1835–1914) Illinois. Lawyer.

THE CABINET

Secretary of State:
Walter Q. Gresham (1893–1895)
Richard Olney (1895–1897)

Secretary of the Treasury:
John G. Carlisle (1893–1897)

Secretary of War:
Daniel S. Lamont (1893–1897)

Attorney General:
Richard Olney (1893–1895)
Judson Harmon (1895–1897)

Postmaster General:
Wilson S. Bissell (1893–1895)
William L. Wilson (1895–1897)

Secretary of the Navy:
Hilary A. Herbert (1893–1897)

Secretary of the Interior:
Hoke Smith (1893–1896)
David R. Francis (1896–1897)

Secretary of Agriculture:
Julius Sterling Morton (1893–1897)

SIGNIFICANT EVENTS THAT OCCURRED DURING OFFICE——MARCH 4, 1893–MARCH 3, 1897

Hawaii and Cuba

Cleveland refused to consider a treaty for annexation of the Hawaiian Islands because of American influence in the overthrow of the existing government. He also refused to aid Cuban insurgents in their battle against the Spanish colonial government.

Repeal of the Silver Purchase Act—1893

The Silver Purchase Act allowed for redemption of silver notes for gold. As a result, the treasury's gold reserves were rapidly dwindling, and a national depression, which would become known as the Panic of 1893, was beginning. Cleveland called a special session of Congress and pushed for repeal of the Sherman Silver Purchase Act. While he succeeded in repealing the act, he exhausted his own political capital.

Wilson-Gorman Act—1894

The struggle to reduce tariffs continued to be a political football, with compromises added that diminished or negated the original intentions. As was the usual case, the Wilson-Gorman Act reduced some tariffs but levied higher duties on other goods. Cleveland allowed the bill to become law without his signature.

Pullman Strike—1894

In a dispute over reduced wages, railway workers struck against the Pullman Car Company. When work stoppages turned violent, Cleveland followed the advice of his attorney general and sent federal troops to Illinois to take control on the grounds that interruption of railroad traffic obstructed the mail. Cleveland's action was extremely unpopular.

Venezuela and British Guiana

In 1895 Cleveland issued a warning that the United States would not tolerate British intervention in the dispute over the boundary between Venezuela and British Guiana. Ex-president Harrison represented Venezuela in the lawsuit that followed.

CONTRIBUTIONS TO AMERICAN HISTORY WHILE PRESIDENT

Cleveland was never comfortable with the give-and-take of political compromise. He was personally courageous and moral, but was often unable to recognize these qualities in the opposition and had a difficult time seeing other points of view.

While many of Cleveland's actions, especially his vetoes, may seem negative and self-serving, he left the office of president stronger and gave future chief executives more power to fight with Congress on matters of national interest.

POST PRESIDENCY

After leaving the presidency, Cleveland moved to an estate he named Westland near Princeton, New Jersey. He removed himself from mainstream Democratic ideology and refused to support nominee William Jennings Bryan. He resumed his legal practice and served as a member of Princeton University's board of trustees.

DIED

In his later years, Cleveland suffered from acute rheumatism. He died at his home in Princeton on June 24, 1908, of complications from chronic stomach problems.

(For personal background on Grover Cleveland see Chapter 22.)

CHAPTER TWENTY-FIVE
☆　☆　☆

WILLIAM MCKINLEY

1843–1901

25th President of the United States

SECTION ONE

BORN

McKinley was born on January 29, 1843, in the family home in Niles, Ohio.

TERMS SERVED AS PRESIDENT

1897–1901
March–September 1901 (Assassinated while in office at beginning of his second term.)

POLITICAL PARTY

Republican

PUBLIC LIFE BEFORE PRESIDENCY

After his admission to the bar he opened a law office in Canton, Ohio, in 1867 and was elected prosecuting attorney of Stark County from 1869 to 1871. After being defeated for reelection, he returned to private practice.

U.S. Representative—1877–1883, 1885–1891

McKinley served in Congress for almost fourteen years. He supported protective tariffs. He served as chairman of the Ways and Means Committee and created the McKinley Tariff of 1890.

Governor of Ohio—1892–1896

In his two terms as governor, McKinley was effective and popular. He continued to gain national recognition and left office as a front-runner for the 1896 Republican presidential nomination.

CAMPAIGNS

First Election—1896

When the Republican convention met in St. Louis, the country was in the third year of a severe economic depression brought on by the Panic of 1893. Hard times were worst for the farmers and small businessmen, who had big mortgages and other debt payments to make. McKinley was the almost uncontested choice, supporting the gold standard and winning the nomination on the first ballot by a huge margin.

Because the majority of the people most affected by the depression were Democrats, it was no surprise when they embraced the "free silver" movement. Nebraska congressman William Jennings Bryan, a brilliant orator, was nominated by the Democrats on the fifth ballot. Bryan gave the famous "Cross of Gold" speech on the convention floor, warning Republicans and wealthy bankers and industrialists, "You shall not press down upon the brow of labor this crown of thorns, you shall not crucify mankind on a cross of gold." Gold and silver standards became the major issue of the campaign.

While McKinley campaigned from his front porch, Bryan traveled more than eighteen thousand miles, gave more than six hundred speeches to more than five million people, and the Democrats took an early lead. But the economy began to improve dramatically in the fall of 1896, shifting enough support back to the Republicans to give McKinley a comfortable victory.

Electoral Votes:
McKinley 271
Bryan 176

Second Election—1900

The campaign of 1900 was a rematch between McKinley and Bryan, who were both renominated easily, but the improved economy and discovery of gold in Alaska pushed the currency issue to the background, and foreign policy was the battle ground. The Democrats, now the champion of the little people, accused the Republicans of blatant imperialism, forgetting the principles of freedom on which the country was founded. The Republicans answered that the United States had the almost divine mission of bringing order and civilization to less fortunate peoples everywhere.

McKinley let vice presidential nominee Teddy Roosevelt carry his message and once again remained at home. Bryan took to the road, but, in the end, McKinley won easily.

Electoral Votes:
McKinley 292
Bryan 155

VICE PRESIDENTS

Garret Augustus Hobart (1844–1899) New Jersey. Lawyer. (Died in office.)
Theodore Roosevelt (1858–1918) New York. Rancher, writer. (Succeeded McKinley.)

THE CABINET

Secretary of State:
John Sherman (1897–1898)
William R. Day (1898)
John Hay (1898–1901)

Secretary of the Treasury:
Lyman J. Gage (1897–1901)

Secretary of War:
Russell A. Alger (1897–1899)
Elihu Root (1899–1901)

Attorney General:
Joseph McKenna (1897–1898)
John W. Griggs (1898–1901)
Philander C. Knox (1901)

Postmaster General:
James A. Gary (1897–1898)
Charles Emory Smith (1898–1901)

Secretary of the Navy:
John D. Long (1897–1901)

Secretary of the Interior:
Cornelius N. Bliss (1897–1899)
Ethan A. Hitchcock (1899–1901)

Secretary of Agriculture:
  James Wilson (1897–1901)

SIGNIFICANT EVENTS THAT OCCURRED DURING
OFFICE——MARCH 4, 1893—SEPTEMBER 21, 1901

Dingley Tariff Act—1897

This Republican-sponsored measure restored the tariff to a new high of 46 percent.

Annexation of Hawaii—1898

McKinley abandoned the Cleveland policy of not recognizing the revolutionary government and signed a joint resolution to annex the islands.

Spanish-American War—1898

The brief war (April to August 1898) between the United States and Spain was fought over Spanish refusal to allow Cuba to govern itself. Spanish methods used to quash the rebellion were considered brutal and offensive to Americans, who were also angry about the blowing up of the battleship *Maine* in Havana harbor (February 1898) and there was a general clamor for war. When it was over, Spain had lost most of its colonial interests in the Western Hemisphere, and the United States had become a legitimate world power. Negotiations with Spain resulted in American occupation of Cuba until its independence in 1902 and the acquisition of Puerto Rico. McKinley also overcame anti-imperialist opposition and claimed the Philippines as a U.S. possession. After the signing of the Paris Peace Treaty in December of 1898 the United States had become a colonial power.

Open Door Policy—1899

The Open Door Policy called for an end to discriminatory tariffs to help maintain access to a country's trade.

Boxer Rebellion—1900

American soldiers in conjunction with forces from Britain, France, Germany, Russia, and Japan went into China to rescue Western hostages caught in the middle of nationalist turmoil.

Gold Standard Act—1900

The act backed all paper money by gold held in federal treasuries.

Shortly after his reelection, McKinley was assassinated.

CONTRIBUTIONS TO AMERICAN HISTORY WHILE

PRESIDENT

McKinley strengthened the presidency, traveled widely, and gave the press greater access to the White House. He was comfortable with the rough-and-tumble of politics and worked well with Congress, using the power of office skillfully to promote his programs. The evolution of the strong modern presidency was continued during his terms of office.

SECTION TWO

PERSONAL PROFILE

McKinley, of average height, was stocky and broad and tended to heaviness. One of the most open and accessible men to serve as president, he was courteous, friendly, and well liked—even by the opposition.

FAMILY BACKGROUND

Ancestors

McKinley was Scotch-Irish. The family emigrated from Ireland in the mid-eighteenth century and settled in Pennsylvania. McKinleys served in the Revolution and the War of 1812.

Immediate Family

FATHER: William McKinley, Sr. (1807–1892) Businessman. Manufactured pig iron in his foundry. He learned the business from his father.

MOTHER: Nancy Allison McKinley (1809–1897) Born in Ohio, "Mother" McKinley was very close to her son and hoped he would become a minister. She visited him in the White House.

BROTHERS AND SISTERS: David A. McKinley; Anna McKinley; James McKinley; Mrs. Mary May; Helen McKinley; Mrs. Sarah E. Duncan; Abner McKinley.

CHILDHOOD AND EARLY YEARS

From his earliest days, McKinley was an outdoorsman. He loved sports and spent time camping and fishing with friends.

EDUCATION

McKinley began his education at the public school in Niles. When the family moved to Poland, Ohio, he continued at the school there. He entered a Methodist seminary in 1852, where he was first exposed to public speaking and discovered his gift for oratory. In 1860, he enrolled at Allegheny College for his junior year but left because of illness and family finances. He never finished college. After the Civil War he studied law and was admitted to the Ohio bar in 1867.

MILITARY SERVICE

Civil War: 23d Ohio Volunteers (1861–1865)
RANK: Rose from private to brevet major.
Served under Rutherford B. Hayes. Saw action throughout the course of the war including at Antietam and in the Shenandoah Valley.

RELIGION

Methodist

FAMILY LIFE

Marriage:

McKinley was twenty-seven when he married Ida Saxton on January 25, 1871, at the First Presbyterian Church in Canton, Ohio. Daughter of James Saxton, a wealthy banker in Canton, she grew up in a comfortable and supportive environment. She was well educated and well traveled, including a tour of Europe. McKinley met her at a picnic in 1867 and they married four years later. The loss of her mother and both her children in less than two years

(1873–1875) destroyed her health, and she became epileptic and would remain a semi-invalid prone to seizures for the rest of her life. She died in Canton on May 26, 1907.

Children:

Katherine McKinley (1871–1875); Ida McKinley (1873)

HOBBIES

Cards, going to the theater and opera, and cigars.

ASSASSINATED

While standing in a receiving line at the Pan American Exposition on September 6, 1901, McKinley was shot twice, at point-blank range, with a gun wrapped in the bandaged hand of anarchist Leon Czolgosz. Doctors, in a series of operations, were unable to find and remove the bullet lodged in McKinley's abdominal area. For several days doctors were optimistic about his chances for survival, but gangrene had infected the bullet holes and McKinley died on September 14, 1901, at the hospital in Buffalo.

Czolgosz admitted the killing, refused to defend himself at the trial, and, still unrepentant, was electrocuted on October 29, 1901.

CHAPTER TWENTY-SIX
☆ ☆ ☆

THEODORE ROOSEVELT

1858-1919

26th President of the United States
"Teddy"

☆ ☆ ☆

SECTION ONE

BORN

Roosevelt was born on October 27, 1858, at the family home in New York City.

TERMS SERVED AS PRESIDENT

1901–1905 (Succeeded McKinley.)
1905–1909

POLITICAL PARTY

Republican

PUBLIC LIFE BEFORE PRESIDENCY

New York Assembly—1882–1884

In his three terms Roosevelt supported civil service reform, benefits for working people, and government reform in New York City.

Cattle Rancher and Cowboy—1884–1886

Roosevelt worked as a rancher in the Dakota Territory for two years, where he also served as a deputy sheriff. He returned to New York to run for mayor but was defeated and concentrated on writing biographies and historical works.

U.S. Civil Service Commission—1889–1895

Appointed by President Harrison, Roosevelt fought to increase the number of positions that were based on merit and to improve the commission's administrative procedures.

New York City Board of Police Commissioners—1895–1897

As president, he worked to end the ingrained corruption in the police department and forced policemen to comply with and execute laws. His tough reform policies gained him national recognition.

Assistant Secretary of the Navy— 1897–1898

Roosevelt believed strongly in expansionist policies and used his office in whatever way he could to prepare the nation for war with Spain, sometimes overstepping the boundaries of his office to deploy ships. He was not authorized to order Commodore Dewey to take military action in the Philippines.

Governor of New York—1891–1900

Roosevelt continued to advocate reform. He supported a civil service, backed a measure to tax corporations, and ran an active government much to the irritation of party hacks and boss Thomas C. Platt.

Vice President—March–September 1901

To get him out of the way, Republican party boss Thomas C. Platt laid the groundwork for Roosevelt to fill the vice presidential slot left empty by the death of Garret Hobart.

Roosevelt was reluctant, but accepted the nomination as McKinley's running mate in 1900. He campaigned around the country with his usual energy and determination. He succeeded to the presidency in 1901 after the assassination of William McKinley.

CAMPAIGN

Election—1904

Roosevelt was a certainty to win the nomination at the convention in Chicago in June 1904. The platform reflected the successes and concerns of his first term: government reform, keeping the protective tariff in place, maintaining the gold standard, and expanding American influence in the world.

The Democrats ran Alton B. Parker (1852–1926), a New York lawyer who won the nomination easily on the first ballot. After the nomination he came out in favor of the gold standard.

The candidates basically agreed on the major issues of the day, and so the campaign focused on the personalities of the two men, who could hardly have been more different. Parker was cool, efficient, and distant, while Roosevelt was brash, outspoken, and outgoing.

Roosevelt won easily, and Parker retired to his law practice.

Electoral Votes:
Roosevelt 336
Parker 140

VICE PRESIDENT

None (First Term)
Charles Warren Fairbanks (1852–1918) Indiana. Lawyer. (Second Term)

THE CABINET

Secretary of State:
John M. Hay (1901–1905)
Elihu Root (1905–1909)
Robert Bacon (1909)

Secretary of the Treasury:
Lyman J. Gage (1901–1902)
Leslie M. Shaw (1902–1907)
George B. Cortelyou (1907–1909)

Secretary of War:
Elihu Root (1901–1904)
William H. Taft (1904–1908)
Luke E. Wright (1908–1909)

Attorney General:
Philander C. Knox (1901–1904)
William H. Moody (1904–1906)
Charles J. Bonaparte (1906–1909)

Postmaster General:
Charles Emory Smith (1901–1902)
Henry C. Payne (1902–1904)
Robert J. Wynne (1904–1905)
George B. Cortelyou (1905–1907)
George von L. Meyer (1907–1909)

Secretary of the Navy:
  James D. Long (1901–1902)
  William H. Moody (1902–1904)
  Paul Morton (1904–1905)
  Charles J. Bonaparte (1905–1906)
  Victor H. Metcalf (1906–1908)
  Truman H. Newberry (1908–1909)

Secretary of the Interior:
  Ethan A. Hitchcock (1901–1907)
  James R. Garfield (1907–1909)

Secretary of Agriculture:
  James Wilson (1901–1909)

Secretary of Commerce and Labor:
  George B. Cortelyou (1903–1904)
  Victor H. Metcalf (1904–1906)
  Oscar S. Straus (1906–1909)

SIGNIFICANT EVENTS THAT OCCURRED DURING

OFFICE——SEPTEMBER 14, 1901–MARCH 3, 1909

The Panama Canal—1904

Construction on the Panama Canal linking the Atlantic and Pacific Oceans began in Roosevelt's first administration. Opened to traffic in 1920, it was one of the largest construction projects ever undertaken.

Foreign Policy and the Big Stick

Roosevelt made it clear to world powers in his annual messages to Congress in 1904 and 1905 that the United States would not hesitate to enforce the Monroe Doctrine in Latin America. "Speak softly and carry a big stick; you will go far."

Russo-Japanese War—1904–1905

Roosevelt won the Nobel Peace Prize for negotiating a peaceful settlement to the conflict between Russia and Japan over control of Manchuria and Korea.

Antitrust and the Square Deal

The Roosevelt administration was committed to balancing free enterprise and unjust corporate practices. His "trust-busting" officials prosecuted combines in the railroad, oil, beef, and tobacco industries protecting the rights of workers and consumers.

Pennsylvania Coal Strike—1902

Mine owners settled a miners' strike after Roosevelt threatened to seize the mines.

Meat Inspection Act and Pure Food and Drug Act—1906

These bills provided for government inspection of consumer products and set standards of quality.

Conservation and the Environment

Roosevelt was active in protecting resources such as water and coal and established national forests and wildlife refuges, earning him the nickname "The Big Conservationist."

Panic of 1907

After the collapse of the Knickerbocker Trust Company threatened to plunge the country into recession, Roosevelt acted quickly to shore up banks in danger of failing with federal funds, and recovery began in 1908.

CONTRIBUTIONS TO AMERICAN HISTORY WHILE PRESIDENT

The Roosevelt administration used the office of president to address the American people's fears of greed and corruption caused by the abuses of big business, of wasting the nation's resources, and the disintegration of social values. He was a human force in a time when government appeared to be controlled by faceless corporate giants and raised the office of president to heights not attained since Lincoln.

☆ ☆ ☆

SECTION TWO

PERSONAL PROFILE

Roosevelt was truly self-made, pushing himself to overcome his early illness and turning himself into a strong and healthy man. He was colorful, witty, robust, outspoken, and humane. He thrived in the public eye and loved the rough-and-tumble of politics. Though privileged from birth, he came to sympathize with the common man, and the focus of his political life was the ideal of making a better life for all Americans. His love for his children was well-known, and he would interrupt meetings to spend time with them every day.

FAMILY BACKGROUND

Ancestors

Of Dutch, Huguenot, Scots, and English stock, Roosevelt's family began settling in America during the mid-seventeenth century. Teddy Roosevelt was distantly related to Martin Van Buren.

Immediate Family

FATHER: Theodore Roosevelt, Sr. (1831–1878) Importer. Liberal and reform-minded, Roosevelt, Sr., supported worthy causes and informed his children of their responsibility to society. Even though his wife was from the South and did not hide her proslavery sentiments, Roosevelt was an active supporter of Lincoln and antislavery. He died of cancer in 1878.

MOTHER: Martha Bulloch Roosevelt (1834–1884) Daughter of a wealthy Georgia planter, Martha grew up in genuine southern comfort. While living in New York during the Civil War she sent money, food, and clothing south through secret channels. Two of her brothers served in the Confederate military. She died of typhoid fever in 1884.

BROTHERS AND SISTERS: Mrs. Anna Cowles; J. Roosevelt Roosevelt; Elliot Roosevelt; Mrs. Corinne Robinson.

CHILDHOOD AND EARLY YEARS

Roosevelt was born into an old, prosperous Dutch family in New York City on October 27, 1858. He was a weak and frail child and suffered from severe asthma. His father's caring but tough influence gave him the determination to overcome his physical obstacles with a program of strenuous exercise. He made an active and full life for himself. The need for quiet and rest gave him a love of reading that lasted his entire life.

EDUCATION

Because he was too ill to go to school full-time, he studied at home with a series of tutors who gave him an eclectic and varied education. By 1875 his health was good enough to consider college, and he entered Harvard after passing the entrance examination in 1876. At Harvard he was an excellent student who loved the sciences, graduating magna cum laude and Phi Beta Kappa in 1880. He was active in campus affairs and boxed as a lightweight.

He entered Columbia Law School in 1880 but left school to run for assemblyman in New York and never completed his degree.

MILITARY SERVICE

New York National Guard (1882–1885)
RANK: Rose from second lieutenant to captain.
Spanish-American War: 1st U.S. Volunteer Cavalry Regiment
RANK: Rose from lieutenant to lieutenant colonel.

As commander of the "Rough Riders" Roosevelt became a national hero for leading his little band of men in the famous charge up San Juan Hill and routing the enemy out of their trenches. He described it as his finest moment.

RELIGION

Dutch Reform

FAMILY LIFE

First Marriage:

On October 27, 1880, Roosevelt, twenty-two, was married to Alice Hathaway Lee, (1861–1884) age nineteen at the Unitarian Church in Brookline, Massachusetts. The daughter of wealthy banker, George Cabot Lee, she met Roosevelt at a friend's home in 1878. She suffered from Bright's disease and died during childbirth in 1884.

Children:

Alice Lee Roosevelt (1884–1980)

Second Marriage:

On December 2, 1886, Roosevelt, twenty-eight, married twenty-five-year-old Edith Kermit Carow (1861–1948) at St. George's Church in London. Daughter of Charles Carow, a New York businessman, she had known Roosevelt since they were children. After the death of Alice, they met again, and he proposed in 1885. She was an active first lady, redecorating the White House and managing its daily affairs. She died on September 30, 1948.

Children:

Theodore Roosevelt, Jr. (1887–1944); Kermit Roosevelt (1889–1943); Ethel Carow Roosevelt (1891–1977); Archibald Bulloch Roosevelt (1894–1979); Quentin Roosevelt (1897–1918)

HOBBIES

Roosevelt was as prolific and active in his personal pursuits as in his public life. He enjoyed wrestling, boxing, tennis, hiking, big-game hunting, polo, horseback riding, sailing and rowing, and nature study. He read a variety of books and magazines and kept a detailed journal.

POST PRESIDENCY

Roosevelt turned over the government to Taft and began an African safari and grand tour of Europe that lasted a year. He returned in 1910 to find that his handpicked successor had been less than successful in managing affairs of government and that the Republicans were divided and in disarray.

After failing in an attempt to reconcile differences, Roosevelt retired to Sagamore Hill but soon decided to run against Taft for the nomination in 1912. He formed the Bull Moose party and campaigned once again on a theme of ambitious reform. The battle against Taft split the Republicans and ensured the election of Democrat Woodrow Wilson. In 1912, a deranged bartender in Milwaukee attempted to assassinate Roosevelt at a speaking engagement. He was shot once in the chest but survived without complications.

After a journey into the jungles of Brazil he wrote his autobiography and attempted one more run at the presidency in 1916.

DIED

Roosevelt died on January 16, 1919, at Sagamore Hill in Oyster Bay, Long Island, of a coronary embolism.

CHAPTER TWENTY-SEVEN
☆ ☆ ☆

WILLIAM HOWARD TAFT

1857–1930

27th President of the United States
"Big Bill"

☆ ☆ ☆

SECTION ONE

BORN

Taft was born on September 15, 1857, at his parents' home in Cincinnati, Ohio.

TERM SERVED AS PRESIDENT

1909–1913

POLITICAL PARTY

Republican

PUBLIC LIFE BEFORE PRESIDENCY

Judge of Ohio Superior Court—1887

While practicing law in Cincinnati, Taft was appointed to the Ohio Superior Court and won a five-year term the next year. President Benjamin Harrison made him U.S. solicitor general in 1890. From 1892 to 1900 he served as a federal circuit judge of the newly created Sixth Circuit Court. Taft was convinced that he was better suited to the judiciary than politics.

Commissioner and Governor-General of the Philippines—1900–1904

In 1900, Taft headed a commission to end U.S. military rule in the Philippines. As commissioner and later as civil governor, he changed military to civil command, instituted land reform, sponsored a road-construction program, and prepared the Islands for self-government.

Secretary of War—1904–1908

Taft succeeded Elihu Root as secretary of war in Roosevelt's cabinet. His support of Roosevelt's reform positions and of the administration in general won Roosevelt's friendship and loyalty, and Roosevelt persuaded Taft to make a run for the presidency

CAMPAIGN

Election—1908

Feeling that he had a popular mandate, Roosevelt, who was committed to not seeking a third term, wanted to handpick his successor. He chose Secretary of the Navy William Howard Taft. Although often dismissed as Roosevelt's puppet, Taft was nominated on the first ballot. Roosevelt convinced Taft to take more progressive positions on issues to counter the Democrats and coached him on public speaking.

The Democrats picked William Jennings Bryan, who was nominated on the first ballot.

Probably because of Roosevelt's popularity, Taft won an unexpectedly large victory and Bryan, stunned by the margin of his loss, retired from politics.

Electoral Votes:
Taft 321
Bryan 162

VICE PRESIDENT

James Schoolcraft Sherman (1855–1912) New York. Lawyer.

THE CABINET

Secretary of State:
  Philander C. Knox (1909–1913)

Secretary of the Treasury:
  Franklin MacVeagh (1909–1913)

Secretary of War:
  Jacob M. Dickinson (1909–1911)
  Henry L. Stimson (1911–1913)

Attorney General:
  George W. Wickersham (1909–1913)

Postmaster General:
  Frank H. Hitchcock (1909–1913)

Secretary of the Navy:
  George von L. Meyer (1909–1913)

Secretary of the Interior:
  Richard A. Ballinger (1909–1911)
  Walter Lowrie Fisher (1911–1913)

Secretary of Agriculture:
  James Wilson (1909–1913)

Secretary of Commerce and Labor:
  Charles Nagel (1909–1913)

SIGNIFICANT EVENTS THAT OCCURRED DURING OFFICE——MARCH 4, 1909–MARCH 3, 1913

Payne-Aldrich Tariff Act—1909

This tariff act lowered the overall rate by 5 percent but actually raised it on some items and, although Taft defended it, the bill was weak and ill-thought-out. His poor handling of the tariff issue caused a split in the Republican party that would eventually cost it control of Congress and him the White House in 1913.

Mann-Elkins Act—1910

Mann-Elkins gave the Interstate Commerce Commission the power to regulate maximum rates charged by railroads and placed the telephone and telegraph under ICC supervision.

Dollar Diplomacy

The Taft administration encouraged American investment in foreign business and used diplomatic channels to smooth the way.

Webb-Kenyon Interstate Liquor Shipments Act—1913

Congress overrode Taft's veto to pass this law prohibiting interstate transportation of liquor into dry states.

Income Tax Amendment—1913

Taft supported and advocated ratification of the Sixteenth Amendment to the Constitution, which gave Congress power to levy an income tax.

Progressive vs. Conservative

Taft's return to conservative politics and policies and his battles with the progressives gradually drew Roosevelt into open opposition to his administration, and soon he felt there was no choice but to challenge Taft for the nomination in 1912. Taft's control of the party machinery won him the nomination, but Roosevelt's action split the party and resulted in the election of Woodrow Wilson.

CONTRIBUTIONS TO AMERICAN HISTORY WHILE

PRESIDENT

Taft was expected to carry on Roosevelt's progressive policies. And, in fact, he instituted and completed more antitrust cases than Roosevelt himself. He also took measures to enforce the employer's liability law for work done on government jobs, made an eight-hour day mandatory for federal employees, and helped enact a system of postal savings. But, in the end, he was unable to live up to the ideals of the Roosevelt administration.

SECTION TWO

PERSONAL PROFILE

When Taft was in office, his weight exceeded three hundred pounds and he struggled with diets his entire life. He had to install a special bathtub in the White House to accommodate his bulk. Taft was an extremely bright man and an excellent lawyer. Although friendly and seemingly outgoing, he was an extremely private man with few confidants. He was a reluctant president, feeling that he was better suited to be a judge than a politician and, in fact, was happier as chief justice of the Supreme Court than he ever was as president. His break with Roosevelt, who was perhaps his closest friend, caused him much pain.

FAMILY BACKGROUND

Ancestors

Taft's family emigrated from England in the late seventeenth century and settled in Massachusetts.

Immediate Family

FATHER: Alphonso Taft (1810–1891) A lawyer and public official, Taft's father spent his life in politics. He served as a judge on the Cincinnati Superior Court. Secretary of war and attorney general under Grant, minister to Austria-Hungry and Russia under Arthur. His first wife, Fanny Phelps, died of tuberculosis.

MOTHER: Louisa Maria Torrey Taft (1827–1907) Alphonso Taft's second wife Louisa was known for her strong will and definite political opinions.

BROTHERS AND SISTERS: Half brothers—Charles Phelps Taft; Peter Rawson Taft. Full brothers and sisters—Henry Waters Taft; Horace Dutton Taft; Mrs. Frances Edwards.

CHILDHOOD AND EARLY YEARS

Taft grew up in a privileged and comfortable atmosphere. He loved baseball, swimming, and ice-skating.

EDUCATION

Always an excellent student, Taft attended public schools in Cincinnati and was accepted at Yale after graduating second in his high-school class. At Yale he continued his scholastic achievements, graduating salutatorian in 1878. He entered Cincinnati Law School immediately after Yale and again excelled, passing the bar before he graduated in 1880.

MILITARY SERVICE

None

RELIGION

Unitarian

FAMILY LIFE

Marriage:

Taft, twenty-eight, married Helen Herron, twenty-five, on June 19, 1886, at her home in Cincinnati. Helen was the daughter of Judge John H. Herron, a law partner of Rutherford B. Hayes. Shortly after Taft took office as president she suffered a stroke from which she never fully recovered. She died on May 22, 1943.

Children:

Robert Alphonso Taft (1889–1953); Helen Herron Taft (1891–1987); Charles Phelps Taft (1897–1983)

HOBBIES

Golf, baseball, and theater.

POST PRESIDENCY

Taft retired to a teaching post at Yale Law School and served as cochairman of the National War Labor Board during World War I. In 1921, President Warren Harding appointed him chief justice of the United States, a position he had sought several times before. His conservatism was reflected in his opinions, although the influence of Roosevelt and reform made him find for liberal causes as well. He stepped down because of poor health in February 1930.

DIED

Taft died on March 8, 1930, at his home in Washington of complications from heart disease and high blood pressure.

CHAPTER TWENTY-EIGHT
☆ ☆ ☆

WOODROW WILSON

1856–1924

28th President of the United States
"Professor"

☆ ☆ ☆

SECTION ONE

BORN

Thomas Woodrow Wilson was born in Staunton, Virginia, on December 28, 1856.

TERMS SERVED AS PRESIDENT

1913–1917
1917–1921

POLITICAL PARTY

Democrat

PUBLIC LIFE BEFORE PRESIDENCY

Educator and Writer—1885–1910

Wilson taught economy and law at Bryn Mawr College from 1885 to 1888 and history at Wesleyan University in Connecticut from 1888 to 1890. In that year he was hired at Princeton as professor of jurisprudence and political economy. He became a popular lecturer on politics and history and wrote many articles and nine books, including *Division and Reunion,* published in 1893, and his *History of the American People,* published in 1902. In 1902 he became Princeton's president.

Governor of New Jersey—1911–1913

George Harvey, an influential magazine editor, with help from New Jersey's Democratic party bosses, persuaded Wilson to run for governor in 1910. Once in office, he turned against the machine and launched a program of progressive legislation that brought him into national prominence.

He was nominated for president in 1912.

CAMPAIGNS

First Election—1912

With the Republican party split in two in the struggle between Roosevelt and Taft, the Democrats knew they had an excellent chance to recapture the White House. But the convention bogged down in a battle between the big-city-machine Democrats, who favored Speaker of the House Champ Clarke of Missouri, and the reform Democrats, led by William Jennings Bryan, who favored liberal New Jersey Governor Woodrow Wilson. The struggle lasted forty-six ballots before Wilson gained a majority.

The infighting between Roosevelt and Taft only helped the Democrats, and Wilson was an unexpectedly effective campaigner. His program, which he called "The New Freedom," promised major social reform.

Roosevelt, the people's favorite, did succeed in punishing Taft, but he couldn't overcome the Democratic vote. Even though he got just 41 percent of the popular vote, Wilson captured forty of the forty-eight states.

Electoral Votes:
Wilson 435
Roosevelt 88
Taft 8

Second Election—1916

After the Germans sank the British liner *Lusitania* in 1915, killing Americans, Wilson had ordered a state of readiness for American forces. However, he was determined to keep America out of the war, and the majority of Democrats agreed with him. He was easily renominated.

Roosevelt sought the Republican nomination, but his third-party candidacy had burned too many bridges, and the party chose Supreme Court Justice Charles Evans Hughes. Still influential, however, Roosevelt advocated U.S. intervention in Europe, and an attack on Wilson's peace policy was part of the Republican platform.

While the Democrats had a clear campaign issue in the peace theme, Roosevelt had placed Hughes in a difficult position, forcing him to walk a narrow line between Republicans hawks and doves, as well as between progressive and conservative elements of the party. Hughes, however, proved to be a good campaigner. The race was close, and many felt he would be the winner.

On Election Day, Wilson needed just twelve electoral votes to assure reelection. California provided them, and Wilson squeaked back into the White House.

Electoral Votes:
Wilson 277
Hughes 254

VICE PRESIDENT

Thomas Riley Marshall (1854–1925) Indiana. Lawyer. (Both terms.)

THE CABINET

Secretary of State:
  William Jennings Bryan (1913–1915)
  Robert Lansing (1915–1920)
  Bainbridge Colby (1920–1921)

Secretary of the Treasury:
  William G. McAdoo (1913–1918)
  Carter Glass (1918–1920)
  David F. Houston (1920–1921)

Secretary of War:
  Lindley M. Garrison (1913–1916)
  Newton D. Baker (1916–1921)

Attorney General:
  James C. McReynolds (1913–1914)
  Thomas W. Gregory (1914–1919)
  Alexander M. Palmer (1919–1921)

Postmaster General:
  Albert S. Burleson (1913–1921)

Secretary of the Navy:
  Josephus Daniels (1913–1921)

Secretary of the Interior:
  Franklin K. Lane (1913–1920)
  John B. Payne (1920–1921)

Secretary of Agriculture:
  David F. Houston (1913–1920)
  Edwin T. Meredith (1920–1921)

Secretary of Commerce:
  William C. Redfield (1913–1919)
  Joshua W. Alexander (1919–1921)

Secretary of Labor:
  William B. Wilson (1913–1921)

SIGNIFICANT EVENTS THAT OCCURRED DURING

OFFICE——MARCH 4, 1913–MARCH 3, 1921

Underwood Tariff—1913

The Underwood Tariff, which established a small income tax, was the first major reduction in tariffs since the Civil War.

Federal Reserve Act—1913

The Federal Reserve Act provided for twelve regional "banker's banks," from which regular banks could borrow money at discount rates set by "The Fed" to adjust to changing economic conditions.

Federal Trade Commission—1914

The commission was designed to be a watchdog to protect small businesses against large corporations and monopolies.

Clayton Antitrust Act—1914

The Clayton Act recognized the rights of workers by legalizing negotiations between labor and management, such as collective bargaining, strikes, and boycotts. It also barred corporations from holding stock in competitors' companies.

Adamson Act—1916

The act set the eight-hour day for railroad workers and averted a strike.

Eighteenth Amendment (Prohibition)— 1919

The states ratified the Eighteenth Amendment, which prohibited the manufacture and sale of alcoholic beverages.

Revolution in Mexico

Mexico was in political turmoil. Wilson refused to recognize the military government of Victoriano Huerta in an attempt to force him into free elections. Huerta resisted, Wilson ordered marines to occupy Vera Cruz and supported constitutionalist Venustiano Carranza. Mediation by Argentina, Brazil, and Chile led to Huerta's resignation in July 1914.

In 1915, Wilson recognized Carranza's provisional government, and in 1916 he sent troops under John J. Pershing into Mexico after Carranza's rival, guerrilla leader Pancho Villa, had raided a town in New Mexico, killing several Americans. Villa eluded capture, and Wilson called the army back in 1917.

In February, British Intelligence produced a message from Mexico's German minister proposing an alliance with Mexico against the United States. The implications pushed America closer to war.

World War I—1914–1918

Wilson did his best to keep America out of World War I. After the *Lusitania* was sunk in May 1915 (with the loss of 128 Americans), he firmly negotiated pledges from Germany to provide for the safety of passengers caught in submarine attacks, and in May 1916 the Germans agreed to abandon unrestricted submarine warfare. But the promise was to be short-lived.

When Germany renewed all-out submarine warfare in 1917, Wilson severed diplomatic relations and asked Congress for a declaration of war, asserting that "the world must be made safe for democracy."

Once committed, Wilson acted quickly, establishing a series of war agencies, extending federal control over industry, transportation, labor, food, fuel, and prices. In May 1917 he signed a Selective Service bill, drafting almost three million men into service. The precedents for presidential action set during this all-out mobilization would give future presidents the means to deal with future conflicts.

The American Expeditionary Force, under the command of John J. Pershing, landed in France in 1918. Fighting outside of Allied control, the AEF was instrumental in bringing an end to the long and brutal war.

"Peace without Victory"

Throughout the war, Wilson attempted to negotiate peace. On January 22, 1917, he called for a "peace without victory" and asked for a League of Nations to settle international disputes.

In January 1918, while the AEF prepared to ship overseas, Wilson presented his Fourteen Points, which set not only a means of peaceful resolution of the war, but an outline of Allied goals if the fighting continued. Eventually Germany agreed to negotiate, hoping for fair treatment under the proposal.

The Treaty of Versailles, signed in 1919, was much harsher on Germany than Wilson had wanted, but he felt it was the best possible solution. The League of Nations would be able to mediate later problems.

But Wilson had made a political blunder by not getting committed bipartisan support for his peace plan and, in the end, his hopes for a just peace and the establishment of his beloved League of Nations were dashed by political infighting. Senate Republicans refused to approve the treaty without significant modifications of U.S. commitment to the league.

Wilson took to the road to convince the American people of the league's value and the importance of U.S. membership. Exhausted, he collapsed on September 25, 1919, after a speech in Pueblo, Colorado. A week later he suffered a stroke.

The Senate rejected the treaty in November 1919 and again in March 1920. Republican Warren G. Harding, who had established a reputation as an opponent of the league, won the presidency in a landslide in 1921. Wilson was awarded the Nobel Peace Prize for 1919.

CONTRIBUTIONS TO AMERICAN HISTORY WHILE

PRESIDENT

Once United States participation in the conflict in Europe became inevitable, Wilson mobilized the forces of war with ruthlessness and determination and worked for a just peace with compassion and humanity. While his dream of a League of Nations would be unfulfilled, the seeds for world cooperation that he planted would grow into the United Nations some twenty-four years later.

SECTION TWO

PERSONAL PROFILE

Wilson considered himself a homely man, shy and awkward, with exaggerated features. He was in poor health most of his life.

He seemed, at times, withdrawn and temperamental, and had difficulties maintaining close friendships. A good public speaker, he was at ease in crowds but uncomfortable in small groups.

FAMILY BACKGROUND

Ancestors

Wilson was Irish on his father's side and Scots on his mother's. Both families emigrated to America in the early nineteenth century and settled in the Philadelphia area, and then Ohio.

Immediate Family

FATHER: Joseph Ruggles Wilson (1822–1903) A Presbyterian minister who sympathized with the South during the Civil War.

MOTHER: Janet Woodrow Wilson (1830–1888) Born in England, she settled with her family in Ohio. Wilson considered her one of the major influences in his life.

BROTHERS AND SISTERS: Mrs. Marion W. Kennedy; Mrs. Anne J. Howe; Joseph R. Wilson, Jr.

CHILDHOOD AND EARLY YEARS

Wilson was raised in a devoutly religious household. The family moved from Staunton to Augusta, Georgia, in 1857, where they lived throughout the Civil War. Wilson grew up during Reconstruction and never forgot the brutality and injustice inflicted on the South by northern policies after the war. Throughout his life he considered himself a Southerner and felt that the South had been justified in secession.

EDUCATION

He attended Davidson College and then entered the College of New Jersey, which would later become Princeton University, graduating in 1879. He studied law at the University of Virginia Law School and was admitted to the bar in 1882. He practiced briefly in Atlanta, and in 1883 entered The Johns Hopkins University for graduate study in political science, where he wrote *Congressional Government*, which was published in 1885, a year before he graduated.

MILITARY SERVICE

None

RELIGION

Presbyterian

FAMILY LIFE

First Marriage:

At age twenty-five, Wilson married Ellen Louise Axson, twenty-two, on June 24, 1885, at the home of the bride's grandfather. A minister's daughter, she was well educated and knowledgeable in the arts. As first lady she was active in social causes. She died of Bright's disease in the White House on August 6, 1914.

Children:

Margaret Woodrow Wilson (1886–1944); Jessie Woodrow Wilson (1887–1933); Eleanor Randolph Wilson (1889–1967)

Second Marriage:

While president fifty-eight-year-old Wilson married Edith Bolling Galt, forty-three, on December 18, 1915, at her home in Washington. The marriage, coming so quickly after the death of his first wife, caused a small scandal in Washington, and the couple considered backing out. She served as a wartime first lady and was a close confidante of the president. She died on December 28, 1961.

HOBBIES

Golf, horseback riding, theater, billiards, cards, yachting, and reading.

POST PRESIDENCY

Partially incapacitated by the stroke he suffered in 1919, Wilson retired to his home in Washington, D.C., where he attempted to practice law but was too ill.

DIED

Wilson died at home on February 3, 1924, of complications from a second stroke.

CHAPTER TWENTY-NINE
☆ ☆ ☆

WARREN GAMALIEL HARDING

1865–1923

29th President of the United States

☆ ☆ ☆

SECTION ONE

TERM SERVED AS PRESIDENT

1921–1923 (Died in office.)

BORN

Harding was born on November 2, 1865, at the family farm in Corsica (now Blooming Grove), Ohio.

POLITICAL PARTY

Republican

PUBLIC LIFE BEFORE PRESIDENCY

After brief, stints as a teacher, law student, and insurance sales-man, Harding and two partners purchased the *Marion Daily Star* in 1884. As editor and publisher, Harding made the newspaper prosper, and he rewarded his employees with shares of the profits. In a Democratic stronghold, Harding was an avid Republican.

Ohio Politics—1899–1903

Elected to the Ohio Senate in 1898, he quickly became a force in the factionalized Republican party, gaining a reputation for being able to resolve conflicts. He served as lieutenant governor from 1903 to 1905. Harding returned to the *Star,* and was nominated for governor in 1910 but lost badly to the Democratic candidate. In 1912, he was booed off the stage at the Republican Convention while nominating Taft for president.

U.S. Senator—1915–1921

Harding spent most of his career in the Senate making sure he made no enemies. He introduced no bills of national importance and had the worst attendance record on the floor. Consequently he missed voting on some of the most important legislation of his time, including the Eighteenth (Prohibition) and Nineteenth (Women's Rights) Amendments. By offending no one he became a leader in the party and his opposition to the League of Nations put him in position for the presidential bid.

CAMPAIGN

Election—1920

Illinois Governor Frank Lowden and General Leonard Wood were the top contenders for the Republican nomination; but after a few ballots the Republicans turned to a dark horse, Ohio Senator Warren G. Harding, whose main qualification was his perceived opposition to the League of Nations and the Treaty of Versailles. He was nominated on the tenth ballot.

The Democrats tried to remain loyal to Wilson's political vision, but it took them forty-four ballots to nominate Ohio Governor James M. Cox. Franklin D. Roosevelt was the nominee for vice president.

Harding ran on a simple campaign slogan: "Return to Normalcy." His speeches dealt with no specific issues and emphasized "old-fashioned American values," a welcome relief to a public tired of messy involvement in foreign wars.

Cox campaigned diligently, but Harding won a landslide victory.

Electoral Votes:
Harding 404
Cox 127

VICE PRESIDENT

Calvin Coolidge (1872–1933) Massachusetts. Lawyer. (Succeeded Harding.)

THE CABINET

Secretary of State:
Charles Evans Hughes (1921–1923)

Secretary of the Treasury:
Andrew W. Mellon (1921–1923)

Secretary of War:
John W. Weeks (1921–1923)

Attorney General:
  Harry M. Daugherty (1921–1923)

Postmaster General:
  William H. Hays (1921–1922)
  Hubert Work (1922–1923)
  Harry S. New (1923)

Secretary of the Navy:
  Edwin Denby (1921–1923)

Secretary of the Interior:
  Albert B. Fall (1921–1923)
  Hubert Work (1923)

Secretary of Agriculture:
  Henry C. Wallace (1921–1923)

Secretary of Commerce:
  Herbert C. Hoover (1921–1923)

Secretary of Labor:
  James J. Davis (1921–1923)

SIGNIFICANT EVENTS THAT OCCURRED DURING OFFICE——MARCH 4, 1921–MARCH 3, 1923

Scandals in Office

Scandal, bribery, and graft overshadowed most of the accomplishments of the Harding administration. Harding relied heavily on advisors, preferring to leave most of the details of governing to others. He stocked his cabinet with some of the best men of his time including Charles Evans Hughes (State), Herbert Hoover (Commerce), and Andrew Mellon (Treasury). However, his hands-off policy allowed other members, notably Albert Fall (Interior), to dip deep into the till.

Teapot Dome Oil Reserve

Fall arranged for the private development of federally owned oil fields on the Teapot Dome reserve in Wyoming, in exchange for a $308,000 bribe. He arranged a similar deal in California and accepted $100,000. Fall was sentenced to a year in prison in 1929. Attorney General Harry Daugherty, a longtime Harding confidant, was also implicated in kickbacks. Other acts of corruption were exposed.

League of Nations—1921

Harding announced to Congress that he would not support U.S. membership in the League of Nations, although he did favor membership in the World Court. Without American involvement the fledgling league was doomed.

Formal End of World War I—1921

On July 2, 1921, Harding was summoned from the golf course to sign the paper that brought an end to World War I. He returned to the course to finish his round.

Washington Conference for the Limitation of Armament—1921–1922

The United States, Great Britain, France, Italy, and Japan agreed to limitations on ships of war and to respect each other's holdings in the Pacific.

Budget Bureau—1921

In order to monitor federal spending, Harding established the Bureau of the Budget.

Civil Rights

Perhaps the most notable social act of the Harding administration came when he spoke to a segregated audience at the University of Alabama in October of 1921. In his address, he called for an end to racial injustice and asked for blacks to become full members of American society.

The Emergency Tariff Act—1921 Fordney-McCumber Tariff Act—1922

These tariffs raised duties and protected certain war-related industries.

CONTRIBUTIONS TO AMERICAN HISTORY WHILE

PRESIDENT

Although Harding himself was never implicated in the scandals that rocked his administration, he placed enough greedy men in positions of power without supervision that his presidency is forever suspect.

SECTION TWO

PERSONAL PROFILE

Handsome and charming, President Harding's only qualification for office, as noted by a close associate, was that "he looked like a president."

FAMILY BACKGROUND

Ancestors

A mix of English, Scots, Irish, and Dutch heritage, his family emigrated to America in the early seventeenth century and worked as fishermen in Massachusetts. Throughout his life, right up to the White House, Harding was the subject of rumors that his family had Negro blood.

Immediate Family

FATHER: George Tyron Harding (1843–1928) Born in Ohio, Harding's father was a farmer and a doctor with a small practice in Marion, Ohio.

MOTHER: Phoebe Elizabeth Dickerson Harding (1843–1910) A midwife, she was an assistant to her husband, George. She was accused of malpractice in the death of a child and, although proven innocent, her reputation as well as her husband's suffered.

BROTHERS AND SISTERS: Mrs. Charity Malvina Remsberg; Mary Clarissa Harding; Mrs. Abigail Victoria Lewis; George Tyron Harding; Mrs. Phoebe Caroline Votaw.

CHILDHOOD AND EARLY YEARS

Harding spoke of his childhood with pleasure. He enjoyed physical work on the farm and also hired out as a laborer on the local railroad. He learned the printers' trade while working part-time for the local newspaper and played cornet in the local band.

EDUCATION

Harding was a product of the local school system. At fifteen, he enrolled at Ohio Central College in Iberia and graduated in 1882. While at college he started a campus paper.

MILITARY SERVICE

None

RELIGION

Baptist

FAMILY LIFE

Marriage:

Harding, age twenty-five, married Florence Kling DeWolfe, thirty, on July 8, 1891. She was the daughter of a wealthy local banker, Amos Kling, and a divorceé with a son. Her father was violently opposed to the marriage, convinced that the rumors of Negro bloodlines in the Harding family were true. The union was an unhappy one from the beginning and although they worked together on Harding's newspaper, and she was instrumental in making it a success, their lives were quite separate. She died on November 21, 1924, of kidney disease.

Children:

Elizabeth Ann Christian (Illegitimate. Mother: Nan Britton)

AFFAIRS

Carrie Phillips: Wife of his friend James Phillips, she and Harding were involved for over fifteen years. She threatened to make the affair public unless Harding voted against the declaration of war in 1917, but backed down only to threaten exposure again while he was running for president. She accepted a lump sum and a monthly payment from the Republican party to keep quiet.

Nan Britton: The affair with Britton began in 1917 and lasted until 1923. She met him at hotels and at the White House, where their daughter, Elizabeth Ann, was conceived. After failing to convince the Harding estate to grant Elizabeth a trust fund, she wrote a best-selling exposé in 1927 called *The President's Daughter* to provide for her care.

HOBBIES

Golf, poker, baseball, fishing, sailing, and driving.

DIED IN OFFICE

While returning from a trip to Alaska, Harding died suddenly of a heart attack on August 2, 1923, and Calvin Coolidge succeeded to the presidency. It is suspected that the implications of scandal and corruption in his administration proved too stressful.

CHAPTER THIRTY
☆ ☆ ☆

CALVIN COOLIDGE

1872-1933

30th President of the United States
"Silent Cal"

☆ ☆ ☆

SECTION ONE

BORN

Coolidge was born on July 4, 1872, at the family home in Plymouth Notch, Vermont.

TERMS SERVED AS PRESIDENT

1923 (Succeeded Harding.)
1925–1929

POLITICAL PARTY

Republican

PUBLIC LIFE BEFORE PRESIDENCY

Coolidge practiced law in Northampton, Massachusetts, after his admission to the bar in 1897.

Massachusetts General Court— 1907–1908

Coolidge pushed a progressive agenda during his two terms, advocating a six-day workweek and labor laws for women and children.

Mayor of Northampton, Massachusetts—1910–1911

Displaying his knack for running government like a business, Coolidge cut taxes and improved services at the same time.

Massachusetts State Senator—1912–1915

Coolidge continued to work for reform of labor laws and supported workers' rights to compensation.

Lieutenant Governor of Massachusetts— 1916–1918

As lieutenant governor he handled appointments to office and pardons, content as usual to remain in the background.

Governor of Massachusetts—1919–1920

Continuing his agenda of workers' rights, Coolidge urged and got the forty-eight-hour workweek for women and children. He took a stand on law and order and gained national recognition when he backed the mayor of Boston and sent in troops to quell the Boston police strike of 1919. "There is no right to strike against the public safety by anybody, anywhere, anytime," he told union boss Samuel Gompers.

Vice President—1921–1923

As vice president, Coolidge set the tone for his demeanor in high public office. He rarely involved himself in Senate debates or in cabinet meetings. He was vacationing at home in Vermont when news reached him of Harding's death on August 2, 1923.

CAMPAIGN

Election—1924

In August 1923, Vice President Calvin Coolidge, untouched by the Harding scandals, became president. Because the country's economy was booming, Coolidge's nomination in 1924 was a certainty.

The Democrats, on the other hand, took nine intense days of brutal infighting and 102 ballots before settling on John W. Davis, a New York lawyer. The primary issue was over a resolution strongly to condemn the Ku Klux Klan and their increasingly violent activities in the South and Midwest, both Democratic strongholds. In the end, the Klan was condemned but only mildly.

A bipartisan third party grew out of dissatisfaction with both candidates and nominated Republican Wisconsin Senator Robert ("Fighting Bob") LaFollette for president and Democratic Montana Senator Burton K. Wheeler for vice president. The Progressives hoped to get enough votes to throw the election into the House of Representatives.

Despite vigorous campaigning, neither Davis nor LaFollette

was able to come up with an issue that captured the imagination of a contented, prosperous nation. On Election Day, Coolidge polled more popular votes than his two opponents combined.

Electoral Votes:
Coolidge 382
Davis 136
LaFollette 13

VICE PRESIDENTS

None (First Term)
Charles G. Dawes (1925–1929) Illinois. Lawyer. (Second Term)

THE CABINET

Secretary of State:
Charles E. Hughes (1923–1925)
Frank B. Kellogg (1925–1929)

Secretary of the Treasury:
Andrew W. Mellon (1923–1929)

Secretary of War:
John W. Weeks (1923–1925)
Dwight F. Davis (1925–1929)

Attorney General:
Harry M. Daugherty (1923–1924)
Harlan F. Stone (1924–1925)
John G. Sargent (1925–1929)

Postmaster General:
Harry S. New (1923–1929)

Secretary of the Navy:
Edwin Denby (1923–1924)
Curtis D. Wilbur (1924–1929)

Secretary of the Interior:
Hubert Work (1923–1928)
Roy O. West (1929)

Secretary of Agriculture:
Henry C. Wallace (1923–1924)

Howard M. Gore (1924–1925)
W. M. Jardine (1925–1929)

Secretary of Commerce:
Herbert C. Hoover (1923–1928)
William F. Whiting (1928–1929)

Secretary of Labor:
James G. Davis (1923–1929)

SIGNIFICANT EVENTS THAT OCCURRED DURING
OFFICE——AUGUST 3, 1923–MARCH 3, 1929

Immigration Act of 1924

This act limited the numbers of Italians and Jews that could enter the country, raised quotas on northern Europeans, but excluded Japanese and put a ceiling on the total number of immigrants allowed.

Revenue Acts—1924–1926

These tax reductions on income and inheritance also eliminated many excise taxes left over from World War I. Suddenly, huge amounts of money were available for speculation and the stock market began its meteoric rise.

Veterans' Bonus Act—1924

Coolidge vetoed legislation to give paid-up life insurance to veterans of World War I that would be redeemable in twenty years, but Congress overrode the veto and the bill became a law.

Air Commerce Act—1926

This act awarded transcontinental commercial air routes to TWA and Southwestern Airway.

McNary-Haugen Bill—1927

Coolidge twice vetoed legislation to form a government corporation to purchase farmers' surpluses, calling it nothing more than 'price fixing."

Pact of Paris—1928

The Kellogg-Briand Pact of 1928 was a joint agreement between most of the countries of the world to settle international disputes peacefully.

CONTRIBUTIONS TO AMERICAN HISTORY WHILE
PRESIDENT

Calvin "the business of America is business" Coolidge believed that the nation and the government needed to focus attention on private affairs rather than being pressed to institute public policies. The general sense of prosperity that existed in the 1920s supported his view, although signs of the depression to come were in the air.

SECTION TWO

PERSONAL PROFILE

Coolidge, chronically shy, small, and somewhat frail, was plagued with respiratory problems throughout his life. He was a frugal and industrious man who admired businessmen and corporations. He had a dry wit and loved practical jokes, which he played on close friends and advisors. Known as a man of few words, he would speak to the issue at hand and no more. Ironically, for a man who spent his life in the public eye he had to force himself to meet strangers and learn to be cordial and friendly.

FAMILY BACKGROUND

Ancestors

Coolidge's family emigrated from England and settled in Massachusetts and eventually in Vermont.

Immediate Family

FATHER: John Calvin Coolidge (1845–1926) A successfu farmer, storekeeper, and active public official in Vermont Coolidge's father, as notary public and justice of the peace, gave hin the oath of office when Harding died.

MOTHER: Victoria Josephine Moor Coolidge (1846–1885) A Vermont native, she died of tuberculosis in 1884.

BROTHERS AND SISTERS: Abigail Gratia Coolidge. She died when Coolidge was fifteen years old.

CHILDHOOD AND EARLY YEARS

Coolidge grew up working in his father's store and doing regular chores on the family farm. From childhood he was serious, hardworking, and trustworthy. He shared his father's interest in politics and local affairs. He was known for a dry and satiric sense of humor.

EDUCATION

Coolidge attended local schools where he was an average student. He enrolled at Amherst College and again, was only an average student until his junior and senior years when his grades suddenly began to improve. He graduated cum laude in 1895. He was considered the campus wit, but spent most of his time alone. Coolidge studied law in Northampton and was admitted to the bar in 1897.

MILITARY SERVICE

None

RELIGION

Congregationalist

FAMILY LIFE

Marriage:

Coolidge, thirty-three, married Grace Anna Goodhue, twenty-six, on October 4, 1905, at her home in Burlington, Vermont. She was the daughter of Andrew I. Goodhue, an engineer and inspector. Mrs. Coolidge was as outgoing and charming as her husband was reserved and reclusive. She was a popular first lady. She died on July 8, 1957.

Children:

John Coolidge (1906–?); Calvin Coolidge (1908–1924)

HOBBIES

Practical jokes, target shooting, horseback riding, and the circus.

POST PRESIDENCY

In 1928 Coolidge announced to a surprised nation that he would not seek reelection. He retired with his wife to Northampton, Massachusetts, where he wrote his autobiography, newspaper columns, and magazine articles.

DIED

He died of a coronary thrombosis in Northampton, Massachusetts, on January 5, 1933.

CHAPTER THIRTY-ONE
☆ ☆ ☆

HERBERT HOOVER

1874–1964

31st President of the United States
"The Great Humanitarian"
"The Great Engineer"

☆ ☆ ☆

SECTION ONE

BORN

Hoover was born on August 10, 1874, in West Branch, Iowa.

TERM SERVED AS PRESIDENT

1929–1933

POLITICAL PARTY

Republican

PUBLIC LIFE BEFORE PRESIDENCY

Mining Engineer—1896–1914

After working in California mines as a laborer, he was hired to inspect gold mines in Australia. During the next twenty years he traveled through much of Asia, Africa, and Europe as a mining developer and made a fortune. At the outbreak of World War I in August 1914 he was in London.

World War I—1915–1919

Hoover, who was a pacifist, volunteered to help American tourists get out of Europe and then was appointed head of the Commission for Relief in Belgium and later the American Relief Administration. Hoover was responsible for the distribution of millions of dollars in aid, food, and clothing and set aside funds for Belgian postwar reconstruction. The work he did earned him the nickname "the great humanitarian," and national recognition. When the United States entered the war in April 1917, Hoover was called to Washington to serve as food administrator.

By the end of the war, Hoover was a potential presidential candidate, but he had never participated in partisan politics. In 1920 he became a Republican.

Secretary of Commerce—1921–1928

As secretary of commerce, Hoover was active in policy as well as domestic affairs. He was concerned not only with business but with workers and their quality of life as well. He asked corporations to join together in trade associations and thereby develop and share vital information about costs of production and distribution and about available markets. He expanded the Bureau of Standards and authorized the testing of a wider range of commercial products, increased the role of the Census Bureau as a collector of data for business, and lobbied to improve working conditions.

CAMPAIGN

Election—1928

When Calvin Coolidge declined to seek reelection in 1928, the Republican favorite was clearly Herbert Hoover, his highly respected secretary of commerce. Hoover was a strong believer in big business, small government, and Prohibition. He was nominated for president on the first ballot.

The Democratic nominee was Al Smith of New York City who had dropped out of school and made his living on the streets until, as member of Tammany Hall, he worked his way up to the governorship of New York. A Roman Catholic, he was a witty and charismatic man who was against Prohibition and pro states' rights.

The vicious campaign centered on Smith's religion and Prohibition. The Klan burned crosses at Democratic rallies across the South and West in protest. Millions of people believed that Smith was under the influence of the pope and that all Protestant religious ceremonies would be banned. He was portrayed as a president who would set the country on a drunken binge.

The mudslinging, although brutal, was unnecessary. The public believed that Hoover, "great engineer," would maintain prosperity and he won in a landslide.

Electoral Votes:
Hoover 444
Smith 87

VICE PRESIDENT

Charles Curtis (1860–1936) Kansas. Lawyer.

THE CABINET

Secretary of State:
  Henry L. Stimson (1929–1933)

Secretary of the Treasury:
  Andrew W. Mellon (1929–1932)
  Ogden L. Mills (1932–1933)

Secretary of War:
  James W. Good (1929)
  Patrick J. Hurley (1929–1933)

Attorney General:
  William DeWitt Mitchell (1929–1933)

Postmaster General:
  Walter F. Brown (1929–1933)

Secretary of the Navy:
  Charles F. Adams (1929–1933)

Secretary of the Interior:
  Ray L. Wilbur (1929–1933)

Secretary of Agriculture:
  Arthur M. Hyde (1929–1933)

Secretary of Commerce:
  Robert P. Lamont (1929–1932)
  Roy D. Chapin (1932–1933)

Secretary of Labor:
  James J. Davis (1929–1930)
  William N. Doak (1930–1933)

SIGNIFICANT EVENTS THAT OCCURRED DURING

OFFICE——MARCH 4, 1929–MARCH 3, 1933

The Great Depression

The result of overspeculation in financial markets, severe drought in the Midwest, high tariffs, and surpluses of agricultural products that depressed prices, the Great Depression was the worst economic disaster in American history. Lasting for over ten years, it plunged the country into a spiral of despair that would not end until World War II.

Agricultural Marketing Act—1929

In order to combat the decade-long agricultural depression, the act promoted the idea of marketing cooperatives to increase their efficiency while the government purchased surplus commodities for a limited time.

Prohibition Reexamined—1929

Hoover established a commission to examine law enforcement and to take a look at the real effects of Prohibition on the country. While the commission decided that the soaring crime rate was linked to sales of illegal alcohol, it did not suggest repeal.

The Stock Market Crash—1929

On Black Thursday, October 29, 1929, the stock market collapsed and the country was plunged into the Great Depression, from which it would not recover until the beginning of World War II.

Hawley-Smoot Tariff—1930

With the highest general level of duties in history, the tariff caused a global trade war.

London Naval Treaty–1930

This treaty revised the limitations set on naval vessels in the Washington Conference of 1922. Japan was allowed to increase its fleet and began the buildup that led to World War II in the Pacific.

Bonus March—May 1932

Fifteen thousand veterans marched on the Capitol Building to demand immediate payment of the bonus voted them by Congress in 1924 even though it was not due to be paid until 1945. Most left when Congress voted down the bill, but several thousand remained camped out near the Capitol. In July, Hoover ordered the army to remove them, and many were injured in the ensuing action, which was perceived by the nation as heartless and brutal.

End of the Lame Duck—1933

The Twentieth Amendment moved the inauguration of the president from March 4 to January 20 and called for Congress to convene on January 3.

CONTRIBUTIONS TO AMERICAN HISTORY WHILE

PRESIDENT

Hoover and his advisors were unable to recognize the implications of the stock market crash of 1929 and essentially did nothing to save the collapsing economy. Instead, fearing that too much government intervention would hinder the process of recovery, he took a conservative stance, counting on the strength of individuals and private initiative to solve the country's problems. As the crisis spiraled out of control, Hoover's perceived lack of action ruined his excellent reputation and eclipsed his brilliant political career before the presidency.

SECTION TWO

PERSONAL PROFILE

Hoover, tall and stocky, was a shy man who was deeply committed to his Quaker beliefs and practiced them in his public and private life. He believed in hard work, efficiency, and organization, and demanded it from everyone he associated with.

FAMILY BACKGROUND

Ancestors

Of Swiss-German heritage, Hoover's (originally Huber) family emigrated to Pennsylvania in the early seventeenth century and settled in North Carolina.

Immediate Family

FATHER: Jesse Clark Hoover (1846–1880) A successful blacksmith and salesman in West Branch, Hoover's father died of heart trouble while Herbert was a child.

MOTHER: Huldah Minthorn Hoover (1848–1883) She took in sewing and hoarded her husband's life insurance money to raise the family, but was to die of pneumonia only three years after her husband's death.

BROTHERS AND SISTERS: Theodore Jesse Hoover; Mrs. Mary Leavitt.

CHILDHOOD AND EARLY YEARS

After Hoover was orphaned at the age of eight, he lived with relatives around the country, including an uncle who was superintendent of the Osage reservation in Oklahoma. He settled eventually with his uncle John Minthorn, a doctor in Newberg, Oregon, where he spent most of his childhood.

EDUCATION

After elementary school in West Branch, Hoover attended a Quaker school in Oregon but never graduated. He passed an entrance and was the youngest student in his class at Stanford University where he studied mining engineering, graduating in 1895.

MILITARY SERVICE

None

RELIGION

Society of Friends (Quaker)

FAMILY LIFE

Marriage:

Hoover, twenty-four, married Lou Henry, twenty-four, on February 10, 1899, at her home in Monterey, California. Hoover met Lou when they were geology students at Stanford. She became a Quaker. From the beginning she was an active part of Hoover's political career. She died of a heart attack in 1944.

Children:

Herbert Clark Hoover (1903–1969); Alan Henry Hoover (1907–)

HOBBIES

Exercise, fishing, and reading fiction.

POST PRESIDENCY

After leaving office Hoover remained an important advisor in the Republican party. After World War II he served as coordinator of the European Food Program in 1946 and 1947. From 1947 to 1949 and later from 1953 to 1955, he headed two commissions on the organization of the executive branch of the government. In his reports, he recommended changes to make the government more efficient and the executive branch more accountable to the Congress and the public.

DIED

Hoover died in New York City on October 20, 1964, of massive internal bleeding, a complication of his bouts with intestinal cancer.

CHAPTER THIRTY-TWO
☆ ☆ ☆

FRANKLIN DELANO ROOSEVELT

1882–1945

32nd President of the United States
"FDR"

☆ ☆ ☆

SECTION ONE

BORN

FDR was born on January 30, 1882, at the family estate at Hyde Park, New York.

TERMS SERVED AS PRESIDENT

1933–1937
1937–1941
1941–1945
January–April 1945 (Died in office.)

POLITICAL PARTY

Democrat

PUBLIC LIFE BEFORE PRESIDENCY

New York State Senator—1911–1913

During his two terms, Roosevelt continued the family tradition of reform politics, opposing Tammany Hall, and supporting labor and women's suffrage.

Assistant Secretary of the Navy—1913–1920

Roosevelt worked to expand the navy, making early preparations for American entrance into WWI. He was a firm supporter of the League of Nations.

Polio—1921

Roosevelt was struck with polio after his unsuccessful campaign for the Democratic vice presidential nomination in 1920. For three years, he struggled to overcome the disease, and by 1924 had resumed his law practice and begun his political comeback with his nominating speech for Al Smith.

Governor of New York—1929–1933

As the country sank deeper into the Great Depression, Roosevelt worked during his two terms as governor to deal with mounting problems of unemployment, aid programs to farmers and businesses, and attempt to create public jobs.

CAMPAIGNS

Election—1932

Because Hoover, who was blamed for plunging the country into depression and economic chaos, seemed doomed to defeat, the contest for the Democratic nomination was fiercely fought. Al Smith had strong party support, as did Speaker of the House John Nance Garner. But progressive and popular FDR was the front-runner. Although many professionals considered him unfit for office because of his health and his experience, Roosevelt and his advisors, known as the "Brain Trust," orchestrated his nomination on the fourth ballot.

Roosevelt flew to Chicago to give his acceptance speech in which he said, "I pledge you, I pledge myself, to a new deal for the American people."

The Republicans had no choice but to renominate Hoover; not doing so would have admitted responsibility for the Depression. Hoover was renominated on the first ballot at a convention that was dreary and lackluster.

The "New Deal" captured the imagination of the voters, and Roosevelt soared. Hoover's campaign floundered and sank under the weight of the country's problems, and he won just six states in a humiliating defeat.

Electoral Votes:
Roosevelt 472
Hoover 59

Election—1936

The 1936 election was a referendum on Franklin D. Roosevelt. The Democratic convention was essentially a pep rally for the incumbent president, and he was renominated by acclamation. In his acceptance speech, Roosevelt promised an expansion of the New Deal, proclaiming that Americans had a "rendezvous with destiny."

The Republican nominee was Kansas Governor Alfred M. Landon, a fiscal conservative who favored some New Deal measures such as unemployment relief and subsidies for agriculture.

While the Republicans attacked what they perceived as flagrant spending, taxes, and waste in Roosevelt's administration, FDR simply asked the voters if they'd like to go back to the conditions in 1932 or if they thought they were better off after four years of the New Deal. He won all but two states in another landslide victory.

Electoral Votes:
Roosevelt 523
Landon 8

Election—1940

Although the country had not fully recovered from the Depression, the economy and the New Deal were only minor issues in 1940. The real question on people's mind was whether or not the United States should enter the war in Europe.

FDR would probably not have bucked tradition, retiring after his two full terms. But there was no real successor in the Democratic ranks, and eventual entrance into the war was becoming very likely. Roosevelt finally decided he would run for an unprecedented third term—if he was drafted by the convention as he was on the first ballot.

The Republicans couldn't decide between professional politicians Thomas Dewey or Robert Taft. On the sixth ballot, they settled on a man who had no previous political experience and who had been a Democrat until 1939, an Indiana lawyer and businessman named Wendell Willkie. Willkie proved to be an able and persuasive campaigner without a viable issue on which to base a campaign.

Roosevelt, boosted by an upsurge in the economy based on defense spending, his record, and his popularity, won by his third landslide.

Electoral Votes:
Roosevelt 449
Willkie 82

Election—1944

By the time campaigning began, World War II was reaching its conclusion. Roosevelt agreed to run for a fourth term to finish the job, and he was nominated on the first ballot. The real business of the convention was the choice of vice president. Wanting to replace Wallace, Roosevelt's advisors settled on Missouri Senator Harry S. Truman, who was extremely reluctant to leave the Senate for what he considered a powerless position. In the end he agreed to accept the nomination.

After General Douglas MacArthur refused the Republican nod, the party chose Wendell Willkie, who was unable to gather the necessary support in the primaries and lost to New York Governor Thomas A. Dewey. Dewey won an overwhelming first ballot victory.

Dewey campaigned on the position that the Democrats had held office for so long that they were unable to govern effectively. The Republicans also quietly suggested that Roosevelt was too ill to continue to run the country.

Roosevelt had decided not to campaign and focus on ending the war, but rumors about his health finally forced him to make public appearances and defend his record and his ability to continue to govern. He won again in a landslide, but died two and a half months later of a cerebral hemorrhage.

Electoral Votes:
Roosevelt 432
Dewey 99

VICE PRESIDENTS

John N. Garner (1868–1967) Texas. Farmer.
Henry A. Wallace (1888–1965) Iowa. Editor.
Harry S. Truman (1884–1972) Missouri. Farmer, haberdasher. (Succeeded Roosevelt.)

THE CABINET

Secretary of State:
Cordell Hull (1933–1944)
Edward R. Stettinius, Jr. (1944–1945)

Secretary of the Treasury:
William H. Woodin (1933–1934)
Henry Morgenthau, Jr. (1934–1945)

Secretary of War:
  George H. Dern (1933–1936)
  Harry H. Woodring (1937–1940)
  Henry L. Stimson (1940–1945)

Attorney General:
  Homer S. Cummings (1933–1939)
  Frank Murphy (1939–1940)
  Robert H. Jackson (1940–1941)
  Francis B. Biddle (1941–1945)

Postmaster General:
  James A. Farley (1933–1940)
  Frank C. Walker (1940–1945)

Secretary of the Navy:
  Claude A. Swanson (1933–1939)
  Charles Edison (1940)
  Frank Knox (1940–1944)
  James V. Forrestal (1944–1945)

Secretary of the Interior:
  Harold L. Ickes (1933–1945)

Secretary of Agriculture:
  Henry A. Wallace (1933–1940)
  Claude R. Wickard (1940–1945)

Secretary of Commerce:
  Daniel C. Roper (1933–1938)
  Harry L. Hopkins (1939–1940)
  Jesse H. Jones (1940–1945)
  Henry A. Wallace (1945)

Secretary of Labor:
  Frances Perkins (1933–1945)

SIGNIFICANT EVENTS THAT OCCURRED DURING OFFICE——MARCH 4, 1933–APRIL 12, 1945

The Great Depression and the New Deal

The New Deal was a sweeping reorganization of federal policy geared to rebuilding the economy and putting governmental safeguards in place to prevent future collapses. The concept of government being directly responsible for the general welfare of its citizens would forever change the nature of American politics.

The Banking Crisis—1933. The day Roosevelt prepared to take office, the nation's banking system was near collapse. Panicked depositors were withdrawing savings at an alarming rate. Roosevelt, saying that "the only thing we have to fear is fear itself," forced the passage of emergency banking legislation that provided funding so that banks could reopen. In his first "fireside chat" he urged Americans to trust their institutions and not to hoard cash, thus beginning the long process of rebuilding confidence in the economy.

Abandonment of the Gold Standard—1933. To free up currency, Roosevelt abandoned the gold standard or "hard money" and reduced the gold content of the dollar.

The Alphabet Acts—1933-1935. Roosevelt instituted a series of broadly based programs to rebuild the economy and hasten recovery, including: the Civilian Conservation Corps (CCC)—jobs; the Agricultural Adjustment Act (AAA)—reducing crop surplus; the National Industrial Recovery Act (NIR)—grants for large construction projects; Unemployment Insurance and Social Security; the Home Owners Loan Corporation and Farm Credit Administration; the Works Progress Administration (WPA); the Tennessee Valley Authority (TVA)—electrical power from the Tennessee River, and the Rural Electrification Administration (REA)—providing power to farm homes.

While these programs "primed the economy's pump," and set the country moving again they would lead to record federal deficits and dissatisfaction with Roosevelt's "New Deal" by the end of the decade.

Repeal of Prohibition—1933

The Twenty-first Amendment to the Constitution was ratified in 1933 and Prohibition came to an end.

Recognition of the Soviet Union—1933

In exchange for diplomatic recognition, the Soviet Union agreed to stop subversive activities in the United States and recognize the rights of American residents in Russia.

Good Neighbor Policy—1936

Because of the economic problems at home, foreign policy in the 1930s was placed in a secondary position. But Roosevelt's administration effected some changes in relations with Latin America. Replacing the policy of Dollar Diplomacy with a more hands-off approach, Roosevelt withdrew troops from Haiti, removed the United States from Cuba's internal affairs, promised more aid, and agreed to the defense of the Western Hemisphere. The Good Neighbor Policy would pay dividends during World War II.

Court Packing Plan—1937

After the U.S. Supreme Court declared much of the early New Deal legislation unconstitutional, Roosevelt tried to increase the size of the court and "pack" it with younger, more liberal justices. But pressure from his opponents and from his own advisors convinced Roosevelt to abandon the idea.

Hatch Act—1939

This law barred federal employees from taking part in partisan politics.

World War II—1939–1945
(American Participation—1941–1945)

Roosevelt wanted to keep the United States out of World War II, although he believed the United States should be prepared to fight and should provide military aid to its allies. But the Lend-Lease program, which provided arms for Britain and the Soviet Union and sending convoys of supply ships to England would soon make it impossible for the United States to remain neutral, and Roosevelt knew that war was inevitable. The Japanese attack on Pearl Harbor on December 7, 1941, and Germany's declaration of war forced the issue. Americans ceased to be divided and put their entire focus on the war, mobilizing a massive and effective effort.

Roosevelt and Winston Churchill, Great Britain's prime minister, were responsible for Allied military and naval strategy. While they engaged the Japanese in the early years of the war, their focus was on defeating Hitler and forcing the Axis powers into unconditional surrender.

Roosevelt insisted on limiting the Allied effort to military victory. Although concerned about Stalin's ambitions in Eastern Europe, he formed an uneasy alliance with the USSR, in order to hasten the end of the war. He hoped that there might be a possibility of Soviet-American cooperation through a United Nations.

The brutal and devastating conflict would last for five years, and Roosevelt would die before it ended.

CONTRIBUTIONS TO AMERICAN HISTORY WHILE

PRESIDENT

Roosevelt served as president during one of the most difficult periods of American history. In the process of fighting the Great Depression and then World War II, he redefined the position of the federal government on both foreign and domestic policy. Facing the potential collapse of American capitalism, he put the government in the business of social welfare and of managing the economy to promote recovery and public goals.

By coming to the aid of Western Allies before formally entering World War II, he sent a message that the United States was vitally interested in the preservation of democracy on a global level.

The successes he achieved in both arenas made the Democrats the majority party and the champions of the working class, taking the banner of reform from the Republican party.

As president, Roosevelt pioneered the political use of media. He used the radio to address issues facing the country. His fireside chats, broadcast in a relaxed and familiar manner, managed to assuage the fears of Americans who were uncertain and frightened about the future. His unique political style, charm, and charisma made him one of the most revered and beloved presidents in history.

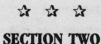

SECTION TWO

PERSONAL PROFILE

Roosevelt, at 6´ 1″ and 180 pounds, was a handsome and athletic figure with a ready smile and friendly manner. Even after he was stricken with polio in 1921, he remained spirited and confident. Three years of physical therapy and hard work made it possible for him to stand with braces and walk short distances with a cane or crutches. He adjusted well to his handicap and went out of his way to make people feel at ease around him. A gifted public speaker, his self-confidence and certainty served him well as president during, perhaps, the most difficult twelve years in American history.

FAMILY BACKGROUND

Ancestors

Roosevelt's family was comprised of Dutch, French Huguenot, Swiss, Swedish, and English elements. His family emigrated from the Netherlands and settled in the New York area around the mid-seventeenth century. The early Roosevelts did well in the new country and were politically active and prosperous.

Immediate Family

FATHER: James Roosevelt (1828–1900) Lawyer, financial speculator, and prosperous landowner. His success helped the Roosevelts become one of the wealthiest and most socially exclusive families on the East Coast. He lived most of his life at the estate in Hyde Park, New York, where he involved himself in business matters and oversaw his huge estate.

MOTHER: Sara Delano Roosevelt (1854–1941) James Roosevelt's second wife was the daughter of a wealthy importer and trader. Franklin was the focus of her entire life. She discouraged his efforts to get into politics as well as his marriage to Eleanor, wishing him to live a simple gentleman's life at Hyde Park.

BROTHERS AND SISTERS: Half brother—James Roosevelt.

CHILDHOOD AND EARLY YEARS

Roosevelt was an only child and grew up in the wealthy, insulated, and extremely comfortable lifestyle of a country squire. He traveled frequently with his parents, both in America and abroad. His doting mother saw that he lacked for nothing. The sailboat he was given at age sixteen instilled in him a lifelong love of the water, and his earliest dreams were to become a naval officer.

EDUCATION

Roosevelt learned the basics from a series of private tutors at the family estate and in Europe. His mother saw to it that he also learned the social graces, dancing, and the arts. At Groton, which he entered in 1896, he was active in sports and extracurricular activities. His cousin, Governor Teddy Roosevelt, spoke at his graduation. He enrolled at Harvard in 1900 and graduated in 1904 with a major in political history and government. He was an average student with an active social life. He entered Columbia Law School in 1904, but passed the bar while he was in school and never graduated, instead taking a job with a Wall Street firm from 1907 to 1910.

MILITARY SERVICE

None

RELIGION

Episcopalian

FAMILY LIFE

Marriage:

On March 17, 1905, Roosevelt, twenty-three, married twenty-year-old Anna Eleanor Roosevelt (1884–1962) at the home of her aunt in New York City. She was his fifth cousin and the niece of Theodore Roosevelt. Roosevelt's mother was opposed to the marriage and did her best to dissuade her son. Active in social issues from an early age, Eleanor opened Roosevelt's eyes to the problems that existed outside the gates of his Hyde Park estate. When he was stricken with polio, Eleanor helped with his recovery and encouraged him to reenter political life. Although they had great affection for each other, they began to grow apart, and while they remained close, lived essentially separate lives. Eleanor became the most active first lady in history, pursuing causes such as women's rights and civil rights. She became a model for independent women everywhere, remaining involved in public life until she died of tuberculosis in 1962.

Children:

Anna Eleanor Roosevelt (1906–1975); James Roosevelt (1907–1991); Elliott Roosevelt (1910–1990); Franklin Delano Roosevelt, Jr. (1914–1988); John Aspinwall Roosevelt (1916–1981)

AFFAIR

Lucy Page Mercer was hired as Eleanor Roosevelt's social secretary in 1913. She and Roosevelt began an affair that was discovered by Eleanor, who demanded that he break it off or face a divorce.

Roosevelt agreed, but resumed seeing Lucy sometime later and continued to do so until he died in 1945.

HOBBIES

Swimming, stamp collecting, sailing, poker, and bird watching.

DIED

FDR died while in office. After the Yalta Conference in 1945, Roosevelt, whose health was steadily failing, journeyed to his home in Warm Springs, Georgia, for rest and recuperation. He died there on April 12 of a cerebral hemorrhage and was succeeded by Harry S. Truman.

CHAPTER THIRTY-THREE
☆ ☆ ☆

HARRY S. TRUMAN

1884-1972

33rd President of the United States
"Give 'Em Hell Harry"

☆ ☆ ☆

SECTION ONE

BORN

Truman was born on May 8, 1884, at his family home in Lamar, Missouri.

TERMS SERVED AS PRESIDENT

1945–1949 (Succeeded Franklin Delano Roosevelt.)
1949–1953

POLITICAL PARTY

Democrat

PUBLIC LIFE BEFORE PRESIDENCY

After his graduation from high school, Truman worked a series of odd jobs in Kansas City including mailroom and bank clerk, and timekeeper for the railroad. In 1906 he returned to the farm to help his father, which he did until World War I. After the war he went into the clothing business, which initially did well but folded during the recession in 1922, leaving Truman in bankruptcy.

Judge of Jackson County—1922–1924

When the business failed in 1921, he entered politics with the help of Thomas J. Pendergast's Kansas City Democratic machine and won election to the Jackson County Court (county commission) in 1922.

Presiding Judge of Jackson County— 1926–1934

Defeated in 1924, he was elected presiding judge in 1926 and held the office for eight years. He proved himself to be reform-minded and a friend of the lower and middle classes.

U.S. Senator—1935–1945

In 1934 Truman was elected to the U.S. Senate, where he was an active supporter of the New Deal. In 1941 Truman became chairman of a special Senate committee investigating inefficiency and corruption in World War II military spending programs, where he gained recognition for his integrity and solid work.

Vice President—March–April 1945

Well liked, and with strong support in the Democratic party, he reluctantly accepted the Democratic vice presidential nomination in 1944, replacing Henry A. Wallace. Eighty-two days later, Truman became president when Roosevelt died on April 12, 1945.

CAMPAIGN

Election—1948

In 1946, after the end of World War II, the Republicans captured control of Congress for the first time since 1932, and most political observers believed that the Republicans would capture the White House in 1948. People were ready for a change. Both parties approached General Eisenhower, commander in chief of Allied forces in Europe and national hero, but he declined, preferring to wait for a better political climate.

The Democrats unenthusiastically nominated Truman for president. Splinter parties had formed which opposed Truman's stand on civil rights and blamed the growing "Cold War" between the United States and the Soviet Union on his foreign policy. Strom Thurmond was the opposition nominee. The polls showed Republican nominee Thomas Dewey leading Truman by a wide margin.

Truman and his advisors decided not to run against the popular Dewey, but against the Republican Congress, which had refused to pass any of the social reform programs he had proposed. "Give 'em hell, Harry" Truman attacked Congress as the "worst in history" and labeled the Republicans "bloodsuckers with offices on Wall Street."

Dewey, with the polls showing him comfortably ahead, refused to answer the charges and spent the last days of the campaign planning his inauguration. The *Chicago Tribune,* in one of the most famous journalistic gaffs ever, printed a post–Election Day headline that read "Dewey Beats Truman." But, against all odds, Truman was victorious.

Electoral Votes:
Truman 303
Dewey 189
Thurmond 39

VICE PRESIDENT

None (First Term)
Alben William Barkley (1877–1956) Kentucky. Lawyer. (Second Term)

THE CABINET

Secretary of State:
  Edward R. Stettinius (1945)
  James F. Byrnes (1945–1947)
  George C. Marshall (1947–1949)
  Dean G. Acheson (1949–1953)

Secretary of the Treasury:
  Henry Morgenthau, Jr. (1945)
  Frederick M. Vinson (1945–1946)
  John W. Snyder (1946–1953)

Secretary of War:
  Henry L. Stimson (1945)
  Robert P. Patterson (1945–1947)
  Kenneth C. Royall (1947)

Secretary of Defense:
  James V. Forrestal (1947–1949)
  Louis A. Johnson (1949–1950)
  George C. Marshall (1950–1951)
  Robert A. Lovett (1951–1953)

Attorney General:
  Francis B. Biddle (1945)
  Thomas C. Clark (1945–1949)
  J. Howard McGrath (1949–1952)

Postmaster General:
  Frank C. Walker (1945)
  Robert E. Hannegan (1945–1947)
  Jesse M. Donaldson (1947–1953)

Secretary of the Navy:
  James V. Forrestal (1945–1947)

Secretary of the Interior:
  Harold L. Ickes (1945–1946)
  Julius A. Krug (1946–1949)
  Oscar L. Chapman (1950–1953)

Secretary of Agriculture:
  Claude R. Wickard (1945)
  Clinton P. Anderson (1945–1948)
  Charles F. Brannan (1948–1953)

Secretary of Commerce:
  Henry A. Wallace (1945–1946)
  William Averell Harriman (1946–1948)
  Charles Sawyer (1948–1953)

Secretary of Labor:
  Frances Perkins (1945)
  Lewis B. Schwellenbach (1945–1948)
  Maurice J. Tobin (1949–1953)

SIGNIFICANT EVENTS THAT OCCURRED DURING OFFICE—APRIL 12, 1945–JANUARY 20, 1953

The End of World War II—1945–1946

When Germany surrendered on May 8, 1945, it became clear that the Soviet Union was determined to continue to occupy Eastern Europe and control the eastern portion of Germany. In July of 1945, Truman met with Stalin at the Potsdam Conference to discuss the issue, but there was no resolution. During this meeting, Truman gave the go-ahead to use the atomic bomb at Hiroshima and, if necessary, Nagasaki, to hasten Japanese surrender in the Pacific. The bombings, on August 6 and August 9, forced the Japanese into unconditional surrender on August 14, 1945. From 1945 to 1946 the Nuremberg Trials were held to prosecute twenty-two top Nazi leaders for war crimes, focusing on the Holocaust.

The Cold War and the Truman Doctrine

By 1946 Western fears of Communist occupation of Eastern Europe proved to be correct, and the "Iron Curtain" descended over Europe. Truman responded in what became known as the Truman Doctrine, that it was the job of free peoples to help others remain free. When the Soviets isolated West Berlin in 1948, the Allies undertook a massive airlift to get food and supplies into the city. The Cold War, which would last for almost fifty years, was born. The United States and Western European nations negotiated the North Atlantic Treaty (NATO) in 1949. And, Truman introduced the Four Point Program to release technical aid for impoverished countries, intended to check the spread of communism.

Marshall Plan—1948–1952

Truman authorized Secretary of State Marshall to implement his ambitious and far-reaching plan for the recovery of Europe. The United States would spend billions of dollars to set Europe back on its feet.

The United Nations—1945

Truman bucked the traditional United States policies of isolationism and championed the creation of the United Nations. He used the world body to support the creation of Israel in 1948 and to help conduct the Korean War.

The Korean War—1950–1953

The event that sparked the Korean War was the invasion of South Korea by North Korea in 1950. The larger political issue was the emergence of China as a world power and the spread of communism versus the United States' wish to contain it. Truman led the fight in the United Nations to assemble a "police" force to remove the North Koreans from South Korean soil. Under General MacArthur, the United Nations army, comprised mostly of American and South Korean forces, began a conflict that would last for four years. When China sent troops over the border in 1950, MacArthur fought with Truman to declare war. But Truman, fearful of nuclear conflict with the Soviet Union, refused. When their differences became public, he replaced MacArthur, causing a political firestorm. Peace talks began in 1951 and dragged on for years.

Seizure of the Steel Mills—1952

Truman lost his fight to take over the nation's steel mills to stop a strike that might impede the war effort when the Supreme Court ruled his action unconstitutional.

The Hydrogen Bomb—1952

The first test of the "H" bomb took place at Eniwetok, in the Marshall Islands.

The Red Scare and Joe McCarthy

The anticommunist frenzy reached its height in the United States when it was announced that the USSR had successfully tested its first atomic bomb. Shortly thereafter came a series of communist espionage cases, including those of Alger Hiss and Julius and Ethel Rosenberg, involving the theft of atomic secrets and possible penetration of government offices. Truman authorized a program of loyalty investigations of federal employees in 1947, but he was attacked for being soft on communists. In 1950, Republican Senator Joseph R. McCarthy became the leader of the anticommunist movement, using his committee to charge communist infiltration at every level of American life.

Presidential Succession Act of 1947

This law reshuffled the order of succession as put down in the Succession act of 1886, making the Speaker of the House and president pro tem of the Senate in direct line after the vice president and ahead of the cabinet.

Taft-Hartley Act—1947

An antiunion act, passed over Truman's veto, the law eliminated the "closed shop," allowing workers the right not to have to join a union, and made it illegal for unions to contribute to political campaigns.

Fair Deal

Truman's domestic proposals, or the Fair Deal, were extensions of the New Deal and included broad social welfare reforms. Truman supported economic controls in times of crisis and promoted underwriting full employment by government intervention. In 1948, he ordered desegregation of the armed forces, authorized the Justice Department to support blacks in civil rights cases, and was the first president since Reconstruction to have a legislative civil rights program. He lost his bid for a program of national health insurance

Attempted Assassination—1950

Two Puerto Rican nationalists attacked the Blair House, where Truman was staying while the White House was under repairs, on November 1. The president watched the gunfight between the revolutionaries and White House guards from an upstairs window. One guard and one assassin were killed. The surviving assassin was sentenced to death, but Truman commuted his sentence to life imprisonment in 1951.

Term Limits—1951

The Twenty-second Amendment limiting presidents to two terms of service was ratified.

CONTRIBUTIONS TO AMERICAN HISTORY WHILE

PRESIDENT

Truman inherited the presidency in a time of national crisis. While the end of World War II was in sight, it was far from over, and he was faced with difficult decisions. The use of the atomic bomb to hasten Japanese surrender brought a mix of praise and criticism. His decision to remove the popular MacArthur from command during the Korean War cost him dearly, but Truman's personal integrity and "the buck stops here" attitude gave him the strength to do what he believed was right. His struggle with postwar inflation, social problems, and the rising threat of communism in Europe made his terms as president very demanding.

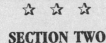

SECTION TWO

PERSONAL PROFILE

Truman, who wore tailored suits, was 5´ 10˝ and weighed around 180 pounds. He was very nearsighted. Like Andrew Jackson and

Abraham Lincoln, he was truly a president for the common man. His language was rough and direct, and he won respect for sticking to and taking responsibility for his decisions. Possessing great personal integrity and absolute incorruptibility, he loved the game of politics and had the ability not to take the inevitable attacks and criticism personally.

FAMILY BACKGROUND

Ancestors

Truman was descended from English, Irish, and German stock. His family arrived in the mid-seventeenth century, settling first in Connecticut, and then in Kentucky.

Immediate Family

FATHER: John Anderson Truman (1851–1914) Born in Jackson County, Missouri, Truman's father was a farmer and salesman. A small but aggressive man, he had a fighting temper and was an active Democrat. Although a hard worker, he had bad luck in his investments and was continually starting over. After he lost a small fortune in speculations in 1901, Truman had to return to help on the farm.

MOTHER: Martha Ellen Young Truman (1852–1947) Born near Kansas City, she was a doting mother whose family had been badly treated by Union soldiers during the Civil War, and was pro-Confederate and pro-South for all of her life.

BROTHERS AND SISTERS: Mr. Vivian Truman; Mary Jane Truman.

CHILDHOOD AND EARLY YEARS

Truman's childhood was affected by his poor vision and limited physical abilities. Forced to wear very thick glasses, he was unable to participate in sports. He spent a great deal of time learning the piano, reading, and helping around the house. He was strongly influenced by his father's politics and committed himself to the Democratic party at an early age.

EDUCATION

Truman learned to read from his mother and attended local grade schools and high school in Independence, Missouri. He was an average student but had real potential as a pianist. He was encouraged by his instructors to consider it as a career, but when his father went broke in 1901, Truman was forced to give up his dreams of college and a life in music. After making the decision to enter politics, Truman entered Kansas City Law School in 1923.

MILITARY SERVICE

General Service: Missouri National Guard (1905–1911)
RANK: Lieutenant
World War I: 129th Field Artillery (1917–1919)
RANK: Rose from lieutenant to major.

Truman served and saw action in France as commander of a field artillery unit at St. Mihiel, the Meuse-Argonne offensive, and Verdun.

RELIGION

Baptist

FAMILY LIFE

Marriage:

Truman, age thirty-five, married Elizabeth "Bess" Virginia Wallace (1885–1982) on June 28, 1919 at Trinity Episcopal Church in Independence, Missouri. She was thirty-four. She was Truman's childhood sweetheart. She did not enjoy her role as first lady, limiting social activities and hostessing few events.

Children:

Mary Margaret Truman (1924–)

HOBBIES

Playing piano, poker, and walking for exercise. (Truman was famous for his early-morning walks.)

POST PRESIDENCY

Truman revealed his decision not to run for a third term in 1952 and retired to Independence. Over the next twenty years, Truman remained active in politics as an emissary and advisor. He campaigned for national and local figures, wrote his memoirs, lectured extensively, and helped establish the Truman Library. His country wit and Midwestern integrity made him a popular and sought-after ex-president.

DIED

Truman died on December 26, 1972, of complications from kidney failure and generally poor health.

CHAPTER THIRTY-FOUR
☆ ☆ ☆

DWIGHT DAVID EISENHOWER

1890–1969

34th President of the United States
"Ike"

☆ ☆ ☆

SECTION ONE

BORN

Eisenhower was born on October 14, 1890, in Denison, Texas.

TERMS SERVED AS PRESIDENT

1953–1957
1957–1961

POLITICAL PARTY

Republican

PUBLIC LIFE BEFORE PRESIDENCY

President of Columbia University— 1948–1950

Although Eisenhower spent almost his entire public life in the army, he served as president of Columbia University after resigning his military command. (See Military Service)

CAMPAIGNS

First Election—1952

Eisenhower became the favorite for the Republican nomination when he declared himself a Republican in early 1952. The Democrats were plagued by the bloody stalemate in Korea, and the "Red Scare" dominated the headlines at home—giving the Republicans perfect issues on which to base a campaign. Eisenhower easily defeated Taft for the nomination.

The Twenty-first Amendment, ratified in 1951, prohibited a president from serving more than two terms. Although Truman was exempt, he chose to retire. The Democrats nominated Senator Adlai E. Stevenson of Illinois over his own objections, but eventually he agreed to accept the nomination.

Eisenhower went against conservative factions in the party and adopted moderate positions on domestic affairs. He believed that the U.S. should continue its leadership in world affairs. He remained above the rough-and-tumble of campaign politics and the job of appeasing the conservatives and anticommunists was left to vice presidential nominee Richard Nixon.

Stevenson campaigned hard, and his speeches were widely admired. But, in the end, he couldn't fight Eisenhower's status as a national hero, and he never captured the voters' imagination. Eisenhower's landslide victory was a personal referendum, however, because the Republicans were unable to take full control of Congress.

Electoral Votes:
Eisenhower 442
Stevenson 89

Second Election—1955

The 1950s were a time of great prosperity for middle-class and wealthy Americans, and Dwight Eisenhower was an extremely popular president. The problem was his health. He had suffered a heart attack in September 1955, and had undergone colon surgery. But after being cleared by his doctors, Eisenhower sent word to the convention that he would run and was nominated by acclamation.

On the Democratic side, after a number of closely contested primaries, Stevenson won a convincing victory in California over Tennessee Senator Estes Kefauver. Stevenson was nominated on the first ballot, and the convention chose Kefauver over Massachusetts Senator John F. Kennedy for his running mate.

Again Stevenson campaigned hard on his vision for a "New America," which included specific proposals ranging from a nuclear testing ban to health programs for low-income Americans. But once again he was unable to overcome Eisenhower's popularity, and the incumbent, running on his record, won the most one-sided victory since 1936.

Electoral Votes:
Eisenhower 457
Stevenson 73

VICE PRESIDENT

Richard Milhous Nixon (1913–1994) California. Lawyer. (Both terms)

THE CABINET

Secretary of State:
John Foster Dulles (1953–1959)
Christian A. Herter (1959–1961)

Secretary of the Treasury:
George M. Humphrey (1953–1957)
Robert B. Anderson (1957–1961)

Secretary of Defense:
Charles E. Wilson (1953–1957)
Neil H. McElroy (1957–1959)
Thomas S. Gates, Jr. (1960–1961)

Attorney General:
Herbert Brownell, Jr. (1953–1957)
William P. Rogers (1957–1961)

Postmaster General:
Arthur E. Summerfield (1953–1961)

Secretary of the Interior:
Douglas J. McKay (1953–1956)
Frederick A. Seaton (1956–1961)

Secretary of Agriculture:
Ezra Taft Benson (1953–1961)

Secretary of Commerce:
Sinclair Weeks (1953–1958)
Lewis Strauss (1958–1959)
Frederick H. Mueller (1959–1960)

Secretary of Labor:
Martin P. Durkin (1953)
James P. Mitchell (1953–1961)

Secretary of Health, Education, and Welfare:
Oveta Culp Hobby (1953–1955)
Marion B. Folsom (1955–1958)
Arthur S. Flemming (1958–1961)

SIGNIFICANT EVENTS THAT OCCURRED DURING
OFFICE——JANUARY 20, 1953–JANUARY 20, 1961

End of the Korean War—1953

In his 1952 presidential campaign he had promised to end the Korean War. More interested in making peace than winning a victory, he negotiated a truce in July 1953.

The Eisenhower Doctrine and the Cold War

The Eisenhower administration began a buildup of nuclear weapons to combat the Soviet Union's explosion of missile production. The concept of massive retaliation as a deterrent to war would be United States policy until the Soviet Union collapsed during the Reagan years.

But, while Secretary of State Dulles kept the Cold War hot, he also attempted to lay the groundwork for peaceful negotiations between the hostile superpowers. In 1954 he refused to commit U.S. forces to help the French in Indochina. The U.S. did, however, help set up the anticommunist government in South Vietnam as a buffer against communists in the North. He also spearheaded the Southeast Asia Treaty Organization (SEATO) in 1954, to combat the "domino theory" of communist expansion in the Third World. He and other Western leaders met with a Soviet delegation headed by Nikita Khrushchev in Geneva in 1955 to try and relax political tensions. In 1956, Eisenhower refused to endanger delicate U.S.-Soviet relations by supporting anti-Soviet rebels forces during the Hungarian Revolution. He mediated the end of the Suez Crisis between Egypt and an Anglo-French-Israeli coalition.

Behind the scenes the CIA was at its most covertly active, working to establish anticommunist regimes in Iran, Guatemala, Indonesia and Laos. By the end of his administration the CIA had begun to consider assassinating Cuba's Fidel Castro, who had overthrown the pro-American Batista government in 1959.

The End of Joe McCarthy—1954

Senator McCarthy's reign of terror ended with a Senate vote of censure in 1954. Although Eisenhower was criticized for not taking a more public position on the senator's destructive and largely unsubstantiated bullying of public figures.

Civil Rights

Eisenhower used federal troops to enforce school desegregation at Little Rock, Arkansas in 1957 and signed civil rights acts in 1957 and 1960, providing for penalties for obstructing voter registration and voting rights for Black Americans.

Interstate Highway System—1956

Eisenhower put the wheels in motion to build a system of federally sponsored interstate highways that would provide over forty thousand miles of connecting roads.

St. Lawrence Seaway—1959

The project to open the Great Lakes to the Atlantic Ocean, funded and built jointly with Canada, was begun in 1954 and completed in 1959.

Gary Powers and the U-2 Spy Plane—1960

In May 1960, just as a critical summit conference in Paris was about to begin, the Soviets shocked the world by announcing that they had shot down an American plane and captured its pilot. Eisenhower took full responsibility for the espionage, but the Paris conference deteriorated into a Soviet shouting match.

CONTRIBUTIONS TO AMERICAN HISTORY WHILE

PRESIDENT

Congress was dominated by Democrats during both his terms of office, and Eisenhower, who was a very moderate Republican, continued to entrench the foreign and domestic programs of Roosevelt and Truman. His personal popularity helped make them part of the American political fabric. At the same time, he returned the Republican party to a position of power it had not known since the pre-Hoover days.

In the difficult early years of the Cold War, his sense of control and authority calmed the nation's jitters, and he became one of the most loved presidents in history.

☆ ☆ ☆

SECTION TWO

PERSONAL PROFILE

Eisenhower was 5′ 10″ and weighed around 180 pounds. He was of fair complexion with bright blue eyes and possessed an easy grin that inspired confidence. Friendly, open, and fair-minded, he insisted on looking on the bright side of the darkest issues and refused to hold grudges.

FAMILY BACKGROUND

Ancestors

Eisenhower was of Swiss-German extraction. Members of his family emigrated to America in the mid-eighteenth century, settling in Pennsylvania and later in Kansas.

Immediate Family

FATHER: David Jacob Eisenhower (1863–1942) An engineering mechanic and company manager, Eisenhower's father lost his savings and his business when his partner in a general store left with the money. The resulting bankruptcy affected him for the rest of his life.

MOTHER: Ida Elizabeth Stover Eisenhower (1862–1946) Possessing deeply pacifist views, she was extremely upset when Eisenhower accepted his appointment to West Point.

BROTHERS AND SISTERS: Arthur Eisenhower; Edgar Eisenhower; Roy Eisenhower; Milton Eisenhower; Earl Eisenhower.

CHILDHOOD AND EARLY YEARS

When he was two years old, Eisenhower's family moved from Denison, Texas, to Abilene, Kansas. The family was poor, and the Eisenhower boys were teased relentlessly, learning to fight at an early age. Eisenhower grew up doing odd jobs to help support the family and became a student of military history.

EDUCATION

Eisenhower was a bright but average product of the Abilene public school system, where he played baseball and football and acted in school plays. When he passed the entrance exam for the U.S. Naval Academy but was too old to be eligible, he accepted an appointment to the U.S. Military Academy at West Point, graduating as a second lieutenant in 1915. At the academy he was well liked but somewhat of a disciplinary problem and a strong halfback for the football team, until he injured his knee.

After graduation he was assigned to the 19th Infantry and later attended the Command and General Staff School and the Army War School, graduating with honors.

MILITARY SERVICE

Career Soldier: United States Army (1915–1948)
RANK: Rose from second lieutenant to five-star general.

General Service—1915–1941

Eisenhower requested, but did not receive, an overseas combat assignment during World War I. Instead he was assigned to a series of training camps, where he became widely recognized as an excellent staff officer. He served as administrative assistant to Army Chief of Staff Douglas MacArthur in 1933. During this time he developed the ability to serve loyally without alienating powerful rivals. Eisenhower accompanied MacArthur to the Philippines in 1935.

World War II—1941–1945

Eisenhower moved upward in the military command becoming chief of staff of the Third Army in 1941 and, after Pearl Harbor, being assigned to Army Chief of Staff George C. Marshall. In June of 1942 he was sent to England as U.S. commander in Europe.

In Europe, Eisenhower served as a brilliant planner, conciliator, and compromiser—all essential qualities for running a vast war machine. He was regarded also as a tough, decisive military leader able to handle the egos of the volatile mix of commanding Allied officers.

As the war progressed, he was recognized as the best candidate to organize the invasion of France and was assigned to that task in 1943. On June 6, 1944, Allied forces invaded Normandy in a military offensive unparalleled in the history of warfare. The German Army began a fighting retreat that would end in their unconditional surrender on May 8, 1945.

Eisenhower returned to the United States a true American hero.

Post War—1945–1952

After World War II, he served a term as army chief of staff, then resigned his commission in 1948. He wrote his famous memoir, *Crusade in Europe,* and served briefly as president of Columbia University. In December 1950, President Truman named him military commander of NATO, and he served in that post until 1952.

RELIGION

Presbyterian

FAMILY LIFE

Marriage:

Eisenhower, twenty-five, married Mary ("Mamie") Geneva Doud (1896–1979) on July 1, 1916, at her home in Denver, Colorado. Although the product of a wealthy home, the attractive and spunky Mamie adjusted with enthusiasm to the less than opulent and mobile lifestyle of a career military officer and was a gracious and charming first lady. She died of a stroke at the Eisenhower farm in Gettysburg, Pennsylvania, on November 11, 1979.

Children:

Doud Dwight Eisenhower (1917–1921); John Sheldon Doud Eisenhower (1923–)

HOBBIES

Golf, hunting, fishing, poker, oil painting, cooking, cards, reading, and television.

POST PRESIDENCY

Retiring to his farm in Gettysburg, Pennsylvania, in 1961, Eisenhower spent the last eight years of his life writing books and playing golf. He remained interested in the political scene but was reluctant to involve himself personally. He did endorse Barry Gold-water in 1964, and, although his relations with Nixon were always strained, he endorsed him for president in 1968.

DIED

He died in Washington, D.C., on March 28, 1969, at Walter Reed Hospital, of congestive heart failure.

CHAPTER THIRTY-FIVE
☆ ☆ ☆

John Fitzgerald Kennedy

1917–1963

35th President of the United States
"JFK"

☆ ☆ ☆

SECTION ONE

BORN

Kennedy was born on May 29, 1917, at his family home in Brookline, Massachusetts.

TERM SERVED AS PRESIDENT

1961–1963 (Assassinated while in office, November 22, 1963.)

POLITICAL PARTY

Democrat

PUBLIC LIFE BEFORE PRESIDENCY

After his discharge, Kennedy worked briefly as a reporter, for the *Chicago Herald-American* and the *International News Service.*

U.S. Representative—1947–1953

Kennedy served two terms as a Boston congressman during which he involved himself in foreign policy debates and advocated social policies, such as low-cost public housing. He remained his own man and continued positioning himself as a moderately liberal Democrat.

U.S. Senator—1953–1961

Although the Republicans benefited from Eisenhower's landslide in 1952, Kennedy successfully challenged incumbent Republican Henry Cabot Lodge, Jr., winning a convincing victory. During periods of 1954 and 1955 his back ailments made it difficult for him to play much of a senatorial role. He was criticized for not voting to censure McCarthy, but avoided the issue by arguing that he was too ill to vote. During this time, Kennedy wrote *Profiles in Courage,* which won a Pulitzer Prize for biography in 1957.

In 1956, Kennedy bid unsuccessfully for the Democratic vice presidential nomination. From that point on, he focused on becoming president. He continued to be firmly anticommunist and modestly liberal, backing a compromise civil rights bill in 1957 and firming up his ties to labor.

CAMPAIGN

Election—1960

Kennedy's opponent for the Democratic nomination was Senator Hubert Humphrey of Minnesota. In order to win the bid he had to overcome some severe liabilities: his family wealth and influence, his age (43) and his Roman Catholic faith. But his charisma and appeal overcame Humphrey in the later primaries, and he was nominated on the first ballot. To appease the power base in the party and to guarantee support in the South, he picked Lyndon Johnson of Texas, a political veteran, as his running mate

Eisenhower endorsed his vice president, Richard Nixon, as the Republican presidential nominee. Nixon was shedding his hardline anticommunist stance and working to establish himself as a statesman who provided the experience and the skills to lead America into the new decade. With Eisenhower's blessing, the Republican convention nominated him on the first ballot.

Kennedy and Nixon engaged in heated debates on the issues of the economy and the communist threat. For the first time, candidates faced each other on television in a series of press-conference-style debates. Kennedy, with his youthful good looks, wit, and clear responses, soared out of the first debate as the front-runner when Nixon, who appeared nervous and ill at ease, was unable to successfully play the experience card.

But the race remained tight, and the most difficult issue for Kennedy to shake was his Catholicism. Although he confronted the issue directly, observers believed that anti-Catholic sentiment would be his downfall. Predictions of the closest race in American history were proven to be correct—the popular vote was almost too close to call, and razor-thin margins of victory in Illinois and Texas made the difference.

Electoral Votes:
Kennedy 303
Nixon 219

VICE PRESIDENT

Lyndon Baines Johnson (1908–1973) Texas. Senator, rancher. (Succeeded Kennedy.)

THE CABINET

Secretary of State:
Dean Rusk (1961–1969)

Secretary of the Treasury:
C. Douglas Dillon (1961–1965)

Secretary of Defense:
Robert S. McNamara (1961–1968)

Attorney General:
Robert F. Kennedy (1961–1968)

Postmaster General:
J. Edward Day (1961–1963)
John A. Gronouski, Jr. (1963)

Secretary of the Interior:
Stewart L. Udall (1961–1969)

Secretary of Agriculture:
Orville L. Freeman (1961–1969)

Secretary of Commerce:
Luther H. Hodges (1961–1964)

Secretary of Labor:
Arthur J. Goldberg (1961–1962)
W. Willard Wirtz (1962–1963)

Secretary of Health, Education, and Welfare:
Abraham A. Ribicoff (1961–1962)
Anthony J. Celebrezze (1962–1963)

SIGNIFICANT EVENTS THAT OCCURRED DURING OFFICE——MARCH 4, 1961–NOVEMBER 22, 1963

Bay of Pigs—1961

Kennedy signed off on a plan involving Cuban expatriates in conjunction with the CIA launching an amphibious assault on Cuba to liberate the island. The plan was developed during the Eisenhower administration. The actual invasion, which was a disaster, was Kennedy's decision, however, and he took the blame for its embarrassing failure.

Alliance for Progress

In an attempt to lessen anti-American feeling in Latin and South America, Kennedy backed development projects and aid packages. Although billions were promised, little was actually delivered.

Peace Corps—1961

The call to public service so simply stated in Kennedy's inaugural address—"Ask not what your country can do for you—ask what you can do for your country" was answered with the Peace Corps. The idealistic and ambitious program placed more than eighty-five thousand young men and women as volunteers around the world.

Southeast Asia and Vietnam

Even after the ill-fated Bay of Pigs, Kennedy remained committed to covert fighting of communist advances. He continued to build American nuclear capability and increased military aid to combat the growing revolution in South Vietnam. By November 1963, there were more than sixteen thousand military personnel in Vietnam. Under his watch the CIA was involved in the plot to overthrow the regime of Ngo Dinh Diem in November 1963.

The Race to the Moon—1961

Russian leadership in the exploration of space prompted Kennedy to promise a man on the moon by the end of the decade. The administration set in motion an ambitious program to develop the technology to beat the Russians in space.

Civil Rights—1962–1963

The Kennedy administration became active in the Civil Rights Movement during 1962 and 1963 after unsuccessful attempts by Governors Barnett of Mississippi and Wallace of Alabama to bar black students from enrolling at their state universities. Riots followed, and "freedom riders" poured in from around the country to press for desegregation and racial equality. Although reluctant to involve the federal government in the beginning, Kennedy came to realize the potential catastrophe and pushed for legislation, used executive action, and spoke eloquently in support of the movement.

The Berlin Wall—1961

As part of the saber rattling that was becoming a test of nerves between himself and Kennedy, Soviet Premier Khrushchev threatened to sign a treaty with East Germany giving them control over western access routes to Berlin. Kennedy responded that he would go to war to keep West Berlin free. The Soviets then erected a wall between East and West Berlin almost overnight. Kennedy visited the wall in June of 1963, where he stated, "All free men, wherever they may live, are citizens of Berlin, and, therefore, as a free man, I take pride in the words, *'Ich bin ein Berliner.'* "

Cuban Missile Crisis—1962

In October 1962, U.S. intelligence revealed that the Russians were building nuclear missile sites in Cuba. Although the Russians claimed that the sites were for defensive purposes only, aerial photos made it clear that the missiles were aimed at the United States. Kennedy demanded their removal; Khrushchev refused. Kennedy ordered a naval and air quarantine on shipping to Cuba and promised to search all ships for weapons and threatened military invasion of Cuba. After several tense days, the Soviets agreed to remove the missiles.

Nuclear Test Ban Treaty—1963

Perhaps as a result of bringing the world to the brink of nuclear war, the United States and the Soviet Union signed a treaty along with Great Britain barring atmospheric testing of nuclear weapons.

CONTRIBUTIONS TO AMERICAN HISTORY WHILE PRESIDENT

Kennedy's charm and eloquence brought a whole generation of young men and women into the political arena. The vision of a caring, compassionate and strong America inspired a burst of faith in the potential of government and the people working together to promote positive change. His assassination was the catalyst for a generation of violence and political unrest and the end of an era in which the United States seemed invincible and far above the problems that beset the rest of the world.

SECTION TWO

PERSONAL PROFILE

Kennedy was a handsome, vibrant man with eternally poised, innocent, and youthful looks that belied the back pain and bouts of illness from which he suffered for most of his adult life. His instinctive wit and sense of grace combined with his all-American good looks to create a lasting image for millions of Americans of what the country could be. Beneath the projection of idealism and goodwill, however, was a shrewd and skilled politician, pragmatic and logical and used to getting his way.

FAMILY BACKGROUND

Ancestors

Kennedy was of Irish descent. His great-grandfather emigrated from Ireland in 1848 and settled in Boston. The Kennedy family was heavily involved in Boston and Massachusetts politics from the late eighteenth century.

Immediate Family

FATHER: Joseph Patrick Kennedy (1888–1969) A businessman and public official, who served as ambassador to Great Britain, Joseph made a fortune in the stock market and got out before the crash in 1929. He used his influence and money to aid politicians and causes in which he held an interest. He was tough and demanding, believing in winning no matter what the cost.

MOTHER: Rose Fitzgerald Kennedy (1890–1995) Born in Boston to a family active in politics, she married Joseph in 1914 and became the matriarch of a political dynasty. She remained active in her children's public lives throughout her life.

BROTHERS AND SISTERS: Joseph P. Kennedy, Jr.; Rosemary Kennedy; Mrs. Kathleen Cavendish; Mrs. Eunice M. Shriver; Mrs. Patricia Lawford; Robert F. Kennedy; Mrs. Jean Smith; Edward M. Kennedy.

CHILDHOOD AND EARLY YEARS

Kennedy grew up in wealth and privilege in Brookline, New York City, Hyannis Port, Cape Cod, and Palm Beach, Florida. He was plagued by illness as a child and seemed to be in a constant state of recuperation.

EDUCATION

Kennedy began his education at the Dexter School in Brookline, and then attended Riverdale Country Day School in New York City. He went to prep school at Choate, briefly attended Princeton University, and then entered Harvard University in 1936. At Harvard he became a serious student and wrote an honors thesis on British foreign policies in the 1930s; it was published in 1940, the year he graduated, under the title *Why England Slept*. He was active in sports and graduated cum laude in 1940.

MILITARY SERVICE

World War II: U.S. Navy (1941–1945)
RANK: Rose from ensign to lieutenant.
In 1941, shortly before the United States entered World War II, Kennedy joined the U.S. Navy and was given command of a PT boat in the Pacific. The boat (PT-109) was sunk by the Japanese in 1943 and Kennedy's action in rescuing his crew earned him the Purple Heart and a navy medal and Marine Corps medal. During the action he aggravated an old back injury and would suffer from it for the rest of his life.

RELIGION

Roman Catholic

FAMILY LIFE

Marriage:

Kennedy, thirty-six, married Jacqueline Bouvier (1929–1995), twenty-four, in Newport, Rhode Island, on September 12, 1953. Jacqueline was born into society and wealth in New York City. She met Kennedy at a dinner party in 1951 and they dated on and off until they announced their engagement in 1953. The wedding was a glittering affair. She became one of the most glamorous and popular first ladies in history, bringing a sense of sophistication and society to her life in the White House. Although she played her role with grace and charm, she was shy of publicity and remained so her entire life. After Kennedy's assassination she married Aristotle Onassis who died in 1975. Later in life she became an editor at Doubleday Books in New York City.

Children:

Caroline Bouvier Kennedy (1957–); John Fitzgerald Kennedy Jr. (1960–); Patrick Bouvier Kennedy (1963)

AFFAIRS

Throughout his married life, Kennedy was rumored to have had a constant string of affairs. Women in his life supposedly included Marilyn Monroe, Judith Campbell Exner, Mary Pinchot Meyer, and Blaze Starr.

HOBBIES

Touch football, sailing, tennis, golf, swimming, film, and theater.

ASSASSINATED

During a political swing through Texas to heal a split in the Democratic party, Kennedy and his wife made a stop in Dallas. On November 22, 1963, he was assassinated while they were riding in a motorcade to a rally. He died an hour later of a gunshot wound to the head. The assassination threw the country into turmoil and began a long period of massive political unrest in the United States.

CHAPTER THIRTY-SIX
☆ ☆ ☆

LYNDON BAINES JOHNSON

1908–1973

36th President of the United States
"LBJ"

☆ ☆ ☆

SECTION ONE

BORN

Johnson was born August 27, 1908, on a farm near Johnson City, Texas.

TERMS SERVED AS PRESIDENT

1963–1965 (Succeeded Kennedy.)
1965–1969

POLITICAL PARTY

Democrat

PUBLIC LIFE BEFORE PRESIDENCY

After leaving Georgetown University, Johnson returned to Texas, where he taught for a year in 1930. In 1931 he was hired as secretary to Democratic Representative Richard Kleberg and remained with him until 1934. During that four-year period, Johnson developed a wide network of political contacts in Washington.

Director of the National Youth Administration, Texas—1935–1937

President Roosevelt named Johnson as head of the Youth Administration in Texas. Johnson enjoyed working with young people, helping them to find jobs and complete their educations.

U.S. Representative—1937–1949

In 1937, Johnson sought and won a Texas seat in Congress, which he would keep for six sessions. As a congressman, he supported the New Deal and lobbied for Roosevelt's programs, championing public works, reclamation, and public power programs.

U.S. Senator—1949–1961

In 1948 he ran for the Senate, winning the Democratic party primary by only eighty-seven votes. His opponents accused him of rigging the ballot boxes, and he earned the nickname, "Landslide Lyndon." The election results were challenged in court without success and he won the general election, taking office in 1949. In the Senate, Johnson honed his political instincts, moving quickly into the power elite. He served as Senate majority leader for six years.

Johnson was a politician's politician—shrewd, tough, and skillful. He was an expert at getting things done and sensing where opportunities lay. A hard worker, he gained friends and supporters with his attention to details and his willingness to compromise.

In 1957, he changed his position on civil rights, pushing for and supporting the Civil Rights Acts of 1957 and 1960. In doing so, he began to emerge as a political leader on a national level. He was a favorite son candidate for president in 1956. After losing to Kennedy on the first ballot, in 1960 Johnson was picked as his running mate.

Vice President—1961–1963

Johnson's presence on the ticket was essential if Kennedy had any hopes of winning the Deep South. Although, many of his colleagues in the Senate urged him not to accept the bid, Johnson decided to run.

He was appointed by Kennedy to head the President's Committee on Equal Employment Opportunities. He also served on the National Aeronautics and Space Council and the Peace Corps Advisory Council. As vice president, he also undertook many goodwill tours abroad to gain some insights into foreign affairs.

When Kennedy was assassinated on November 22, 1963, Johnson was given the oath of office aboard Air Force One and assumed the presidency.

CAMPAIGN

Election—1964

Johnson, after assuming the presidency, vowed to continue JFK's legacy, continuing to build on the legislation offered as part of Kennedy's New Frontier to fashion a "Great Society" that would heal America with compassion and justice. He was nominated for reelection on the first ballot at the Democratic convention.

None of the major Republican politicians were anxious to run against the Democrats in what appeared to be a certain Johnson victory, so the ultraconservative Republican faction took control of the convention and nominated Arizona Senator Barry Goldwater on the first ballot.

Johnson, a veteran campaigner, took advantage of Goldwater's conservative and often seemingly simplistic positions on domestic and foreign affairs and crafted a hard-edged negative television campaign that portrayed his opponent as a man whose politics would destroy the world. Goldwater's politics proved too extreme for most Americans, and Johnson, as expected, captured a record 61.1 percent of the popular vote on the way to a landslide victory.

Electoral Votes:
Johnson 486
Goldwater 52

VICE PRESIDENT

None (First Term)
Hubert Horatio Humphrey (1911–1978) North Dakota. Teacher, senator from Minnesota. (Second Term)

THE CABINET

Secretary of State:
  Dean Rusk (1961–1969)

Secretary of the Treasury:
  C. Douglas Dillon (1963–1965)
  Henry H. Fowler (1965–1968)

Secretary of Defense:
  Robert S. McNamara (1963–1968)
  Clark Clifford (1968–1969)

Attorney General:
  Robert F. Kennedy (1963–1965)
  Nicholas Katzenbach (1965–1967)
  Ramsey Clark (1967–1969)

Postmaster General:
  John A. Gronouski (1963–1965)
  Lawrence F. O'Brien (1965–1968)
  W. Marvin Watson (1968–1969)

Secretary of the Interior:
  Stewart L. Udall (1961–1969)

Secretary of Agriculture:
  Orville L. Freeman (1961–1969)

Secretary of Commerce:
  Luther H. Hodges (1963–1965)
  John T. Connor (1965–1967)
  Alexander B. Trowbridge (1967–1968)
  Cyrus R. Smith (1968–1969)

Secretary of Labor:
  W. Willard Wirtz (1962–1969)

Secretary of Health, Education, and Welfare:
  Anthony J. Celebrezze (1963–1965)
  John W. Gardner (1965–1968)
  Wilbur J. Cohen (1968–1969)

Secretary of Housing and Urban Development:
  Robert C. Weaver (1966–1969)
  Robert C. Wood (1969)

SIGNIFICANT EVENTS THAT OCCURRED DURING
OFFICE——NOVEMBER 22, 1963–JANUARY 20, 1969

The Great Society and the War on Poverty—1964

Johnson's victory in 1964 gave him a mandate for the Great Society, as he called his domestic program. In 1964, Congress passed a tax cut to promote economic growth and the Economic Opportunity Act, containing provisions for: a Job Corps, Work Study Program, Work Experience Program, Head Start, and the Community Action Program. The act launched the War on Poverty. Congress passed the Medicare and Medicaid programs, which provided health services to the elderly and the poor. Johnson also created the Department of Housing and Urban Development.

Civil Rights

Johnson pushed for civil rights legislation with teeth, and the Civil Rights Act of 1964 provided legal authority to seek out and prosecute racial and sexual discrimination. The Voting Rights Act of 1965 made discriminatory literacy testing illegal and gave the government the authority to promote voter registration.

But racial tension continued to build in spite of Johnson's efforts, and while the war in Vietnam escalated, race riots and urban violence broke out all over the country between 1965 and 1968. With the assassination of Martin Luther King, Jr., in 1968, the breakdown of the civil rights movement seemed inevitable as Republican victories in Congress would take away Johnson's mandate.

The Environment

Johnson introduced sweeping legislation to clean up the air and water including: the Water Quality Act of 1965 (establishing water standards), the Clean Water Restoration Act of 1966 (matching funds for sewage treatment), the Clean Air Act of 1965 (auto emissions), and the Air Quality Act of 1967 (enforcement).

Vietnam

When North Vietnamese torpedo boats attacked U.S. naval vessels in the Gulf of Tonkin in 1964, Johnson ordered air strikes in retaliation and pressed Congress for authorization to "repel and . . . prevent aggression." The Gulf of Tonkin Resolution gave him that authority and, by 1964, Johnson had increased the number of U.S. military personnel there—16,000 at the time of Kennedy's assassination—to nearly 25,000. In February 1965, U.S. planes began to bomb North Vietnam, and American troop strength in Vietnam increased to more than 180,000 by the end of the year and to 550,000 by 1968. But the huge troop deployment was unable to bring down North Vietnam, and the Viet Cong's Tet Offensive on Saigon in 1968 was a psychological blow. Some of Johnson's closest advisors now began to call for a de-escalation policy in Vietnam and negotiations for a peaceful settlement.

Johnson's "credibility gap" with American voters was too wide to bridge. With mounting domestic opposition to the war and domestic policy at a standstill, Johnson announced on March 31, 1968, that he would stop the bombing in most of North Vietnam and seek a negotiated end to the war, and he would not run for reelection.

Dominican Republic

Johnson sent the marines to the Dominican Republic in 1965 to "protect American lives" during a communist takeover.

CONTRIBUTIONS TO AMERICAN HISTORY WHILE PRESIDENT

As president, Johnson's shrewd and sure political instincts failed him, and his administration became a mass of contradictions instead of a positive benchmark in social history. He came into office with a mandate to develop one of the most progressive social agendas in history, but it was the policy of military escalation in Vietnam that proved to be his undoing as president. It deflected attention and drew resources from legitimate domestic concerns, created sharp inflation, enlarged the deficit, and prompted social rebellion and class warfare among the American public.

Johnson, in the end, was unable to resolve either the domestic or foreign issues that faced his administration, and his dream of social reform and equality was shattered in the jungles of Vietnam.

SECTION TWO

PERSONAL PROFILE

Johnson, who loved power almost for its own sake, was bigger than life. At 6´3˝, 210 pounds, and large of frame, he was a dominating presence in any situation he found himself in. Energetic, headstrong, confident, shrewd, skillful, and open, he was a force to be reckoned with as a negotiator and dealmaker. A skilled debater, he was persuasive and had a gambler's instinct for the win. But he was also secretive, stubborn, devious, and dogmatic—unable to change a course once he had set his mind to it, no matter what the consequences.

FAMILY BACKGROUND

Ancestors

Johnson's ancestry was a mix of English, Scots, and German. His family emigrated to North Carolina in the mid-eighteenth century and some settled in Texas in the mid-1840s. Many of his relatives fought on the Confederate side during the Civil War. His paternal great-grandfather, cattleman, Sam Ealy Johnson, Sr., founded Johnson City, Texas.

Immediate Family

FATHER: Sam Ealy Johnson, Jr., (1877–1937) Johnson's father was a farmer, teacher and served in the Texas House of Representatives. A liberal Democrat, he was against the Klan and fought for the rights of German-American citizens during World War I.

MOTHER: Rebekah Baines Johnson (1818–1958) After working her way through college, she taught school and edited a local newspaper. She died while Johnson was in the Senate.

BROTHERS AND SISTERS: Mrs. Rebekah L. Bobbit; Mrs. Josefa H. Moss; Sam Houston Johnson; Mrs. Lucia H. Alexander.

CHILDHOOD AND EARLY YEARS

The Johnson family was poor, and, as a child, Lyndon worked odd jobs and hired out to neighbors to earn extra money. He loved baseball and politics, going with his father on the campaign trail and to sessions of the state legislature.

EDUCATION

Johnson was a quick study, learning to read by the age of four. He attended public schools in and around Johnson City. In high school he was a star member of the debate team. After graduation in 1924, Johnson and some his friends hit the road for California in an old Model T Ford. He returned two years later and enrolled in Southwest Texas State Teachers College and graduated in 1930. After two years of law at Georgetown University, he returned to Texas and began teaching speech and debate first, in Pearsall, and then in Houston.

MILITARY SERVICE

World War II: Navy (1940 [Reserves]; 1941–1942 Regular Navy)

RANK: Lieutenant commander (Pacific Theater of War)

Johnson, who was awarded the Silver Star, resigned his commission in 1942 when Roosevelt ordered all serving congressmen back to Washington.

CHAPTER THIRTY-SEVEN
☆ ☆ ☆

RICHARD MILHOUS NIXON

1913–1994

37th President of the United States

SECTION ONE

BORN

Nixon was born on January 9, 1913, in Yorba Linda, California.

TERMS SERVED AS PRESIDENT

1969–1973
1974 (January–August) Resigned from office.

POLITICAL PARTY

Republican

PUBLIC LIFE BEFORE PRESIDENCY

U.S. Representative—1947–1950

Nixon upset liberal Democratic incumbent Jerry Voorhis in a campaign that reflected the rabid anticommunist feeling of the period. Nixon suggested that Voorhis had dangerous left-wing tendencies and won easily. From that point on, anticommunist activism became his major political theme. He served on the House Un-American Activities Committee and was part of the team that investigated spies in the government. He helped convict Alger Hiss in 1950.

U.S. Senator—1951–1953

In 1950 he defeated Democratic Congresswoman Helen Gahagan Douglas, using the same "Red Scare" tactics he had successfully employed to beat Voorhis. He was clearly a rising star in the Republican party. His speaking skills and willingness to stump at party fund-raising dinners around the country helped him build a strong base of political support. In 1952, he was nominated to run on Eisenhower's ticket as vice president.

Electoral Votes:
Nixon 520
McGovern 17
Hospers 1 (Libertarian Party—California)

VICE PRESIDENTS

Spiro T. Agnew (1918–) Maryland. Lawyer.
Gerald R. Ford (1913–) Michigan. Lawyer. (Succeeded to the presidency after Nixon resigned.)

THE CABINET

Secretary of State:
William P. Rogers (1969–1973)
Henry A. Kissinger (1973–1974)

Secretary of the Treasury:
David M. Kennedy (1969–1970)
John B. Connally, Jr. (1971–1972)
George P. Shultz (1972–1974)
William E. Simon (1974)

Secretary of Defense:
Melvin R. Laird (1969–1972)
Elliot L. Richardson (1973)
James R. Schlesinger (1973–1974)

Attorney General:
John N. Mitchell (1969–1972)
Richard G. Kleindienst (1972–1973)
Elliot L. Richardson (1973)
William B. Saxbe (1974)

Postmaster General:
Winton M. Blount (1969–1971)

Secretary of the Interior:
Walter J. Hickel (1969–1970)
Rogers C. B. Morton (1971–1974)

Secretary of Agriculture:
Clifford M. Hardin (1969–1971)
Earl L. Butz (1971–1974)

Secretary of Commerce:
Maurice H. Stans (1969–1972)
Peter G. Peterson (1972)
Frederick B. Dent (1973–1974)

Secretary of Labor:
George P. Schultz (1969–1970)
James D. Hodgson (1970–1972)
Peter J. Brennan (1973–1974)

Secretary of Health, Education, and Welfare:
Robert H. Finch (1969–1970)
Elliot L. Richardson (1970–1973)
Caspar W. Weinberger (1973–1974)

Secretary of Housing and Urban Development:
George W. Romney (1969–1972)
James T. Lynn (1973–1974)

Secretary of Transportation:
John A. Volpe (1969–1973)
Claude S. Brinegar (1973–1974)

SIGNIFICANT EVENTS THAT OCCURRED DURING OFFICE—JANUARY 20, 1969–AUGUST 9, 1974

Vietnam

Nixon kept his campaign promise and reduced troop strength steadily in Vietnam. But he also expanded the war into Laos and Cambodia, causing an explosion of antiwar protests around the country, including the incident at Kent State University in which National Guard troops fired on student demonstrators, killing four and wounding nine. Hoping to force the peace talks to bear fruit, Nixon launched a massive bombing effort and mined Haiphong Harbor. After four years of waging war in Vietnam and with growing resistance in Congress, Nixon and Secretary of State Henry Kissinger managed to arrange a cease-fire that would last long enough to permit total U.S. withdrawal. The last American ground troops left Vietnam in 1972, leaving only support personnel and prisoners behind.

The formal peace agreement was signed in Paris in 1973. Although the truce allowed for the release of all POWs, fighting between the North and South resumed quickly and led to a communist victory. Hostile relations between Vietnam and the United States made discovering the fates of American MIAs impossible, creating an issue that would continue to plague succeeding administrations.

China—1972

Nixon and Kissinger produced a "realpolitik" diplomatic coup when they established limited relations with Communist China. Nixon had supported Chinese admission to the United Nations in 1971 and, in a historic trip to Beijing in 1972, he met with Mao Tsetung. They agreed to broaden scientific and cultural exchanges and increase trade.

Arms Limitations

Seabed Treaty—1970
The United States and the Soviet Union agreed to ban nuclear weapons from the ocean floor in international waters.
Chemical Weapons Treaty—1971
The United States and the Soviet Union agreed to destroy stockpiles of chemical and biological weapons and ban their further development.
SALT (Strategic Arms Limitation Talks) Agreement—1972
The United States and the Soviet Union agreed to defensive ballistic missile sites and to freeze the number of offensive missiles at the current levels.

The War on Crime

Nixon introduced major crime bills to authorize more severe penalties for violent offenders and increase penalties for drug traffickers. Part of the effort was the "no knock" provision that allowed enforcement to enter premises to recover evidence that might otherwise be destroyed.

The Environment

The Nixon administration created the Environmental Quality Policy Act—environmental impact statements; the Environmental Protection Agency (EPA)—pollution control; the National Air Quality Standards Act—auto emissions; the Resource Recovery Act—recycling; the Water Pollution Act—waste treatment plants (over Nixon's veto).

Landing on the Moon—1969

Kennedy's promise of 1961 was kept when Apollo 11 landed on the moon on July 20, 1969.

Watergate—1972–1974

During the 1972 campaign, a group of burglars working for the Committee to Reelect the President broke into the headquarters of the Democratic National Committee at the Watergate office-apartment complex in Washington, searching for political intelligence. Attempts by the White House to impede the investigation failed when it was revealed that Nixon had tapes of conversations he had made in the Oval Office which would reveal the degree to which the president and his men had obstructed justice.

Even though evidence was building against the president at a furious rate, Nixon continued to deny any wrongdoing and became obsessed with remaining in office, refusing to turn over the unedited recordings.

Impeachment Proceedings—July 27–30, 1974

The Supreme Court, in a unanimous decision, required that Nixon turn the tapes over to Special Prosecutor Leon Jaworski. With evidence in hand, the House Judiciary Committee voted to recommend approval by the full House of three articles of impeachment against the president if he did not resign.

Resignation—August 9, 1974

On August 9, 1974, Nixon resigned. He was succeeded by Vice President Gerald R. Ford, whom he had selected to replace Agnew after he had been forced to step down in the wake of a corruption and bribery scandal. Ford pardoned Nixon a month after his resignation. While he accepted, Nixon continued to insist that his actions were political, not criminal.

CONTRIBUTIONS TO AMERICAN HISTORY WHILE

PRESIDENT

During Nixon's administration the United States withdrew its military forces from Vietnam. He informally recognized the government of the People's Republic of China, initiating an era of global politics and the end of isolationism in the United States. The Watergate scandal that occurred at the beginning of his second term brought Nixon to the verge of impeachment by the House of Representatives and led to the first resignation of an American president. His brilliant achievements in foreign policy will be forever clouded by the scandal of his resignation.

☆ ☆ ☆

SECTION TWO

PERSONAL PROFILE

Nixon was of average height, 5′ 11″, and weighed approximately 180 pounds. Stiff and uncomfortable in public, he most often appeared nervous and uneasy. He was a mysterious and complex personality, driven to succeed and extremely ambitious but constantly suspicious and distrustful of advisors and friends. He loved the rough-and-tumble of politics and was willing to go to any length to achieve personal and public victory.

FAMILY BACKGROUND

Ancestors

Nixon's ancestry was Scots, Irish, German, and English. He was descended from King Edward III (1312–1377). Nixons emigrated to America as early as 1753. Family served in the Revolutionary and Civil Wars.

Immediate Family

FATHER: Francis Anthony Nixon (1887–1956) Owner of a grocery store and a gas station, Francis Nixon, who dropped out of grade school to go to work, held many jobs before settling in Yorba Linda, California. He possessed a quick temper and was outspoken on political issues. He started as a Democrat but became a Republican during McKinley's administration.

MOTHER: Hannah Milhous Nixon (1885–1967) Nixon's mother, born in Indiana, was a devout Quaker with strong humanitarian views. She wanted Richard to become a Quaker missionary.

She died while Nixon was campaigning for his second bid to become president.

BROTHERS AND SISTERS: Harold S. Nixon; Francis Donald Nixon; Arthur B. Nixon; Edward C. Nixon.

CHILDHOOD AND EARLY YEARS

Born into poverty in Yorba Linda, Nixon and his family moved to Whittier, California, in 1922. He was a hardworking and well-mannered child, helping in his father's store when not in school. Watching the Teapot Dome scandal unfold during the Harding administration, he decided to become a lawyer. The most significant and difficult event of Nixon's childhood was the death of his older brother, Arthur, of tuberculosis.

EDUCATION

Despite the poverty and resulting family tension in which he grew up, Nixon was an excellent student, graduating first in his high-school class, second from Whittier College in 1934, and third from Duke University Law School in 1937. His academic abilities earned him scholarships, which he had to supplement with part-time work. He was admitted to the California bar in November of 1937.

MILITARY SERVICE

World War II: U.S. Navy (1942–1946)

RANK: Rose from lieutenant junior grade to lieutenant commander.

Nixon served as a supply officer in the South Pacific, receiving commendations for his work. He also honed his skill as a poker player, reportedly winning several thousand dollars while in the navy.

RELIGION

Quaker

FAMILY LIFE

Marriage:

Nixon, twenty-seven, married twenty-eight-year-old Thelma Catherine "Pat" Ryan on June 21, 1940, at the Mission Inn in Riverside, California. Orphaned by seventeen, Pat worked her way through college by doing a variety of jobs including: clerking, secretarial work, X-ray technician, and movie extra. She attended several different schools, finally graduating cum laude from the University of California in 1937. She met Nixon while teaching typing and shorthand at Whittier High School. He proposed quickly, but they dated for two years before announcing their engagement. She died in 1993.

Children:

Patricia Nixon (1946–); Julie Nixon (1948–)

HOBBIES

Golf, bowling, poker, and swimming.

POST PRESIDENCY

After retiring to San Clemente, California, Nixon moved to New York City, then to Saddle River, New Jersey. In 1981 he joined former presidents Ford and Carter as members of the official U.S. delegation to the funeral of Egyptian president Anwar al-Sadat. Nixon remained popular abroad and traveled frequently. He slowly made his way back into the role of elder statesman and by the end of his life had regained a bit of his former public status.

DIED

Nixon died on April 22, 1994, in New York City.

CHAPTER THIRTY-EIGHT
☆ ☆ ☆

GERALD RUDOLPH FORD

1913-

38th President of the United States
"Jerry"

☆ ☆ ☆

SECTION ONE

BORN

Ford was born on July 14, 1913, in Omaha, Nebraska. His birth name was Leslie Lynch King, Jr., but after his adoption he took the name of his stepfather, Gerald Rudolph Ford, Sr.

TERM SERVED AS PRESIDENT

1974–1977 (Succeeded to presidency after Nixon resigned.)

POLITICAL PARTY

Republican

PUBLIC LIFE BEFORE PRESIDENCY

After his discharge from the navy after World War II, Ford returned to his law practice in Grand Rapids, Michigan.

U. S. Representative—1949–1973

Ford easily won election to the House of Representatives in November of 1948. Once elected, he became a professional politician and served twelve consecutive terms of office. He was House minority leader from 1965 until he resigned in 1973 to become vice president.

He was a moderately conservative, hardworking, and completely partisan Republican. While by no means a brilliant legislator, he was an effective advocate for his Michigan constituents. In 1965 he was chosen as House Republican leader. After Nixon was elected, Ford became one of his biggest supporters, endorsing his position on domestic issues and on Vietnam.

Vice President—1973–August 9, 1974

When Vice President Spiro Agnew was forced to resign in October of 1973, Nixon nominated Ford as vice president under the

Twenty-fifth Amendment to the U.S. Constitution, the first time that the procedures outlined in the amendment were used. Following congressional approval of his appointment, Ford was sworn in as vice president on December 6, 1973. He assumed the presidency on August 9, 1974, when Nixon resigned rather than face certain impeachment.

He remains the only president to serve both as president and vice president in the same term without having been elected to either office.

VICE PRESIDENT

Nelson A. Rockefeller (1908–1979) New York. Public official.

THE CABINET

Secretary of State:
Henry A. Kissinger (1973–1977)

Secretary of the Treasury:
William E. Simon (1973–1977)

Secretary of Defense:
James R. Schlesinger (1974–1975)
Donald H. Rumsfeld (1975–1977)

Attorney General:
William B. Saxbe (1974–1975)
Edward H. Levi (1975–1977)

Secretary of the Interior:
Rogers C. B. Morton (1974–1975)
Stanley K. Hathaway (1975)
Thomas S. Kleppe (1975–1977)

Secretary of Agriculture:
Earl L. Butz (1974–1976)
John A. Knebel (1976–1977)

Secretary of Commerce:
Frederick B. Dent (1974–1975)
Rogers C. B. Morton (1975)
Elliot L. Richardson (1976–1977)

Secretary of Labor:
  Peter J. Brennan (1974–1975)
  John T. Dunlop (1975–1976)
  W. J. Usery, Jr. (1976–1977)

Secretary of Health, Education, and Welfare:
  Caspar W. Weinberger (1974–1975)
  F. David Matthews (1975–1977)

Secretary of Housing and Urban Development:
  James T. Lynn (1974–1975)
  Carla Anderson Hills (1975–1977)

Secretary of Transportation:
  Claude S. Brinegar (1974–1975)
  William T. Coleman, Jr. (1975–1977)

SIGNIFICANT EVENTS THAT OCCURRED DURING
OFFICE——AUGUST 9, 1974–JANUARY 20, 1977

Ford engaged in a running battle with the Democratic Congress. During his two and a half years as president, he vetoed sixty-one bills. Only twelve of the vetoes were overridden. The impression that the government in Washington was deadlocked would hurt Ford's reelection chances.

The Pardon of Richard Nixon—1974

Although he received a bitter storm of criticism, Ford chose to grant Nixon a full pardon for his part in the Watergate scandal rather than have the country go through the protracted legal proceedings sure to come. While many felt he showed favoritism, Ford felt it was important to put Watergate behind.

Clemency for Draft Evaders and Deserters—1974

Ford offered clemency to the thousands of young men who had evaded the draft or deserted rather than fight in Vietnam. Veterans denounced the act as too lenient and antiwar groups felt that accepting the terms of the clemency was the same as admitting wrongdoing in protesting the war.

The Fall of Saigon—1975-1976

The American embassy was evacuated in 1975 as communist forces completed the takeover of the south, ending more than twenty years of revolution.

Assassination Attempts

Two attempts were made on Ford's life while he was president, both by women, in September 1975. The first was on September 5 by Charles Manson disciple Lynette "Squeaky" Fromme, and the second on September 22 by political activist Sara Jane Moore. Both incidents took place in California.

CONTRIBUTIONS TO AMERICAN HISTORY WHILE

PRESIDENT

Perhaps the most important contribution Gerald Ford made was to remain himself during a transition of power that many believed could bring the country down. Ford's unaffected personal style was well received by people needing relief from the political and social unrest of the preceding decade.

While the Ford administration was faced with a major economic slump, with its unique combination of inflation and recession, it also presided over the celebration of the country's two hundredth anniversary.

His intention was to begin the process of healing the country, and in that he succeeded.

SECTION TWO

PERSONAL PROFILE

Tall, fit, athletic, and handsome, Ford took a lot of ribbing for his apparent lack of coordination and a tendency to send golf balls into crowds. Friendly, open, accessible, compassionate, and caring, he is the classic example of "what you see is what you get." These qualities plus determination and stubbornness, allowed him to survive thirty years in Congress and remain generally well liked and trusted.

FAMILY BACKGROUND

Ancestors

Ford is of English ancestry.

Immediate Family

FATHER: Leslie Lynch King (1882–1941) A wealthy wool merchant in Omaha, Nebraska. Ford only saw him twice after the reportedly violent marriage between his mother and father ended.

ADOPTIVE FATHER: Gerald Rudolph Ford, Sr. (1890–1962) Owner of a paint store in Grand Rapids, Michigan, Ford married Dorothy Gardner King in 1916 and adopted her son, giving him his name.

MOTHER: Dorothy Ayer Gardner Ford (1892–1967) When her brief marriage to King became too much in 1915 she moved to her parents' home in Grand Rapids, where she met Ford, Sr.

BROTHERS AND SISTERS: King's second marriage—Half brothers and sisters; Leslie H. King; Mrs. Marjorie Werner; Patricia King. Mother's second marriage—Thomas G Ford; Richard A. Ford; James F. Ford.

CHILDHOOD AND EARLY YEARS

Ford grew up in an average middle-class, middle-American environment. He did not find out that he was adopted until he was in his early teens and one of the most difficult experiences in his young life was meeting his biological father. He helped around the house and worked in his adoptive father's store. Athletically inclined from an early age, he showed an interest in competitive sports.

EDUCATION

In the local school system, Ford was a good student, named to the National Honor Society. He was also the star of the football team. After graduating high school in 1931 he went to the University of Michigan, where he became a star center on the University of Michigan football team and graduated from the university in 1935 with a B average. He was offered pro football contracts from the Detroit Lions and the Green Bay Packers but turned them down to study law at Yale. He was soon admitted to the Yale Law School, finishing in the top third of his class. He was admitted to the Michigan bar in 1941.

MILITARY SERVICE

World War II: U.S. Navy (1942–1946)
RANK: Rose from ensign to lieutenant commander.
Ford received ten Battle Stars for his service aboard the aircraft carrier USS *Monterey* in the Pacific.

RELIGION

Episcopalian

FAMILY LIFE

Marriage:

On October 15, 1948, Ford, thirty-five, married thirty-year-old Elizabeth Anne "Betty" Bloomer (1918–) at Grace Episcopal Church in Grand Rapids, Michigan. Ford's future wife danced professionally with Martha Graham's New York Concert Group and worked as a Powers Model. She met Ford after her divorce from a local salesman and they married a year later. As first lady she revealed her struggle with alcohol and drugs and spoke out for abortion rights and treatment for alcohol and drug dependency around the country.

Children:

Michael Gerald Ford (1950–); John Gardner Ford (1952–); Steven Meigs Ford (1956–); Susan Elizabeth Ford (1957–)

HOBBIES

Golf, swimming, tennis, skiing, weight-lifting, and sports.

POST PRESIDENCY

Although disappointed by his defeat by Carter in 1976, he accepted it with good grace and retired from public office to his home in Rancho Mirage, California. He remains active, serving on various boards and committees, keeps a busy speaking schedule, and plays golf.

CHAPTER THIRTY-NINE
☆ ☆ ☆

JAMES EARL (JIMMY) CARTER
1924–

39th President of the United States
"Jimmy"

SECTION ONE

BORN

Jimmy Carter was born on October 1, 1924, at the local hospital in Plains, Georgia.

TERM SERVED AS PRESIDENT

1977–1981

POLITICAL PARTY

Democrat

PUBLIC LIFE BEFORE PRESIDENCY

After resigning his naval commission and taking over his father's farming business in 1953, Carter survived the worst drought in Georgia's history and turned the family peanut business into a solid financial success. He became the largest peanut wholesaler in the state and began to expand his contacts and influence in the political arena.

Sumter County Board of Education— 1955–1962

He became active in local affairs, and, along with serving on the board of education, he was chairman of the county hospital, and president of the Georgia Planning Association and the Georgia Crop Improvement Association.

Georgia State Senator—1962–1966

Carter ran for the state senate in 1962. After successfully challenging the results of a rigged election in court he had the results reversed and took office. He proved to be an effective and moderately liberal public official, taking strong stands on issues of racial discrimination and educational reform. He gained national notoriety when he voted against excluding blacks from the congregation of his local church.

He ran unsuccessfully for governor in 1966.

Governor of Georgia—1971–1975

After his election as governor, Carter began what was essentially a four-year campaign for the presidency. In his inaugural address he went against the grain of business-as-usual southern state politicians and enhanced his national reputation by saying, "No poor, rural, weak, or black person should ever have to bear the additional burden of being deprived of the opportunity of an education, a job, or simple justice." Using his forum a seated governor, he traveled the country, building his political base and his reputation as a viable alternate Democratic candidate for president.

CAMPAIGN

Election—1976

When he began campaigning for the presidency only 3 percent of the American people knew who Jimmy Carter was. But as he traveled the country, the peanut farmer and "born again" Christian attracted increasing attention by raising issues of morality and calling for a return to honesty in government. He ran as an "outsider" uncompromised and not tied to the business of political life in bureaucratic Washington. While political insiders refused to accept his viability as a candidate he campaigned furiously and, in a stunning and unexpected series of victories, captured nineteen of the thirty-one Democratic primaries. He was nominated on the first ballot.

On the other hand, the Republican nominee, Gerald Ford, had become the first chief executive who was not elected either president or vice president. Although a respected and veteran public servant whose honesty was unquestioned, Ford's unconditional pardon of Richard Nixon raised many questions about whether he had become president because he struck a deal. After his narrow first-ballot victory over Ronald Reagan at the Republican convention, Ford began his campaign with a lot to prove.

Carter's lack of experience in the national political arena and Ford's tendency to appear uninformed and physically clumsy in public resulted in a tight but uninspired race in which neither candidate seemed to generate real enthusiasm. But in the end the outsider, Carter, seemed less tainted by the brush of scandal and political intrigue and was elected in an extremely close race.

Electoral Votes:
Carter 297
Ford 240

VICE PRESIDENT

Walter F. Mondale (1928–) Minnesota. U.S. Senator

THE CABINET

Secretary of State:
  Cyrus R. Vance (1977–1980)
  Edmund S. Muskie (1980–1981)

Secretary of the Treasury:
  W. Michael Blumenthal (1977–1979)
  G. William Miller (1979–1981)

Secretary of Defense:
  Harold Brown (1977–1981)

Attorney General:
  Griffin B. Bell (1977–1979)
  Benjamin R. Civiletti (1979–1981)

Secretary of the Interior:
  Cecil D. Andrus (1977–1981)

Secretary of Agriculture:
  Robert S. Bergland (1977–1981)

Secretary of Commerce:
  Juanita M. Kreps (1977–1979)
  Philip Klutznick (1979–1981)

Secretary of Labor:
  F. Ray Marshall (1977–1981)

Secretary of Health, Education, and Welfare:
  Joseph A. Califano, Jr. (1977–1979)
  Patricia R. Harris (1979–1981)

(Department divided in 1980 into the Department of Health
and Human Services and the Department of Education)

Secretary of Education:
Shirley Hufstedler (1980–1981)

Secretary of Housing and Urban Development:
Patricia R. Harris (1977–1979)
Moon Landrieu (1979–1981)

Secretary of Transportation:
Brock Adams (1977–1979)
Neil E. Goldschmidt (1979–1981)

Secretary of Energy:
James R. Schlesinger (1977–1979)
Charles W. Duncan, Jr. (1979–1981)

SIGNIFICANT EVENTS THAT OCCURRED DURING
OFFICE——JANUARY 20, 1977–JANUARY 20, 1981

Pardon of Vietnam Draft Evaders—1977

Carter's first act as president was to pardon the nearly ten thousand men who had evaded the draft for the Vietnam War. He did
not, however, pardon deserters.

Creation of the Department of Energy—1977

Carter recognized concerns about resources and energy by creating a cabinet-level post to deal with the concerns.

Panama Canal—1977

Honoring a campaign promise, Congress agreed to turn the
Panama Canal over to Panamanian authorities in December of 1999.

Three Mile Island—1979

On March 28, 1979, the nuclear reactor at Three Mile Island in
Pennsylvania malfunctioned, emitting radiation and became the catalyst that would downgrade the U.S. nuclear energy program into
oblivion.

Camp David Accords: Israel and Egypt— 1979

Carter's personal diplomacy led to the signing of a peace treaty between Sadat of Egypt and Begin of Israel at Camp David. Without Carter's personal involvement it is unlikely that the two mortal enemies would have agreed to settle their differences.

The Iranian Hostage Crisis—1979

In November, sixty-three Americans were taken hostage at the embassy in Teheran by Iranian student militants. The hostages would be held for the remainder of the Carter administration and become the single major issue of his presidency, overshadowing the success of the Camp David Accords. The failure of a rescue mission, authorized by Carter in 1980, brought American prestige in world affairs to the lowest point in modern political history and crippled his leadership. Even though he was able, through Algerian intermediaries, to free the hostages, the actual release did not come until January 20, 1981, minutes after the inauguration of Ronald Reagan.

Reaction to Soviet Invasion of Afghanistan—1980

In retaliation for the Soviet invasion of Afghanistan, Carter placed an embargo on sales of grain and technology and later pressured the U.S. Olympic Committee to boycott the Summer Olympics in Moscow. While the committee agreed to boycott, the decision was unpopular and weakened the already struggling Carter administration.

CONTRIBUTIONS TO AMERICAN HISTORY WHILE

PRESIDENT

Carter arrived in Washington as a political unknown. No governor since Franklin Roosevelt had gone on to become president, and Carter was the first Southerner since Polk to be elected to office without succeeding first (as did Andrew and Lyndon Johnson). He ran a campaign not so much about issues as about his lack of political ties and his commitment to clean up government and put it back in the hands of the people.

While this was an appealing message, it would prove to be his undoing while in office. Having alienated most of the establishment on Capitol Hill during the campaign, he had almost no political credit, and his inexperienced staff were unable to bridge the practical gaps of doing business in Washington. Carter's domestic policies were, for the most part, a failure.

Carter's most lasting contributions to the presidency were his honesty and strong moral beliefs. Seemingly unable to find a middle ground, he will be remembered both for his failure to release the hostages in Iran and his success at taking the first steps to peace in the Middle East.

SECTION TWO

PERSONAL PROFILE

Carter is of average height and weight and favors comfortable clothing and conservative suits. Warm and charming in public and loyal to his friends, he is a devout Christian and firm in his beliefs. Carter possesses extraordinary ambition and self-confidence. His warm, broad smile contrasts with a toughness in private and a demanding demeanor with his aides.

FAMILY BACKGROUND

Ancestors

Carter is of English ancestry.

Immediate Family

FATHER: James Earl Carter, Sr., was a small farmer, managed a grocery store, owned the local icehouse and dry cleaning store. He was a hardworking and liberal man who took strong positions against racial discrimination. He died in 1953, forcing Carter to return to Georgia and take over the family business.

MOTHER: Lillian Gordy Carter. A woman of great courage and outspoken in her views, she instilled in Carter his humanitarian point of view. During the Carter presidency she became a public figure and was the subject of a segment on CBS's *60 Minutes*.

BROTHERS AND SISTERS: William "Billy" Carter.

CHILDHOOD AND EARLY YEARS

The Great Depression shaped and defined Carter's early years. The family lived in a small farmhouse without running water and electricity. As a child he worked the land, driving a team of mules to help raise food for the family. He was a bright and gifted young man with an ability for hard work and a ready smile.

EDUCATION

After attending local Plains schools, Carter graduated from Plains High School in 1941, where he played basketball and was a disciplined and active student. He applied to the U.S. Naval Academy in 1941 but needed further academic qualifications to be accepted. He enrolled at Georgia Southwestern College and then spent a year at the Georgia Institute of Technology, receiving his appointment to the Academy in 1942.

Because of the need for officers during World War II, he was placed in an accelerated program at Annapolis and graduated as an ensign with a degree in engineering in 1946 with honors, placing fifty-ninth in a class of 820.

MILITARY SERVICE

Post–World War II: U.S. Navy (1946–1953)

RANK: Rose from ensign to lieutenant commander.

Carter began his career as a senior officer on the USS *Wyoming* and in 1948 was assigned to submarine school. In 1951, after active service in Hawaii and the Pacific, he joined Admiral Hyman Rickover and became part of the team building the arsenal of nuclear submarines. He had expected to become a career military officer until the death of his father forced him to resign his command in 1953 and return to Plains.

RELIGION

Baptist

FAMILY LIFE

Marriage:

July 7, 1946, to Rosalynn Smith (1927–). A native of Plains, Georgia, Rosalynn had known Jimmy since childhood. She enjoyed the life of a navy wife and was reluctant to return to rural Georgia and the family business. She strongly supported his political ambitions and would become one of his most trusted advisors and constant companion.

Children:

John William "Jack" Carter; James Earl "Chip" Carter III; Donnel Jeffrey "Jeff" Carter; Amy Lynn Carter

HOBBIES

Fishing, reading, and political activism.

POST PRESIDENCY

Although his administration was responsible for the ultimate release of the hostages, Carter retired from the presidency with the cloud of the hostage crisis hanging over his head. He devoted himself to writing, teaching at Emory University, and becoming involved in humanitarian causes such as building housing for the poor. He travels extensively as an advocate for human rights and has become one of the most active ex-presidents in American history, involving himself in foreign affairs as an emissary for peace and a negotiator in such places as the Middle East, Haiti, and Panama. His wife Rosalynn remains his active partner.

CHAPTER FORTY
☆ ☆ ☆

RONALD REAGAN

1911-

40th President of the United States
"The Great Communicator"

☆ ☆ ☆

SECTION ONE

BORN

Reagan was born at home on February 6, 1911, in Tampico, Illinois.

TERMS SERVED AS PRESIDENT

1981–1985
1985–1989

POLITICAL PARTY

Republican

PUBLIC LIFE BEFORE PRESIDENCY

Broadcasting Career—1932–1937

After failing to land a broadcasting job in Chicago, Reagan was hired as a weekend sportscaster in Davenport, Iowa, and in 1934 became staff announcer. He was transferred to Des Moines, where he became regionally famous as the voice of Big Ten football and Major League baseball. Using only information on scores coming in over the telegraph, he was able to flesh out the details and convince listeners that they were listening to live broadcasts.

Film and Television Career—1937–1965

Through a friend he was given a screen test with Warner Brothers and signed to a seven-year contract. Reagan appeared in fifty-three films and was gaining fan popularity prior to his service in World War II. After the war he slid into a long series of forgettable roles. He moved into television in the 1950s and became the popular host of *Death Valley Days* and a spokesman for the General Electric Company.

A loyal Democrat for most of his life, he discovered his interest in conservative politics when he served as president of the Screen Actors Guild from 1947–1952 and 1959–1960. In 1947, he testified as a friendly witness before the House Un-American Activities Committee and was an FBI informant. Although he privately disagreed with the way the committee ran the investigation, his anticommunist sentiments prevailed. Reagan switched parties in 1962, becoming a conservative Republican and campaigning for Goldwater in 1964. While a popular and sought-after speaker, he was dismissed by the Republican power brokers as an ex-actor with no solid political base until he easily defeated Pat Brown and became governor of California in 1966.

Governor of California—1967–1975

Reagan's two terms as governor would catapult him into national prominence and win the support of conservative-minded politicians across the country. Initially opposing state spending and tax increases, he adjusted to the needs of the state when California's explosive growth required expansion of government services. When he left office in 1974 the state's budget showed a $550-million surplus.

Reagan was mentioned as a presidential contender in every campaign since 1968. He tirelessly traveled the lecture circuit, skillfully delivering what was called "the speech," an unvarying recitation of the evils of liberalism and building his political base. Eventually the hard work paid off. Although many in the party thought him too old to run in 1980, Reagan swept through the primaries and won the nomination.

CAMPAIGNS

First Election—1980

Reagan's campaign had a simple, two-part theme—"get the government out of our lives" domestically while pursuing a hard line against communism abroad. Reagan promised to stop inflation and promote economic growth by lowering taxes. He was nominated on the first ballot, and chose Bush to be his running mate. Reagan proved to be perhaps the best television candidate of all time, doing especially well in the television debates

Even though Edward "Ted" Kennedy mounted a strong challenge, the Democrats felt they could not abandon Carter during the hostage crisis and rallied around the struggling president, renominating him on the first ballot.

When the ill-fated effort to rescue the American hostages held in Iran failed. Carter's candidacy was doomed. Reagan went on to win a landslide victory.

Electoral Votes:
Reagan 489
Carter 49

Second Election—1984

Ronald Reagan looked pretty much unbeatable as the 1984 elections approached. His program of cutting taxes and increasing defense spending had stimulated the economy and stopped inflation but had also resulted in a stunning increase in the budget deficit. The Republican position was that the deficit would take care of itself as prosperity increased. He was easily renominated.

The Democratic primaries featured a three-way race between Colorado Senator Gary Hart, former vice president Walter Mondale, and the first major black candidate, the Rev. Jesse Jackson. Hart was dropped out of the race after it was discovered he was having an affair. Jackson ran a spirited campaign but was unable to extend his support far enough into the white community. Mondale won the nomination on the first ballot and chose New York Congresswoman Geraldine Ferraro, as his vice presidential candidate.

The Democratic campaign was chaotic and unfocused, and although Mondale tried to debate the deficit and hawkish foreign policy, Reagan's great skill as a communicator brought his message home. He won one of the greatest landslide victories in history.

Electoral Votes:
Reagan 525
Mondale 13

VICE PRESIDENT

George Herbert Walker Bush (1924–) Texas. Oil man. Public official.

THE CABINET

Secretary of State:
Alexander M. Haig, Jr. (1981–1982)
George P. Schultz (1982–1989)

Secretary of the Treasury:
  Donald T. Regan (1981–1985)
  James A. Baker (1985–1988)
  Nicholas F. Brady (1988–1989)

Secretary of Defense:
  Caspar W. Weinberger (1981–1987)
  Frank C. Carlucci (1987–1989)

Attorney General:
  William French Smith (1981–1985)
  Edwin Meese (1985–1988)
  Dick Thornburgh (1988–1989)

Secretary of the Interior:
  James G. Watt (1981–1983)
  William P. Clark (1983–1985)
  Donald P. Hodel (1985–1989)

Secretary of Agriculture:
  John R. Block (1981–1986)
  Richard E. Lyng (1986–1989)

Secretary of Commerce:
  Malcolm Baldrige (1981–1987)
  C. William Verity (1987–1989)

Secretary of Labor:
  Raymond J. Donovan (1981–1985)
  William Brock (1985–1987)
  Ann Dore McLaughlin (1987–1989)

Secretary of Health and Human Services:
  Richard S. Schweiker (1981–1983)
  Margaret M. Heckler (1983–1985)
  Otis R. Bowen (1985–1989)

Secretary of Housing and Urban Development:
  Samuel R. Pierce, Jr. (1981–1989)

Secretary of Transportation:
  Andrew L. Lewis, Jr. (1981–1983)
  Elizabeth H. Dole (1983–1987)
  James H. Burnley (1987–1989)

Secretary of Energy:
  James B. Edwards (1981–1982)
  Donald P. Hodel (1982–1985)
  John Herrington (1985–1989)

SIGNIFICANT EVENTS THAT OCCURRED DURING

OFFICE——JANUARY 20, 1981—JANUARY 20, 1989

Supply-Side Economic Policy ("Reaganomics")

Immediately after his inauguration, Reagan launched his supply-side economics program to revitalize an economy that conservative thinkers felt was in deep crisis. Reagan's plan offered $43 billion in budget cuts to shrink the government, tax cuts especially in the high-income and business brackets, to release investment capital and a speedy pullback quickly from government regulation of businesses and social programs. Despite opposition, Reagan used his immense popularity to push his program through Congress in 1981, promising inflation would decrease.

Reagan's economic policy was in trouble by the fall of 1981, as the economic recession deepened. But the picture had brightened in 1983, with a boom in the stock market, low inflation, new jobs resulting for the most part from the buildup in defense, and rising production. Although the deficit continued to grow at an alarming rate, recovery continued in 1984. Reagan would call for a Balanced Budget Amendment to the Constitution to combat the deficit throughout his time in office, but he never submitted a balanced budget of his own. When he retired, the budget deficit was in the trillions of dollars and remains a major American political issue to this day.

Assassination Attempt—March 30, 1981

As Reagan left the Hilton Hotel in Washington, D.C., John Hinckley, Jr., stepped through security and fired six shots, wounding the president in the chest, hitting Press Secretary James Brady in the head, and seriously wounding two Secret Service men. Reagan, minutes away from death, was taken to George Washington University Hospital, where the bullet, that had lodged an inch from his heart, was removed. He recovered quickly. Brady was severely paralyzed, and Hinckley was committed to a mental institution in Washington.

The War on Terrorism

Reagan campaigned on the promise of quick retribution against terrorist acts and a policy of nonnegotiation with terrorist groups, but as global terrorism increased and many Americans died, the administration found the promises difficult to keep. In 1981, the government listed five nations that actively supported terrorism and harbored terrorists. They were: Iran, Libya, North Korea, Cuba, and Nicaragua, and Reagan named Libya's Mu'ammar Qaddafi as the world's most active terrorist. In 1986 U.S. fighters attacked Libya in retaliation for the bombing of a West Berlin disco.

Iran-Contra

The most damaging scandal of the Reagan administration involved an agreement to sell arms secretly to Iran in exchange for American hostages. As the story unfolded, it was discovered that money from the arms sales was being diverted to revolutionaries in Nicaragua called the "contras." The investigation moved closer and closer to the White House as a commission took testimony to discover who had given the original orders. Reagan, in videotaped testimony in a closed Los Angeles courtroom, testified that he had not ordered any illegal actions, but the testimony was marked by numerous memory lapses. It was decided that Reagan was unaware of the operation, but several of his closest advisors were deeply involved and eventually prosecuted.

The Arms Race

Reagan took a tough stance against the Soviet Union, accelerating defense spending. Arms control talks were stalled as Reagan began a new deployment of U.S. nuclear missiles in Europe in November 1983. The president's rationale was the necessity to counter Soviet advances, but this strategy worried many observers.

In October 1986 Reagan met with Soviet leader Mikhail Gorbachev in Iceland, apparently to conclude an agreement on drastic reductions in nuclear missile strength, but Reagan resisted the Soviet demand that the U.S. Strategic Defense Initiative (Star Wars) be limited to laboratory research, and talks were broken off.

In retrospect it is likely that the aggressive buildup hastened the collapse of the Soviet Union by forcing them to allocate huge amounts of money to remain at military parity with the United States.

CONTRIBUTIONS TO AMERICAN HISTORY WHILE
PRESIDENT

Ronald Reagan, who, at seventy-eight, was the oldest man to hold office, was one of the most popular chief executives in American history. While it is possible to question the success of his domestic, economic, and certain of his foreign policies, it is clear that his tough stand against the Soviet Union hastened its collapse and brought down the iron curtain that had divided Europe for almost fifty years. Reagan had a boundless energy and limitless belief in simple, small-town family values. His ability to communicate his enthusiastic commitment to the American dream was infectious, and for millions of Americans he was one of the most beloved presidents since Eisenhower.

SECTION TWO

PERSONAL PROFILE

At 6′ 1″ and 175 pounds, Reagan retained his movie star good looks even as he approached his late seventies. Trained as an actor and broadcaster, he possessed skills of communication that served him extremely well when presenting his agenda and policies to the American public. He had the ability to seem secure, knowledgeable, and confident in any public situation and possessed a knack for anecdotes that charmed even his most persistent critics.

FAMILY BACKGROUND

Ancestors

Reagan's heritage is predominantly Irish with a mix of Scots and English. His great-grandfather emigrated from London to farm in Illinois in 1856.

Immediate Family

FATHER: John Edward Reagan (1883–1941) Reagan's father was a shoe salesman who, for a while, ran his own business but the Depression cost him his store and the family struggled, until John, an avowed liberal Democrat, found work running New Deal programs under the Roosevelt administration. He was a hard worker with a weakness for alcohol, which caused problems in the family. He died of heart failure.

MOTHER: Nelle Wilson Reagan (1885–1962) Born in Fulton, Illinois, Nelle was a supportive, generous, and forgiving woman who gave time to social causes even as she struggled to hold the family together. She loved the theater and organized local plays. She died in California while Reagan was working in television.

BROTHERS AND SISTERS: Neil Reagan.

CHILDHOOD AND EARLY YEARS

Reagan grew up in a very middle-American setting and because of it embraced the values of small-town life that would shape his political ideology. Although the family had to cope with his father's alcoholism, he remembered his childhood as the happiest time of his life. He worked odd jobs, enjoyed football, baseball, and swimming, collected insects and listened to sports and political events on the radio. Reagan loved the movies and from them, as well as from his mother, came his interest in becoming an actor.

EDUCATION

Reagan, who learned to read from his mother, attended public schools, where he made decent grades and was extremely involved in extracurricular activities, playing sports, acting in plays, and writing for the yearbook. He graduated in 1928. He worked his way through Eureka College, where he admitted to spending more time playing football, performing in plays, and socializing than studying. He graduated in 1932 and went to Chicago to seek a career in radio broadcasting.

MILITARY SERVICE

World War II: Regular Army (1942–1945)

RANK: Rose from lieutenant (Army Reserve) to captain.

Reagan's poor eyesight barred him from combat, and he served most of his tour narrating army training films.

RELIGION

Presbyterian

FAMILY LIFE

First Marriage:

Reagan, twenty-eight, married movie actress, Jane Wyman, twenty-six, on January 25, 1940, in Hollywood, California. They met while shooting a film called *Brother Rat and a Baby* in 1940. The marriage was accompanied by the usual Hollywood ballyhoo and the perfect couple appeared constantly in fan magazines. After Reagan returned from World War II, his acting career stalled while hers skyrocketed. Eventually they went their separate ways, divorcing in 1948.

Children:

Maureen Elizabeth Reagan (1941–); Michael Edward Reagan (1945–)

Second Marriage:

Reagan, forty-one, married Nancy Davis, thirty, on March 4, 1952, at the Little Brown Church in San Fernando Valley, California. Davis was also a movie actress and was a contract player at MGM where she and Reagan met. Their marriage was extremely close and she became a personal protector and advisor during his life in politics. As first lady, she entertained on a lavish scale and returned the White House to a lifestyle that was far grander than the simple tone of the Carter administration. She was active in programs combatting drug abuse, used an astrologer, and had great influence with the president, causing some advisors to consider her a threat.

Children:

Patricia Ann Reagan (1952–); Ronald Prescott Reagan (1958–)

HOBBIES

Working his ranch, horseback riding, and reading.

POST PRESIDENCY

Reagan and Nancy retired to California where he splits his time between his ranch in California and his home in Bel Air (Los Angeles). In 1995 it was revealed that he had begun to suffer from Alzheimer's disease.

CHAPTER FORTY-ONE
☆ ☆ ☆

GEORGE HERBERT WALKER BUSH

1924-

41st President of the United States
"Poppy"

☆ ☆ ☆

SECTION ONE

BORN

Bush was born on June 12, 1924, at the family home in Milton, Massachusetts.

TERM SERVED AS PRESIDENT

1989–1993

POLITICAL PARTY

Republican

PUBLIC LIFE BEFORE PRESIDENCY

The Texas Oil fields—1948–1966

After Yale, Bush surprised his wife and family and moved to Texas to work in the West Texas oil fields. Within two years, he was a partner in the Bush-Overby Development Company trading oil leases and royalties. In less than ten years he became a millionaire in his own right and began to participate in Houston politics.

U.S. Representative—1967–1971

Defeated in a race for the Senate in 1964, Bush was one of two Texas Republicans to go to the U.S. House of Representatives in 1966. He ran as a moderate and supported civil rights legislation, voting for the Civil Rights Act of 1968, even though it was unpopular with the constituents in his district.

U.S. Ambassador to the United Nations—1971–1973

Although Bush had no diplomatic experience, Nixon appointed him to the United Nations after his first choice, Patrick Moynihan, turned the appointment down.

Chairman of the Republican National Committee—1973–1974

Bush was interested in gaining more experience in foreign policy but he agreed to Nixon's request to become chairman of the committee. By default, it became Bush's job to defend the beleaguered president as Watergate heated up, and he was one of the last of his supporters to suggest that he resign.

Chief Liaison to China—1974–1975

He came close to the vice presidential nomination on the Ford ticket. But Ford chose Rockefeller and offered Bush his choice of ambassadorships. He chose China and served there for thirteen months.

Director of the CIA—1976–1977

Again a second choice, Bush was appointed Director of the CIA by Ford when Edward Bennett Williams turned him down. Bush received high marks for his effort to restore morale within the agency. He was replaced by Carter when Carter took office in 1977.

Vice President—1981–1989

Deciding to take the bull by the horns, Bush announced his run for the Republican presidential nomination in 1980. He did well in the early primaries but dropped out after losing Texas and turned his delegates over to Reagan. Again he was the second choice—the convention asked him on the ticket after Ford refused to accept the nomination.

Reagan and Bush worked well together during the eight years they shared the top offices. He traveled extensively for the president and headed the National Security Council's "crisis management team." He took over the reins when Reagan was shot and wounded in March 1981. Using his constitutional authority for the first time in history, Reagan transferred power to Bush before he underwent cancer surgery in July 1985.

CAMPAIGN

Election—1988

Ronald Reagan retained his personal popularity throughout his second term, and his support for Bush set the vice president up to win the nomination on the first ballot. There was serious concern, however that his running mate, Dan Quayle, was unqualified to step into the presidency if something should happen to Bush.

On the Democratic side, Massachusetts Governor Michael Dukakis ran a well organized campaign in the primaries and was easily nominated on the first ballot.

Bush ran one of the most aggressive, negative, and vicious campaigns in recent history. He attacked Dukakis as an East Coast liberal who favored high taxes, coddling the unemployed and criminals, with no knowledge of foreign affairs. He created a very controversial television ad featuring, Willy Horton, a Massachusetts career criminal who had committed rapes and robberies while on a work-release program implying that Dukakis was somehow responsible.

Unable to counter effectively or present himself in a positive light, Dukakis bungled his own publicity. In a mean-spirited campaign, neither candidate generated much enthusiasm, and the votes for Bush were a more a reflection of his connection to Reagan than his particular vision for America. Bush was elected by a landslide.

Electoral Votes:
Bush 426
Dukakis 111

VICE PRESIDENT

James Danforth ("Dan") Quayle (1947–) Indiana. Lawyer.

THE CABINET

Secretary of State:
James A. Baker III (1989–1992)
Lawrence S. Eagleburger (1992–1993)

Secretary of the Treasury:
Nicholas Brady (1989–1993)

Secretary of Defense:
Richard Cheney (1989–1993)

Attorney General:
Dick Thornburgh (1989–1991)
William P. Barr (1991–1993)

Secretary of the Interior:
  Manuel Lujan (1989–1993)

Secretary of Agriculture:
  Clayton Yeutter (1989–1991)
  Edward R. Madigan (1991–1993)

Secretary of Commerce:
  Robert Mosbacher (1989–1992)
  Barbara H. Franklin (1992–1993)

Secretary of Labor:
  Elizabeth Doyle (1989–1990)
  Lynn Morley Martin (1990–1993)

Secretary of Health and Human Services:
  Louis Sullivan (1989–1993)

Secretary of Housing and Urban Development:
  Jack Kemp (1989–1993)

Secretary of Transportation:
  Samuel Skinner (1989–1991)
  Andrew H. Card (1992–1993)

Secretary of Energy:
  James Watkins (1989–1993)

Secretary of Education:
  Lauro Cavazos (1989–1991)
  Lamar Alexander (1991–1993)

Secretary of Veterans Affairs:
  Edward J. Derwinski (1989–1992)

SIGNIFICANT EVENTS THAT OCCURRED DURING
OFFICE——JANUARY 20, 1989–JANUARY 20, 1993

Resolving the Savings and Loan Crisis— 1989

Bush signed a plan to bail out insolvent Savings and Loans that had looted by unscrupulous management or had simply failed during the frenzy created by deregulation in the early eighties. The total cost to taxpayers and banks was expected to reach $500 billion by 2030.

Invasion of Panama—1989–1990

To protect American interests in the Panama Canal Zone and stop the flow of illegal drugs through Panama, Bush sent troops in December of 1989 to depose Panamanian President Manuel Noriega. The military action lasted until Noriega surrendered after four days of sporadic fighting. He was taken to Miami, where he was put on trial for trafficking and sentenced to forty years in prison. It was discovered that he had been in the employ of the CIA.

The Collapse of the Soviet Union

Between 1989 and 1991, the entire Soviet Union collapsed under the weight of seventy years of oppression. The Eastern Bloc fell like a row of dominoes, and the West was presented with an entirely new set of problems centering around the questions of how to help bring almost a third of the world into the market economy and what to do with all the nuclear weapons. Only China, North Korea, and Cuba remain under communist rule.

Persian Gulf War—1990–1991

In August 1990, after Iraq's annexation of Kuwait, Bush formed a coalition of Western powers and effected an economic embargo of Iraq, demanding that they withdraw back across the legally recognized Kuwait-Iraq border. To back it up, he stationed more than 400,000 American troops in the Persian Gulf region to defend Saudi Arabia. He secured congressional approval for the use of force if Iraq refused to withdraw by mid-January 1991. When the deadline came and went, Bush ordered a massive bombing attack on Iraq and its forces in Kuwait to begin on January 16, followed by a ground assault on February 24. Four days later, after sustaining severe casualties, Iraq agreed to withdraw.

Somalia

In December 1992, Bush sent American troops to strife-torn Somalia to feed its starving people. Clinton would inherit the Somalia issue when he took office in 1993.

CONTRIBUTIONS TO AMERICAN HISTORY WHILE

PRESIDENT

Bush achieved hugely positive marks for his efforts in foreign policy, especially the resolution of the Persian Gulf War, but domestic issues would be his downfall. Forced to deal with the pressing problem of a mounting federal deficit, he and moderates of both parties agreed to a compromise that increased taxes, reduced spending, and provided growth incentives for business. While the increase was necessary, the action hurt him politically. "Read My Lips, No New Taxes" would come to haunt him.

In spite of the tax increases, the economy remained stagnant during his last years in office, and productivity slipped to near recession levels during the summer of 1990. Caught between a rock and a hard place, Bush tried to weather the storm with optimism and confidence, but hard times had struck too many Americans, and it was time for a change.

SECTION TWO

PERSONAL PROFILE

Bush stands 6' 2" and weighs between 195 and 200 pounds. He has a ready smile and projects a shy almost gentle quality. Extremely loyal, he is considered warm, generous, and charming. In small groups, where he is more comfortable, he can be witty and playful. After a bout with an ulcer when he was a younger man, Bush learned to slow down and keep a more pragmatic and less emotional perspective on important issues.

FAMILY BACKGROUND

Ancestors

Bush is descended from English stock and his first family member settled in Massachusetts in the mid-seventeenth century.

Immediate Family

FATHER: Prescott S. Bush (1895–1972) A successful businessman, soldier, public official, and U.S. Senator, Prescott Bush was a conservative Republican with some liberal tendencies. He was briefly considered as a candidate for the 1960 presidential nomination. A wealthy man, he believed that it was his responsibility to repay society for the privilege of comfort.

MOTHER: Dorothy Walker Bush (1901–1972) A competitive and gifted athlete, she expected the same level of discipline and commitment from her children that she expected from herself. She kept close track of her son's political career.

BROTHERS AND SISTERS: Prescott Bush; Mrs. Nancy Ellis; Jonathan Bush; William Bush.

CHILDHOOD AND EARLY YEARS

Bush grew up in wealth and privilege. The family split its time between a rambling home in Greenwich, Connecticut, and their vacation house on the ocean in Kennebunkport, Maine. From infancy he loved sports and inherited his mother's competitiveness. He excelled at baseball and tennis and loved ocean fishing and sailing or cruising in the family's motorboat.

EDUCATION

Bush attended Greenwich Country Day School, Phillips Academy in Andover, Massachusetts, then joined the navy and served in World War II. After his discharge he married Barbara Pierce and enrolled at Yale, his father's alma mater, in 1945. While little more than an average student through high school, at Yale he became serious about his studies, making Phi Beta Kappa and graduating with honors in 1948. He also found time to be captain of the varsity baseball team and was known as an excellent first baseman but a below-average hitter. He was tapped as a member of the exclusive secret society, Skull and Bones.

MILITARY SERVICE

World War II: U.S. Navy (1942–1945)

RANK: Rose from seaman second class to lieutenant (junior grade).

Assigned to preflight school, he became the navy's youngest bomber pilot and flew fifty-eight combat missions. In 1944, he was shot down over the Pacific island of Chichi Jima and rescued by a submarine. He was awarded the Distinguished Flying Cross and three Air Medals.

RELIGION

Episcopalian

FAMILY LIFE

Marriage:

Bush, twenty, married Barbara Pierce (1921–), nineteen, on January 6, 1945, at the First Presbyterian Church in Rye, New York. Daughter of Marvin Pierce, a successful magazine publisher, Barbara dropped out of Smith College to marry Bush, whom she had met at a Christmas dance in 1942. After a secret engagement in 1943 the couple married in 1945 and moved to New Haven so Bush could attend Yale. This began a series of moves that became the hallmark of their marriage. Barbara Bush is a very down-to-earth and confident woman. As first lady, she supported educational causes for children and advocated for the homeless. Although she would rarely disagree with her husband in public, she held strong views on women's issues, particularly abortion and gun control, that were often at odds with Republican ideology.

Children:

George Bush, Jr. (1946–); Robin Bush (1949–1953); John Bush (1953–); Neil Bush (1955–); Marvin Bush (1956–); Dorothy Bush (1959–)

HOBBIES

There is probably not a sporting event or activity that Bush has not attended or attempted—golf, fishing, speedboating, tennis, horseshoes, hunting. He also enjoys reading, watching television, and seeing films.

POST PRESIDENCY

Bush retired to Houston, Texas, and rarely appears at public functions or grants interviews. By all accounts, he lives a quiet life, attending sporting events, seeing friends, traveling with his wife, and spending time with his grandchildren.

CHAPTER FORTY-TWO
☆ ☆ ☆

WILLIAM JEFFERSON (BILL) CLINTON

1946-

42nd President of the United States
"Bill"

☆ ☆ ☆

SECTION ONE

BORN

Clinton was born on August 19, 1946, at Julia Chester Hospital in Hope, Arkansas.

TERM SERVED AS PRESIDENT

1993–

POLITICAL PARTY

Democrat

PUBLIC LIFE BEFORE PRESIDENCY

Law Professor, University of Arkansas— 1973–1976

In 1973, after working on George McGovern's presidential campaign and completing law school, Clinton joined the faculty of the University of Arkansas as a law professor with strong political ambitions. By early the next year he was running for the U.S. Congress. Although he narrowly lost to a Republican incumbent, he gained name recognition in Arkansas politics and two years later was elected state attorney general.

Attorney General of Arkansas—1977–1979

His election as attorney general was Clinton's first successful bid for office. He continued to strengthen his political base and gain supporters in the party elite. While serving in that office, he was elected the youngest governor in Arkansas history in 1978, at age thirty-two.

Governor of Arkansas—1979–1981, 1983–1992

Clinton was defeated in a reelection bid in 1980 after raising the state gasoline tax to finance an ambitious highway-building program. He returned to his law practice in Little Rock and reviewed his performance, realizing that he had been too ambitious in his attempts at reform and that it was political suicide to effect change too quickly. After a year in law, 1981 to 1982, he went on to win four consecutive terms (one for four years) during which he practiced more politics of consent than he had in his first term. His special interest, and one shared by Hillary, was improving the state's public education system, which necessitated a bitter struggle with the state's teachers' union and a fight over raising the sales tax. His success gained him national recognition.

Through most of the 1980s, Clinton was a rising star in national Democratic politics. As a founding member of the Democratic Leadership Council, he helped articulate a moderately based strategy for taking the White House. He even briefly considered running for the presidency himself in 1988 but stumped for the Democratic candidate, Michael Dukakis, instead and bided his time.

While governor he would involve himself in some political entanglements and make some decisions of expediency that would surface when he became president. The Whitewater scandal, rumors of womanizing, and his financial involvement with major business interests in the state would surface during the campaign and while in office.

CAMPAIGN

Election—1992

Clinton was an early favorite for the nomination, with all the right credentials, until allegations of adultery began to surface. The candidacy seemed doomed in late 1991, until Bill and Hillary confronted the issue head-on, appearing on national television after the Super Bowl to show their solidarity. It was a masterstroke, and Clinton regained his momentum in the primaries. He was nominated on the first ballot.

Less than a year before, Bush's approval ratings had soared because of the success of the Persian Gulf war. Now, a year later, the president was in deep political trouble because of a lack of confidence in his domestic leadership. Bush, however, won renomina-

tion at the Republican convention and, over the objections of many
advisors, once again chose Quayle as his running mate.

H. Ross Perot, a flamboyant Texas billionaire, used his very deep
pockets to establish a national organization and get on the ballot in
all fifty states. His major theme was an old one: both major-party
candidates were economic amateurs. What the country needed was
a hardheaded businessman at the helm.

Bush campaigned on Clinton's inexperience in foreign affairs
along with the standard Republican theme of battle: Democrats are
genetically inclined to tax and spend. Unfortunately, the label didn't
fit Clinton as well as it had the previous Democratic candidates.
Clinton turned the issue against Bush, pounding away at the theme
that twelve years of Republican rule had made the rich richer while
the middle class and the poor suffered from a prolonged recession
and reminding the public that he had fostered an economic revival
in Arkansas.

H. Ross Perot captured nearly twenty million votes, split the Republican vote, and may have stolen the election from Bush. Although he only received 42 percent of the popular vote, Bill Clinton
became the forty-second president of the United States.

Electoral Votes:
Clinton 370
Bush 168

VICE PRESIDENT

Albert Gore, Jr. (1948–) Tennessee. Lawyer.

THE CABINET

Secretary of State:
Warren M. Christopher (1993–

Secretary of the Treasury:
Lloyd M. Bentsen (1993–1994)
Robert E. Rubin (1994–

Secretary of Defense:
Leslie Aspin, Jr. (1993–1994)
William J. Perry (1994–

Attorney General:
Janet Reno (1993–

Secretary of the Interior:
  Bruce Babbitt (1993–

Secretary of Agriculture:
  Mike Espy (1993–1994)
  Bruce Babbitt (1993–

Secretary of Commerce:
  Ronald H. Brown (1993–1996)
  Mickey Kantor (1996–

Secretary of Labor:
  Robert B. Reich (1993–

Secretary of Health and Human Services:
  Donna E. Shalala (1993–

Secretary of Housing and Urban Development:
  Henry G. Cisneros (1993–

Secretary of Transportation:
  Federico F. Pena (1993–

Secretary of Energy:
  Hazel R. O'Leary (1993–

Secretary of Education:
  Richard W. Riley (1993–

Secretary of Veterans Affairs:
  Jesse Brown (1993–

SIGNIFICANT EVENTS THAT OCCURRED DURING OFFICE——JANUARY 20, 1993—

Gays in the Military—1993

Clinton acted on one of his campaign promises and, over objections of administration and military advisors, attempted to overturn the long-standing ban on gays in the military. He learned one of his first political lessons when he was forced to compromise the issue in such a way that no one was satisfied.

Somalia—1993

Clinton inherited the humanitarian action in Somalia, and while he supported the concept, as the situation became more difficult for troops to handle he demonstrated once again that he had some things to learn about foreign affairs. The last troops would pull out in 1995.

Bosnia—1993–1996

After sanctions failed to secure a truce in Bosnia, Clinton authorized the use of American forces through the United Nations to land on the ground and supervise the transition to peace between Muslims and Serbs.

Whitewater and Other Scandals

Allegations of taking kickbacks and making profits illegally in a real estate venture undertaken while governor of Arkansas would haunt the Clinton presidency. By 1996 an ongoing Republican investigation, while uncovering nothing of substance, would continue under the chairmanship of New York Senator Al D'Amato and shows no signs of abating. Hillary was also implicated in Whitewater and in a stock and commodities scandal.

National Health Care—1993

Hillary Rodham Clinton was named in late January to head the White House task force on national health reform, with the responsibility of examining all available options, creating a consensus on necessary change, and acting as a mediator among all interests concerned. While ambitious, the attempt would stall and die without ever coming to a vote.

Waco

The attorney general, Janet Reno, the Bureau of Alcohol, Tobacco, and Firearms, and the FBI would come under intense scrutiny after a bungled attempt to remove a group of Branch Davidians from their compound outside Waco, Texas. The nation watched as the compound burned out of control, killing everyone inside, including a large number of children.

Foreign Policy

Clinton urged greater Western aid to Russia and the nations of the former Soviet Union.

Protecting the Election in Haiti

Clinton sent troops onto foreign soil to protect and reestablish democracy and guarantee the installation of the duly elected president in Haiti. Ex-president Jimmy Carter helped broker the deal.

The Economy and the Budget

With the Democratic party in power in both the White House and Congress, Bill Clinton urged timely action on programs he had emphasized during the campaign. He outlined his plans for economic revival and deficit reduction in an address to a joint session of Congress. The major proposals over four years included $246 billion in new taxes, expenditures of an additional $169 billion to stimulate the economy, and a general spending cut of $247 billion. Substantial cuts were proposed in defense spending. The deficit, Clinton declared, could be cut by $325 billion over four years. But dissatisfaction with Clinton's position on spending and the deficit caused a Republican revolution in the midterm elections and the conservative faction of the Republican party swept to power, creating a strongly anti-Clinton Congress and Senate and a volatile new leader in Speaker Newt Gingrich.

CONTRIBUTIONS TO AMERICAN HISTORY WHILE

PRESIDENT

The administration of Bill Clinton has been a curious mix of successes and failures. Bad judgments and inexperience in running the government on the national level made for trouble early in his term. But as time went on he seemed to gain some control of the office, and only time will tell what kind of contributions he will make while in office.

SECTION TWO

PERSONAL PROFILE

Clinton is a large man, standing 6′2 1/2″. His weight fluctuates between 200 and 230 pounds because of his self-professed love for junk food. He suffers from severe allergies and introduced the first nonsmoking White House. He is outgoing and carries a ready smile, enjoying the process of campaigning almost as much, if not more, than governing. Because he often takes circular routes of logic to get to his point, he can seem devious and even evasive. He has a tendency to seem to agree with whatever is being said, giving the impression that he agrees with the issue or position that has been presented.

FAMILY BACKGROUND

Ancestors

Clinton is an Anglo-Saxon mix of English, Irish, Scots, and German.

Immediate Family

FATHER: William Jefferson Blythe, III (1917–1946) A traveling salesman, Blythe was returning to Arkansas to pick up his pregnant wife and bring her to Chicago where they had bought a house and intended to live. Driving through Missouri, he blew a tire and skidded off the road, was thrown from the car unconscious, and drowned in a ditch.

STEPFATHER: Roger Clinton (?–1967) A car salesman with a severe drinking problem, he was abusive and subject to alcoholic rages. He and Clinton were never close but made peace just before he died.

MOTHER: Virginia Cassidy Blythe Clinton Dwire Kelly (1923–) A retired nurse, Clinton's mother was born in Bodcaw, Arkansas. After she lost her first husband (Clinton's father) she married Roger Clinton in 1950 and divorced him in 1962. Three months later, they remarried. After his death she married a local hairdresser named Dwire, who died of diabetes in 1974. In 1981 she married Richard Kelly and retired from her nursing career.

BROTHERS AND SISTERS: Half brother—Roger Clinton.

CHILDHOOD AND EARLY YEARS

Clinton grew up in Hope, Arkansas. Times were difficult, and he was sent to live with his grandparents while his mother finished her degree in nursing. His grandparents taught him racial tolerance and helped him learn to read. They were a lasting positive influence on the young man. Clinton overcame the difficulties with his alcoholic stepfather to live a relatively normal small-town life. He sang in the choir, shared his mother's love of Elvis Presley, and learned to play the saxophone, forming a three-piece jazz band. He traveled to Washington as a member of the American Legion's Boys' Nation and shook John F. Kennedy's hand in the Rose Garden. The meeting convinced him that he would pursue a life in politics.

EDUCATION

Clinton attended local public schools and was an excellent student, graduating fourth in his class. He chose Georgetown University because of its foreign service program and graduated in 1968. From 1968 to 1970 he attended Oxford University as a Rhodes scholar and then entered Yale Law School on scholarship in 1970, graduating in 1973. It was at Yale that Clinton met Hillary Rodham, a gifted fellow student from suburban Chicago who would become his wife.

MILITARY SERVICE

None. Clinton was accused of dodging the draft during the Vietnam era. Exactly what happened is not clear, but in any event he did not serve.

RELIGION

Baptist

FAMILY LIFE

Marriage:

Clinton, twenty-nine, married Hillary Rodham, twenty-seven, on October 11, 1975, at the house they had purchased in Fayetteville, Arkansas. Born in 1947, Hillary grew up in Chicago. Her father was the owner of a textile company and a conservative Republican. She was active in causes while still in high school and campaigned for Goldwater in 1964. Her dissatisfaction with the war in Vietnam caused her to switch to the Democratic party and she was an active supporter of Eugene McCarthy in 1968. Brilliant and opinionated, she enrolled at Yale Law School, where she met Clinton and they began dating. Initially, she was not interested in the idea of moving to Arkansas, but by 1975 she had changed her mind. As first lady she champions children's rights and is heavily involved in the policies of the Clinton administration. Clinton considers her one of his best advisors.

Children:

Chelsea Victoria Clinton (1980–)

AFFAIRS

Clinton has been rumored to be a womanizer since his days as governor in Arkansas, allegations and tape recordings of his affair with an Arkansas state employee, Gennifer Flowers, surfaced during the campaign, and Clinton still faces a sexual harassment charge dating from his Arkansas days.

HOBBIES

Jogging, swimming, golf, basketball, cards, collecting, and jazz and blues saxophone.